Complementary medicine today

Complementary medicine consists of a variety of clinical practices, the efficacy of which has been, and continues to be hotly debated. Some members of the orthodox medical profession castigate complementary medicine as useless and dangerous, while others accept that it has a value. Despite this, during the past decade, the practise of alternative medicine has grown rapidly and many patients, dissatisfied with orthodox medicine, are turning to it.

In *Complementary Medicine Today* Ursula Sharma examines the effect of this rise in popularity and the question it raises for the orthodox medical profession. She examines complementary medicine in its social and political context and explores the attitudes of medical practitioners and patients to it. By relating her research to central issues in medical sociology and anthropology she addresses those questions of principle and policy which the growth of the complementary therapies has raised.

This highly topical book will be invaluable to practitioners and students of complementary and orthodox medicine, medical sociologists, and health professionals.

Ursula Sharma is senior lecturer in sociology and social anthropology at the University of Keele.

D0594838

Complementary medicine today

Practitioners and patients

Ursula Sharma

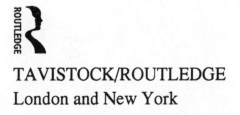

TAVISTOCK/ROUTLEDGE
London and New York

First published 1992
by Routledge
11 New Fetter Lane, London EC4P 4EE

Simultaneously published in the USA and Canada
by Routledge
a division of Routledge, Chapman and Hall, Inc.
29 West 35th Street, New York, NY 10001

© 1992 Ursula Sharma

Typeset in Times by Michael Mepham, Frome, Somerset
Printed and bound in Great Britain by
Mackays of Chatham plc, Chatham, Kent

British Library Cataloguing in Publication Data
Sharma, Ursula, *1941*–
  Complementary medicine today: practitioners and patients.
  1. Alternative therapy
  I. Title
  306.461

Library of Congress Cataloging in Publication Data
  Complementary medicine today: practitioners and
  patients / Ursula Sharma.
  p. cm.
  Includes bibliographical references and index.
  1. Alternative medicine. I. Title.
  [DNLM: 1. Alternative Medicine. 2. Cross-Cultural Comparison.
  WB 890 S531c]
  R733.S52 1991
  615.5—dc20
  DNLM/DLC
  for Library of Congress   91–617
                                                                CIP

ISBN 0–415–04793–5
ISBN 0–415–04794–3 (pbk)

Contents

Tables and figures

FIGURE

Acknowledgements

The research on which this book is based was conducted over a period of five years and in that time I have contracted debts of obligation to more friends and colleagues than I could possibly mention here. However, my first and greatest debt must be to all those individuals who so kindly agreed to be interviewed. I enjoyed talking to them and learnt so much from them – I hope the experience was worthwhile for them also. Without funding, the research would never have been completed, so I would like to express appreciation of the two grants I received from the Nuffield Foundation. I also received a great deal of help and information from officials and employees of various professional and other organisations concerned with complementary medicine. I cannot cite all these by name, but I would particularly like to mention Jane Foulkes of the Institute of Complementary Medicine, who went out of her way to provide me with information and with whom I had many interesting exchanges of ideas.

Colleagues at Keele and elsewhere have been a source of encouragement and support. Thanks are due to Ronnie Frankenberg who was co-applicant for the first grant from the Nuffield Foundation and gave much bibliographic help. Alan Prout, Paul Bellaby (now at the University of East Anglia), John Lloyd and Vincanne Adams patiently listened to me prattle about my fieldwork over coffee, and from their knowledge of medical sociology and anthropology contributed many ideas and insights which helped me in the analysis of my material. In particular, thank you Vincanne for generously taking the trouble of going through the manuscript of this book with a toothcomb and making many constructive suggestions! Mike Savage and Dr Kevan Thorley also read and made helpful comments on portions of the manuscript.

I have exchanged ideas with many scholars in other institutions who are also currently working on the subject of complementary medicine. I have derived particular benefit from discussions with Richenda Power of South Bank Polytechnic, Kate Thomas of Sheffield University, Professor Margaret

Stacey of Warwick University, Guy Sermeus of the Belgian Consumer Association and Joost Visser of the Netherlands Institute of Primary Health Care. Many people have contributed to my thinking about complementary medicine but any errors or shortcomings in this book are of course my own responsibility.

No research project can be undertaken or completed without expert secretarial support. I would like to mention the help I received from Joy Kendrick and Janet Hughes who transcribed the interviews, and to record my gratitude to Doreen Clowes, secretary in the Department of Sociology and Social Anthropology at Keele, for constant encouragement and practical support of so many kinds. I also thank my good friend and neighbour Jill Hall for providing the index.

No book gets written without a lot of support (and forbearance) from family members. My thanks to you all – especially my husband Om Prakash Sharma (student of homoeopathy) – for affectionate interest and encouragement.

Abbreviations

BHMA	British Holistic Medical Association
BMA	British Medical Association
BMJ	*British Medical Journal*
ICM	Institute of Complementary Medicine
JACM	*Journal of Alternative and Complementary Medicine*
JAM	*Journal of Alternative Medicine*
NMS	Natural Medicines Society
Soc Sci and Med	*Social Science and Medicine*

Introduction

The scope of this book

In this book my purpose is to draw together and discuss what is known about the social aspects of complementary or 'alternative' medicine in Britain today, and to present new data from my own field research on the subject. How and why do people use complementary medicine? What kind of people practise it, and why? What political and social issues does its popularity raise and what is its future in this country? Complementary medicine consists of a variety of clinical practices, the efficacy of which has been and continues to be hotly debated. But any system of medicine is practised within a social and political context and involves inter-personal transactions of a more or less institutionalised nature. These social dimensions are as much a part of medical practice as clinical knowledge. I shall try to relate research on these aspects of complementary medicine both to central issues in medical sociology and anthropology and to those questions of principle and policy which the growth of the complementary therapies has raised.

From time to time a major journal or newspaper will run a series of articles on complementary therapies, usually followed by a spate of letters from readers. The reactions generally come from three sources:

a) members of the public who have used complementary medicine, recounting their experiences, good or ill;

b) practitioners, arguing the legitimacy of their therapies, but not necessarily agreeing as to how the future of these therapies is best secured;

c) orthodox doctors, often castigating complementary medicine as useless or dangerous, but sometimes appreciative of particular therapies.

I shall discuss complementary medicine chiefly from the point of view of those who use it and those who practise it. However, I am also interested in the position of the orthodox medical profession and will include a discussion of doctors' attitudes. This selective focus does not exhaust the range of possible viewpoints (I have not, for example, considered the interests of companies who manufacture drugs and medicines) but I believe that I have identified the areas where researchers – especially sociologists and social anthropologists – have collected the kind of data which might contribute to a more informed debate.

In answering the rather straightforward questions posed at the head of this chapter, the more complex theme of control and responsibility will constantly recur. I shall contend that the popularity of complementary medicine raises crucial questions about the balance between the degree of responsibility which patients may be expected to take for decisions about their own treatment and the degree of control over the therapeutic process which therapists, whether orthodox or non-orthodox, may claim. Orthodox medicine, as practised in the National Health Service, is organised on the assumption that the doctor has prime responsibility for therapeutic decision making; this responsibility may be delegated to another practitioner, as when a patient is referred to a specialist, but in general the patient merely 'complies' or 'fails to comply'. But where a plurality of therapeutic systems exist and people exercise deliberate choice in using one system rather than another, a degree of self-responsibility on the part of patients is surely implied. To the extent that some reponsibility must still lie with the therapist, what happens when both orthodox doctors and complementary healers are involved in treatment of the same patient? Is there any way in which therapeutic responsibility may reasonably be divided between them? In the end, who has the right or power to decide who should exercise control or who should take responsibility? The medical professions? The state? The market? A description of the behaviour of users and practitioners of complementary medicine is bound to involve an account of the politics of the therapeutic process.

COMPLEMENTARY MEDICINE: OLD PHENOMENON, NEW ISSUES

What I have called 'orthodox' medicine is orthodox in the sense that it is based on understandings of the body which are widely accepted in western society. The system of medicine practised by doctors asserts its legitimacy with reference to claims to scientificity, claims which are seldom disputed even if their relevance is challenged. But such 'orthodoxy' is a matter of political authorisation as well as cultural acceptability.

In 1858 the state, with the passing of the Medical Act, conferred upon qualified practitioners of what has come to be regarded as orthodox medicine the exclusive right to the term 'medical practitioner', and in the period after the Second World War the National Health Service was built around the institutions of this form of medicine. But orthodox medicine never achieved a total monopoly of medical services in Britain. Homoeopathy, which is at least as old as orthodox medicine, flourished in the first half of the nineteenth century and never entirely disappeared, although it went through a period of eclipse in the mid-twentieth century before its re-emergence in the 1970s. Osteopathy was introduced from America in 1917, naturopathy became popular in the 1930s and herbalism in various forms has been practised from time immemorial in this country. The post-war period, and especially the past twenty years, saw a new wave of interest in existing non-orthodox therapies and the arrival of many new ones – new, that is, to Britain since some of them (such as acupuncture or shiatsu) had long anterior histories in their cultures of origin.

What is new about the situation is the fact that resort to these various therapies is no longer restricted to small groups of enthusiasts. Use of non-orthodox medicine is now widespread and popular in the broad sense of that word. This popularity presents a direct challenge to the authority of the orthodox medical profession as well as raising important policy issues. If consumers – the patients themselves – accord orthodox medicine no privileged role, then should the state not acknowledge this situation and offer non-orthodox medicine some recognition, even provide a choice of therapy on the NHS? Orthodox medicine, however, has bought state recognition at the expense of some state regulation, and social eminence at the price of required conformity to a well policed set of standards of practice. Many practitioners, both orthodox and non-orthodox, are now asking whether complementary medicine should not be subject to the same or comparable controls in order to protect patients and prevent quackery.

These are political questions and will, in the end, be resolved through political processes. Social scientists, however, can make a useful contribution to the current debate. The extent to which patients need protection is discussed more knowledgeably if we know what kind of illnesses people present to non-orthodox practitioners and what degree of authority they accord to the practitioner. The prospect of uniform standards is better debated when we know what kind of people want to become or succeed in becoming complementary practitioners. The likelihood of co-operation between orthodox and non-orthodox practitioners is best discussed when we know something about the ways in which they regard each others' practices and the extent to which they are prepared to network with each other at the local and national level.

I shall present data from my own field research and those collected by other social scientists in as dispassionate a manner as possible. I shall not attempt any conclusions about the efficacy of complementary medicines although I shall refer to this issue in a general way. Obviously I have my own opinions on this, having used a number of non-orthodox therapies myself, but it would be beyond my competence as a social anthropologist to pronounce on the clinical effects of treatments (as opposed to patients' perceptions of these effects, on which I shall have plenty to say).

DEFINING THE FIELD: WHAT CONSTITUTES COMPLEMENTARY MEDICINE?

The expansion of complementary medicine is best seen as one aspect of a much wider movement, a general increase in health options. People who are ill – especially those who have long-term health problems – may draw on all kinds of resources besides those provided by the NHS. The informal advice of friends and kin, the professional services of all kinds of healers and counsellors, the instruction of teachers of yoga, meditation or relaxation techniques, information transmitted through the media, goods sold on the market such as ionisers and dietary supplements – all these may be used in the search for relief from disease and distress, and the range of possibilities continues to increase. This is the context in which the contemporary growth of complementary medicine has taken place. However, in this book I am primarily interested in those forms of therapy which most nearly approximate to a form of medicine as that term is generally understood in western societies. This could be characterised as ideally including:

a) claims to be curative. That is, the therapy claims to do more than simply encourage well-being in a general sort of way, to improve energy levels or promote harmonious living; it claims to be able to cure actual illnesses;
b) some body of knowledge or theory (more or less systematised) about the human person which includes ideas about the causes of illness and health;
c) some kind of technical intervention on the part of an expert practitioner. This might include the administration of substances (as in homoeopathy, orthodox medicine, herbalism), manual techniques (as in osteopathy, chiropractic, reflexology) or mental techniques, whether these involve the consciousness of the patient (hypnotherapy) or the healer (spiritual healing of certain kinds).

Considered as a strict definition, this characterisation is only partially satisfactory, for 'medical' practices can never be sharply distinguished from the 'non-medical' practices in reality. It leaves some therapies or techniques which are often included within the term 'alternative medicine' in popular compendia and scholarly literature in a definitional limbo. Alexander Technique, for instance, does not purport to cure specific diseases, rather to re-educate people into using their bodies more efficiently. Yet many people resort to it because they have heard that it is very useful for those who suffer from back pain, and it does involve a 'technical intervention' of sorts since the teacher uses touch as a means of monitoring muscular tension, and slight manipulations of the body to convey these more economical uses of the body to the pupil. Spiritual healing is also only dubiously a form of complementary 'medicine'. Certainly it is used to cure illness and also involves interventions of various kinds (laying on of hands, prayer, even possession) but some spiritual healers whom I met did not appear to have any highly systematised theory about the body or the way it behaves when they heal a person, and the issue of whether spiritual healers can or should diagnose remains contentious.

In reality there is no impermeable boundary between practices which conform to my model of what a system of medicine looks like and other health-promoting activities. Although I have interested myself primarily in practices at the 'medical' end of this spectrum, the data presented in Chapter 3 will show that it is not possible to discuss the way in which people use complementary medicine without also discussing their exposure to health information provided by the media or their experiments with new kinds of diet, since these are part of the context in which they decide to try out non-orthodox medicine. I do not claim any universal applicability for this model and have used it purely as a focus for research in a particular society, a means of setting limits to a discussion which might otherwise be too diffuse to be productive.

THE VEXED QUESTION OF TERMINOLOGY

I have applied the term 'orthodox' medicine to the kind of medicine practised under the NHS, simply in order to reflect the political reality of its recognition by the state, not in deference to its hegemonic claims. Medical anthropologists and sociologists sometimes use the term 'biomedicine', 'cosmopolitan medicine' or simply 'modern medicine', especially when describing less developed countries where this form of medicine co-exists with other traditional or indigenous forms of healing. Homoeopaths call it 'allopathic' medicine to stress the difference in principle between the two systems; homoeopaths treat an illness with a highly dilute form of some substance which is held to produce similar symptoms to those which the patient manifests, whilst allopathy counters disease with substances which are held to have the opposite effect (e.g. inflammatory disease is treated with anti-inflammatory drugs). Homoeopathy and allopathy, in their extreme forms at least, provide genuinely alternative systems, mutually incompatible views of the human body and the ways in which it can be cured of illness.

I do not know who coined the term 'alternative' medicine but it is consistent with the use of the word 'alternative' to refer to aspects of culture or life style which are regarded as unconventional, less materialistic, more questioning, non-hierarchical, in harmony with nature. As we shall see in a later chapter, some people who use or practise non-orthodox medicine could be said to have espoused an 'alternative' culture to a greater or lesser degree but many are, as one interviewee put it, 'short back and sides types', not notably unconventional in their cultural tastes or political outlook. Nor is it the case that users of non-orthodox therapies necessarily resort to them exclusively, in preference to orthodox medicine. The theory of homoeopathy may provide an alternative view of the human body and the way it works to that of allopathy, but this does not prevent some people from using both, according to their perceptions of their own needs.

Some practitioners nonetheless prefer to describe what they do as 'alternative medicine', conveying as it does the idea of a parallel but independent system. More prefer 'complementary medicine', implying as it does the possibility of co-operation with orthodox medicine. I like the term 'complementary' better, on the grounds that it is a more general reflection of patients' actual behaviour and practitioners' views. Even less prescriptive are the terms 'orthodox' and 'non-orthodox' medicine. In the service of sociological analysis these have the advantage of reflecting the real difference in power base between the two systems while being less politically charged in terms of current disputes in the ranks of the practitioners.

The terms 'orthodox' and 'non-orthodox' medicine also have the merit of not implying anything in particular about the content of the systems of medicine to which they refer. It could, of course, be argued that this is not an advantage at all, that non-orthodox medicine enjoys popularity today precisely because the systems it comprises are substantively different from orthodox medicine. The word 'non-orthodox' is a negative one and implies only deviation from some kind of official norm; is it defensible to define these systems purely in relation to the form of medicine recognised by the state?

The problem is that the systems which I have termed non-orthodox are very various in respect of their understandings of the way the body works, their aetiologies and nosologies, not to speak of the techniques they employ. Some involve direct manipulation of the patient's body (like chiropractic), some do not even require the patient to be present (such as radionics). Some administer substances, others use mental techniques. Some are western in origin, others originate in oriental cultures. As I shall report in a later chapter, many of the practitioners I spoke to did have convergent views about the need for therapies which mobilise the body's own 'natural' healing resources, about patient reponsibility and about the nature of the therapeutic relationship. How far these common features should be regarded as among the original causes of their marginal political status (the state not conferring authority upon systems of medicine in which control and subordination of the patient were not integral to clinical practice) or how far they are a latter-day result of their marginal position (non-orthodox practitioners tending to emphasise what distinguishes them from orthodox therapeutic practice in order to secure a market for their services) I find very difficult to decide.

Many claim to be holistic, i.e. to treat the whole person, and this term is sometimes treated as synonymous with non-orthodox medicine (Stalker and Glymour 1989), especially in America. The practices of most of the practitioners whom I interviewed, as they described them to me, would seem to merit this adjective. But many orthodox practitioners also claim to use a holistic approach, and so this term has too wide a reference to distinguish orthodox medicine from non-orthodox medicine. The term 'natural' is also problematic, although one sees much reference to 'natural' therapies and 'natural' medicines. It seems to me that there is nothing inherently more natural about sticking needles into a person's body (like acupuncturists) than administering steroid drugs or transplanting organs (like orthodox doctors). Many non-orthodox therapies, as they are practised in Britain at least, claim that their techniques simply mobilise the body's natural capacity to heal itself, to defend itself against illness. But from this point of view vaccination (which some therapists see as eminently *un*natural) could be regarded as a mobilisation of the natural process by which the body protects itself from disease. What is 'natural', as Ros Coward has suggested, lies in the eye of the beholder and the term is open to considerable manipulation (Coward 1989: 15ff). Having considered the question of terminology carefully, I decided to use 'complementary' medicine and 'non-orthodox' medicine more or less interchangeably as the least contentious and the least prescriptive terms, using others where I wish to widen the field of reference.

This book would have been much easier to write if it were the case that non-orthodox medicines did have common assumptions and practices, or could be characterised collectively in some economical way. I shall not describe the individual systems in any more detail than is necessary to clarify a point or explain particular data (a glossary of therapies is provided at the end of the text), since there are several excellent books which provide accounts of the history and basic principles of the therapies and their characteristic techniques. Stephen Fulder's *Handbook of Complementary Medicine* (1988), *The Alternative Health Guide* by Brian Inglis and Ruth West (1983), and *Alternative Medicine* by A. Stanway (1986) are particularly recommended, and Roger Cooter's edited volume *Studies in the History of Alternative Medicine* (1988) contains some useful historical accounts.

The material in this book is presented in two main sections, one dealing with the people who use non-orthodox medicine and the ways in which they use it, and the second dealing with its practitioners. Each section is organised along similar lines and begins with a general overview of research in the area, drawing mainly on survey data. This is followed by a consideration of sociological and social anthropological concepts which I have found relevant to the analysis of non-orthodox medicine. Then I present data based on my own empirical research in Midland localities before discussing particular issues which I believe to be important (patients' satisfaction, the politics of complementary medicine). In my conclusion I relate the research data presented in earlier chapters to the political issues which are currently under discussion.

I should point out that this book was written between October 1989 and August 1990. The complementary medical professions are developing very rapidly and whilst I have been careful to report matters as accurately as I could, it is possible that there may have been further developments, even changes in government policy, between the time of writing and the actual publication of this book. It is unfortunate that most of the manuscript was completed before the Bagenal report on the Bristol Cancer Help Centre was published in September 1990. There is therefore very little reference to this major controversy and its impact on public debates about complementary medicine.

I hope, however, that what I have written will be of interest both to social scientists and to those with either a professional or personal interest in health issues (which should of course include us all).

Part I
Using complementary medicine

1 Who uses complementary medicine?

In this chapter I shall discuss what is known about the usage of complementary medicine at the broad statistical level. The past few years have seen a spate of publications and pronouncements on non-orthodox medicine on the part of orthodox practitioners and medical scientists (BMA 1986, Watt and Wood 1988, Stalker and Glymour 1989). Major medical periodicals like the *British Medical Journal* and the *Lancet* have even devoted editorials to the subject. Whilst some of this comment suggests a disposition of curiosity, even appreciation, most ranges from the critical to the bitterly hostile. One senses a degree of professional panic, a fear that 'scientific' medicine may lose its patients to therapies which are regarded as being based on the flimsiest of intellectual foundations.

Is complementary medicine a mass movement, or merely the prerogative of those members of the articulate and informed middle class who can afford private medicine? Is it a national phenomenon or confined as yet to the wealthy south, the trend-setting metropolis? Which demographic groups use it most, and for what kinds of illness?

In the past ten years a number of national surveys and opinion polls have been carried out which have attempted to gauge the extent to which non-orthodox medicine is used. Irritatingly, these surveys have asked different questions about different lists of therapies, with the result that comparisons between consecutive studies are not straightforward, and the rate of increase is not easy to judge.

There are two ways to estimate the level of usage. Either we can calculate it in terms of consultations with practitioners or in terms of persons making consultations. Most courses of treatment with a complementary practitioner involve at least four or five consultations, and, as we shall see in Chapter 3, people who have used complementary medicine for one health problem are quite likely to consult for other problems subsequently. Counting the number of consultations would give us a better picture of changes in the level of demand for non-orthodox practitioners' services as reflected in the amount of money spent on such services, but counting the number of people who use it would give a better idea of how this demand is distributed.

Stephen Fulder and Robin Munro carried out a survey of non-orthodox therapists for the Threshold Foundation in 1980–1, using a sample drawn from seven districts in England and Wales. Practitioners were asked to specify the number of patients they treated per week, and on the basis of these figures, the researchers calculated the number of consultations for the UK to be between 11.7 and 15.4 million per year. This range represents between 6.5 per cent and 8.6 per cent of the number of consultations with GPs per year. From this they extrapolate that the number of people using non-orthodox medicine in a year may be as high as two million, i.e. around 3.7 per cent of the total population (Fulder and Munro 1982: 28). A study of practitioners carried out for the Institute of Complementary Medicine in 1984 came up with the more conservative estimate of 4.6 million consultations per year involving around one million people (Davies 1984: 18). The gap between these two very different estimates may be in part due to the fact that Fulder and Munro considered non-orthodox practitioners of all kinds, whereas Davies drew his sample only from those listed in ten professional registers covering six main therapies. Fulder and Munro also based their calculations on an assumption of an average of 9.7 consultations per course of treatment while Davies seems to have assumed a slightly lower average.

Do studies based on surveys of users produce any more consistent results? An opinion poll carried out by Research Surveys of Great Britain for Swan House Special Events in 1984 found that as many as 30 per cent of a representative sample of 2023 adults had used one or more of a range of non-orthodox therapies. In 1985 the consumer magazine *Which* polled its readers about their use of non-orthodox medicine and found that one in seven of the readers who responded had visited a complementary therapist during the past year (*Which*, October 1986). Whilst this cannot be regarded as a representative sample, it should be remembered that *Which* deals with many other issues besides health; there is no reason to assume that its readers would have more health problems or more hypochondriasis than the readers of any other magazine, though they might well be unrepresentative in other respects.

Various other opinion polls have been commissioned by different organisations, the most recent survey at the time of writing this book being one carried out in 1989 by Market and Opinion Research Information for *The Times* newspaper. Of a sample of 1826 adults in various parts of Britain, 27 per cent said that they had used non-orthodox medicine at one time or another. Unfortunately respondents were asked about only six specific forms of therapy which did not include herbalism (one of the more popular therapies according to the evidence of other surveys) let alone the less established therapies like reflexology or radionics, so 27 per cent is probably a conservative figure based on narrow questioning.

It is unfortunate that researchers studying users have not used more uniform methods, rendering reliable comparisons difficult and preventing the firmer identification of trends. If we are really interested in measuring the growth of complementary medicine it might be easier to do this by tracking changes in the numbers of practitioners, although this does not dispose of the problem of different definitions of what counts as complementary medicine. Fulder calculates that the increase in the number of practitioners during the period 1978–81 has been six times that of the growth in numbers of GPs. No therapy had declined and some, such as acupuncture, had doubled their numbers in this short time (Fulder 1988: 44). This suggests a large increase in consultations, even allowing for the possibility that new practitioners sometimes take patients away from existing ones and not all practitioners are equally busy. Davies asked individual practitioners to estimate the rate at which their numbers of patients had increased or decreased during the period 1982–3, and found a perceived increase of 15 per cent, although there was some variation as between different therapies (Davies 1984: 18).

All these estimates of the national level of usage conceal considerable regional differences. Both the RSBG poll of 1984 and the MORI poll of 1989 suggest a lower rate of use for Scotland and the north of England than for the rest of Britain. Does the greater popularity of complementary medicine in the south of England simply reflect the greater number of people who practise it there (see Chapter 5) and the greater number of training schools in the south? Or does it reflect a higher level of healthcare and training facilities in general? The latter explanation seems unlikely. Fulder points out that studies in both America and the UK have put paid to the notion that alternative practitioners flourish in medically under-served areas, citing material to show that the reverse is true where certain therapies are concerned and that where conventional medicine increases its coverage, complementary medicine follows suit (Fulder 1988: 30).

On the whole, the evidence from patients' own stories (see Chapter 4) suggests that use of non-orthodox medicine tends to be supply-led, to the extent that users resort to it because people they know and who live near them have already done so. Consultations generate more consultations, and so non-orthodox medicine is likely to grow faster in those areas where there are already many established practices. Yet the MORI poll shows that the variations in interest and approval are much narrower than the variations in usage. Given the uneven availability of complementary therapies (see Chapter 5), perhaps there are areas of unsatisfied demand in Scotland and the North?

Aggregated statistics such as those I have cited also conceal variations in usage between different therapies. Yet when we disaggregate the figures the information seems contradictory; I have listed the most popular therapies given in three major polls in Table 1, and although much the same group of therapies appears in each list, there is little consistency as to rank order. Here again there are problems of methodology. The RSBG poll seems to have used the term 'herbal medicine' to include the use of herbal medicines available over the counter as well as actual consultations with a professional herbalist, whilst the MORI poll did not ask about herbalism at all. People who say that they have used homoeopathy may equally be referring to the use of commercially available remedies rather than consultations with a homoeopath. The most we can say is that at the present time the most popular therapies certainly include osteopathy, acupuncture, homoeopathy, herbalism and chiropractic, with hypnotherapy and spiritual healing of different kinds (only dubiously a form of medicine as I defined the term in the Introduction, but included by many researchers) also to the fore. But there is no reason to assume that this 'league table' will not change in future. Reflexology and aromatherapy seem to be growing rapidly in popularity and in terms of the numbers of practitioners being trained, and therapies like radionics and dowsing, though not new, have a higher public profile and are evidently taken more seriously by the public than was the case but a short time ago. Systems of medicine such as Ayurveda and Unani Tibb, which at present are used mainly by people of South Asian origin in this country (see Aslam 1979), are likely to extend their popularity beyond areas of Asian settlement in the future. Also the influence of systems such as anthroposophical medicine and naturopathy may well be greater than might be suggested by the number of people who actually profess to use or practise them.

Table 1 Usage of different kinds of complementary medicine (as measured in three national surveys) showing relative popularity

RSGB 1984		Which 1986		MORI 1989	
Herbal medicine	12%	Osteopathy	42%	Homoeopathy	11%
Osteopathy	6%	Homoeopathy	20%	Osteopathy	10%
Homoeopathy	4%	Acupuncture	23%	Faith healing	5%
Acupuncture	3%	Chiropractic	22%	Acupuncture	4%
Chiropractic	2%	Herbalism	11%	Chiropractic	4%
Spiritual healing	2%			Hypnosis	3%
Hypnotherapy	2%				
(100% = representative sample of 2023)		(100% = random sample of 1942 from unspecified number of readers who claimed to have used complementary medicine)		(100% = representative quota sample of 1826 adults)	

All the evidence indicates that even if we cannot come up with a firm national statistic to express the present level of usage we can confidently agree with Fulder that non-orthodox medicine represents a 'significant second system, apart from conventional medicine' (Fulder 1988: 29). Almost certainly the number of people who are interested in complementary medicine or evince some degree of approval for it, indicates a corona of appreciation and approval beyond the core of those who actually use it. The MORI survey of 1989 asked people which forms of non-orthodox medicine they would seriously consider using; only 23 per cent said they would not consider using *any* of the therapies specified. As well as a substantial and almost certainly growing minority of people who have actually used non-orthodox medicine there is a larger number who are well disposed towards it and might well use it in future.

The popularity of non-orthodox medicine in Britain is not an isolated phenomenon, but appears to be consistent with what is known about other European countries. In Table 2 I have reproduced a very helpful summary of data on usage of non-orthodox medicine in nine European countries, collated by Guy Sermeus for the Belgian Consumers' Association in 1987 (Sermeus 1987). Sermeus has made the useful distinction between the (estimated) proportion of the population who have ever used non-orthodox medicine and those who have used it in a specific twelve-month period (obviously all the studies do not refer to the same twelve months, but the bulk of the data he cites was published since 1979). He is wisely cautious about the significance which can be attached to these figures; his summary is in the nature of an 'overall interpretation'. If different research designs and various definitions of what constitutes non-orthodox medicine complicate attempts to identify trends within the same country, how much more must they bedevil international comparisons. The estimated figures for Switzerland, for instance, look very different if we include statistics for the use of chiropractic, which is offered to patients under the Swiss state health service and is scarcely regarded as non-orthodox in that country, although it is so regarded elsewhere. Iridology has been treated as a separate therapy in some countries; in Britain it is widely practiced by herbalists and others as a diagnostic aid, but not all of the practitioners who use it describe themselves primarily as iridologists and would not therefore be known as iridologists to their patients.

An interesting aspect of Sermeus's estimates is that the differences in the rates of usage are not obviously related to differences in the legal situation of non-orthodox medicine. In Belgium, for instance, the practice of what I have termed non-orthodox medicine is not legally permitted to those who are not also qualified in orthodox medicine, even though training in non-orthodox therapies is not provided in schools of medicine. Yet the level of interest in non-orthodox medicine reported for Belgium is higher than that

Table 2 The extent of the use of complementary medicine in nine European countries, and most frequently occurring forms

	Proportion of population having used alternative medicine (approximate ranges are author's interpretation using data available)		Most frequently occurring forms of alternative medicine (in decreasing order of frequency)
	'ever used'	'twelve-month period'	
Belgium	/	24%	1. homoeopathy
			2. manual healing
	(66–75%)	T	3. acupuncture
			4. chiropractic
			5. osteopathy
			6. naturopathy
			7. herbal remedies
			8. paranormal healing
			9. hypnotherapy
			10. anthroposophical medicine
France	49%	/	1. homoeopathy
		(16%)	2. acupuncture
			3. herbal remedies
			4. water cures
			5. chiropractic
			6. thalassotherapy
			7. osteopathy
			8. iridology
Netherlands	18%	6–7%	1. homoeopathy
		T	2. herbal remedies
			3. manual therapies (chiropractic + osteopathy + manipulation)
			4. paranormal healing
			5. acupuncture
			6. diet therapy
			7. naturopathy
			8. anthroposophical medicine
Great Britain	26–30%	8–10%	1. herbal remedies
		T	2. osteopathy
			3. homoeopathy
			4. acupuncture
			5. chiropractic
			6. healing
			7. hypnotherapy
			8. reflexology
			9. naturopathy
			10. aromatherapy

West Germany	20–30%	5–12% T	1. homoeopathy 2. acupuncture 3. procaine injection therapy 4. chiropractic 5. ozone and oxygen therapy 6. herbal remedies 7. humoral pathology 8. psychotherapy 9. massage 10. cell therapy
Switzerland	13–27% (1) 15–40% (2)	2.8% (1)(4) 3–4% (2)(4) 6–8% T	1. homoeopathy 2. manipulation techniques 3. acupuncture 4. herbal remedies 5. reflexology 6. dowsing 7. sophrology + hypnotherapy + psychotherapy 8. anthroposophical medicine 9. massage
Denmark	20% (3) 25–35% (2)	8–11% (2) T	1. chiropractic 2. acupuncture 3. hypnotherapy 4. massage 5. iridology 6. zone therapy 7. sound therapy
Finland	40–60%	15–20% T	1. herbal remedies 2. massages 3. chiropractic + naprapathy + bone setting 4. acupuncture 5. homoeopathy 6. cupping 7. faith healing 8. anthroposophical medicine
Italy	/	/	1. homoeopathy 2. acupuncture 3. herbal remedies 4. prana therapy 5. chiropractic

(1): not including consultations with qualified chiropractors
(2): including consultations with qualified chiropractors
(3): probably only part of this figure includes chiropractic treatment
(4): excluding qualified MDs
(T): Use of alternative medicine involving the intervention of a practitioner

Reproduced from Sermeus (1987) by kind permission of the author cited for Britain where the legal provision for the practice of non-orthodox medicine is more liberal.

Data is available on the use of complementary medicine in the United States of America and in Australia but not, so far as I am aware, in the form of national rates of usage. (In the case of the United States such statistics would not be very meaningful even if they existed, since the provision and legal situation of non-orthodox medicine varies so much within the Union.) However, we can safely say that medical pluralism is a feature of most industrialised countries just as it is of most non-industrialised countries, where traditional systems of medicine and healing flourish alongside modern biomedicine, though it raises different policy issues and has different antecedents.

WHAT KIND OF PEOPLE USE COMPLEMENTARY MEDICINE?

Stereotypes abound as regards the 'typical' user of non-orthodox medicine. The widespread use of the term 'alternative' medicine suggests an affinity with alternative culture, itself a loose term but generally carrying associations of minority or unconventional taste and life style. Terms like 'fringe' medicine or 'marginal' medicine (see Wallis and Morley 1976) also suggest cultural marginality. Complementary medicine is variously seen as an indulgence of the well-to-do middle classes or (chiefly in America) as the irrational resort of the uneducated, rustics or ethnics who are not 'completely socialized into the middle-class models of physician utilization' (Kronenfeld and Wasner 1982: 119).

Like most stereotypes such conceptions are not without some foundation in reality. But it is clear from survey data that there is no single 'type' of person who uses non-orthodox medicine: patients represent a wide spectrum of people. Fulder asserts, on the basis of his own research, that patients come from all social classes. However, in the UK there are slightly more patients from socio-economic grades A and B (professional, managerial, technical, business, academic, etc.) than the others (Fulder 1988: 31).

The poll carried out by RSGB in 1984 found that people from the lower social classes were substantially more likely never to have used any of the complementary therapies or remedies mentioned in the questionnaire (76 per cent of respondents from social classes C2, D and E as opposed to 60 per cent of respondents from social classes A, B and C1). The more recent MORI poll did not categorise respondents by class, but if we scan the data for indicators of socio-economic status we find that the differences in usage are not startling. The unemployed were as likely to have used one of the six therapies mentioned in the poll at some time or other as those in full-time employment (22 per cent in either case). People who claimed to vote Labour were least likely to have used any one of the six therapies (20 per cent) but their score was nearer to that of Conservative voters (22 per cent) than to those found among supporters of the SDP and SLD (28 per cent and 30 per cent respectively). Telephone ownership and home ownership status seem to be better discriminators, but even here the differences are not great. However, when we look at the responses to a question about which therapies the respondent would 'seriously consider' using, then the differences in response by these variables are even narrower. This suggests that if people who do not own telephones, who rent council houses, vote Labour, etc. are inhibited from using complementary medicine it is because they cannot afford it or because it is not easily available where they live rather than due to class-based attitudes to healthcare.

This kind of data is consistent with that of researchers in other countries. An Australian study of new patients of non-orthodox practitioners carried out in 1977 found a bias in favour of the higher socio-economic groups in the survey sample, but this was not very great (20 per cent of 13,818 adult users were from the professional and managerial class, compared to 18 per cent of the Australian population as a whole (Boven *et al.*1977: 305). The study carried out by the Netherlands Institute of Preventive Medicine and the Technical Industrial Organisation in Holland compared users of non-orthodox medicine with users of orthodox consultants and found that a slightly higher percentage of the former belonged to the top status groups (14 per cent compared with 10 per cent) (Ooijendijk, Mackenbach and Limberger 1981: 11). In Table 3 I have reproduced Sermeus's summary of the findings of European studies about the kind of patients who visit non-orthodox practitioners and this also suggests that the bias in favour of the better paid and the better educated is fairly general in Europe. Sermeus's data also remind us that aggregating information about all types of non-orthodox medicine may conceal differences between particular therapies. In some countries faith healing is more commonly used by the poor (especially when it is offered free of charge) and traditional 'folk' therapies may be more popular among the uneducated. However, in Britain, no very pronounced trends of this kind can be identified on the basis of recent studies.

Most national surveys, both in Britain and in other European countries, indicate a slightly greater number of women among users of non-orthodox medicine than men (the only exception I could find being the patients of hakims who were predominantly male: Aslam 1979: 73). In the RSGB poll of 1984, 73 per cent of the men in the sample had tried none of the therapies mentioned in the questionnaire, while the figure for women was only 67 per cent. In the more recent MORI poll, 71 per cent of the men and 67 per cent of the women claimed never to have used any of a more restricted list of therapies. Complementary practitioners have sometimes suggested to me that

Table 3 Profiles of complementary medicine users in nine western European countries

	Sex	Age	Educational attainment, (occupation or socio-economic class)
1. Belgium	rel. *more*: females; *esp.* for homoeopathy, manipulation techniques, paranormal healing and acupuncture	rel. *more*: 35–55 yrs, rel. *less*: over 65s and under 18s	rel. *more*: higher level of educ. * *exception*: paranormal healing: lower educ. level rel. *more*: higher incomes rel. *more*: higher socio-economic groups * *exception*: paranormal healing: lower socio-economic groups
2. France	rel. *more*: females	rel. *more*: 25–65 yrs *esp.* 40–65 yrs rel. *less*: over 65s and under 18s *esp.* acupuncture: hardly used at all by children and adolescents	rel. *more*: senior & middle management, professions and self-employed with larger businesses rel. *less*: agricultural and horticultural workers rel. *more*: higher education
3. Netherlands	rel. *more*: females	rel. *more*: 30–60 yrs, *esp.* 35–50 yrs rel. *less*: under 30s and over 60s	rel. *more*: higher educ. level * *exception*: herbal remedies and paranormal healing: lower educ. level
4. Great Britain	rel. *more*: females *esp.* herbalism and homoeopathy * *exception*: massage & osteopathy used rel. *more* by males	rel. *more*: 21–65 yrs, *esp.* 35–60 yrs rel. *less*: under 21s *esp.* acupuncture, herbalism & osteopathy	rel. *more*: higher and middle socio-economic groups

5. West Germany	rel. *more*: females	rel. *more*: 18–65 yrs *esp.* 40–45 yrs rel. *less*: under 15s	rel. *more*: higher educ. level rel. *more*: higher income groups rel. *more*: higher occupational groups
6. Switzerland	very few and statistically insignificant differences between sexes *trend towards*: more males in Italian- and French-speaking parts; more females in German-speaking part *preventative use* of alternative medicine: more females	very few and statistically insignificant differences evenly distributed throughout all age groups	few and statistically insignificant differences evenly distributed throughout all socio-economic groups *trend*: rel. *less*: with degree-level qualifications and those of working age but not in the job market
7. Denmark	rel. *more*: females * *exception*: chiropractic used more by males than females	rel. *more*: 30–60 yrs	rel. *more*: middle socio-economic groups *esp.* clerical workers
8. Finland	no very important differences *trend*: more females *esp.* in alternative remedies, acupuncture, traditional massage & bone setters * *exception*: healers consulted more by males than females	rel. *more*: 45–65 yrs *trend*: users of traditional Finnish folk cures are possibly slightly older than users of non-traditional methods	no indications *trends*: lower educ. level and lower income groups for alternative remedies, massage (females), cupping & healing higher educ. level: acupuncture, massage (males)
9. Italy	rel. *more*: females	rel. *more*: 25–50 yrs	*trend*: rel. lower socio-economic groups for prana therapy

Reproduced from Sermeus (1987) by kind permission of the author women are more open-minded where healthcare is concerned, or more receptive to holistic forms of treatment. But women also consult orthodox doctors more frequently than men, a fact for which medical sociologists have found no simple explanation. Women display greater morbidity than men, but live longer. Is this because men are exposed at work to the kinds of hazards which lead to injuries, acute conditions and sudden death, whilst women's social role typically exposes them to the risk of chronic problems, depression in particular (Morgan, Calnan and Manning 1985: 235, Stacey 1988: 140)? The tendency to greater medical supervision of women's reproductive (and contraceptive) activities may go some way to explain the fact that women consult orthodox practitioners more often than men.

To the extent that women are more likely to experience certain chronic conditions than men, and to the extent that it is chronic rather than acute conditions which users present to non-orthodox therapists then we might expect the gender differences with respect to complementary medicine to be even greater than they are. On the other hand, most non-orthodox medicine is private medicine for which insurance cover is still difficult to obtain. If women have access to fewer economic resources (because they tend to be paid less than men and because they often have differential access to or control over household income), then we might expect them to consult non-orthodox practitioners less often than men. Without more information it is not easy to explain the differences in usage between men and women, but gender is a theme to which I shall have reason to return later.

With respect to age, few users of non-orthodox practitioners in Britain appear to be drawn from among the very old or the very young (Fulder 1988: 31) and similar results have been found in other countries (Ooijendijk, Mackenbach and Limberger 1981: 10, Boven *et al.* 1977: 303. See also Table 3). This may be because, as Fulder suggests, old people have fewer resources to pay for private medicine while the very young are less likely to suffer from the kind of illnesses which are commonly taken to complementary practitioners (Fulder 1988: 31). Most of the practitioners whom I interviewed in my local research thought that their particular form of medicine could be used to treat children, indeed several suggested that children were easier to treat because they had fewer inappropriate preconceptions about what medical treatment ought to consist of. Possibly non-orthodox medicine is perceived by parents as less suitable for children, or – to the extent that use of non-orthodox medicine still is seen as experimental or risky – parents are more prepared to experiment or take risks with treatments for themselves than for their children.

There is very little information about the use of complementary medicine by different ethnic groups. Only one survey (to my knowledge) even included a question on race or ethnicity; the MORI poll of 1989 indicated that 29 per cent of the black respondents in the sample reported that they had used one or more of the six specific therapies mentioned in the questionnaire, compared with 31 per cent of the whites. Blacks were more likely to have used acupuncture, homoeopathy or spiritual healing than chiropractic or osteopathy. However, this poll, like others which have used similar methods, failed to include Unani Tibb or Ayurveda among the list of therapies featured in the questionnaire. American studies more routinely feature questions about ethnicity and some do suggest differential rates of usage for certain therapies; e.g. Avina and Schneiderman's study conducted in the San Francisco Bay area indicates over-representation of whites among users of homoeopathy (Avina and Schneiderman 1978: 367).

We cannot assume that the findings of American studies would necessarily apply to this country, but we should be alert to the possibility that members of different ethnic groups have different access to or different attitudes to non-orthodox medicine. Where black people live in depressed inner city zones, they may have fewer resources to pay for private medicine of any kind. Where they have resources and where they are also immigrants, their practice in this country may be shaped in part by experiences in their countries of origin (homoeopathy and Ayurveda are popular in many parts of India, Unani Tibb in Pakistan, acupuncture in most parts of the world where ethnic Chinese have settled). Certainly some groups are known to have a range of folk or home remedies at their disposal which might be considered non-orthodox in the sense that they are not part of the pharmacopoeia recognised by orthodox medicine, though these do not generally require the advice or intervention of a professional practitioner (Donovan 1986: 191).

A hypothesis which has informed some research has been the possibility that users of complementary medicine differ from non-users with respect to psychological traits. Parker and Tupling, in their study of Australian chiropractic patients, conclude that their sample could not be distinguished from the general population in terms of social class, ethnic group or neuroticism. However, they did find a higher level of 'psychological disturbance', which the authors relate to the fact that most of these patients were suffering from painful conditions such as might be expected to generate distress. At a follow-up interview, ten weeks after the initial treatment, the level of psychological disturbance was found to be near to that characteristic of the general population, physical distress having been 'considerably reduced' during the period of treatment (Parker and Tupling 1976: 375). Furnham and Smith (1988) studied homoeopathic patients in a British small town, and found a level of minor psychiatric morbidity significantly higher than the norm, but they too conclude that the patients' long careers of physical illness might account for this degree of disturbance. As we shall see in the next section, people who use complementary medicine tend to suffer from the kind of chronic condition which may well be pathogenic in psychological terms, and a substantial group consult a complementary practitioner with the express purpose of resolving a psychological problem. Those who are antagonistic to non-orthodox medicine would no doubt like to see evidence that users are neurotic hypochondriacs, and those who support it would no doubt be gratified if it could be shown that users are as balanced and sane as everyone else. But given the problems of disentangling the mental and physical manifestations of many kinds of chronic distress, this particular line of enquiry is probably not very fruitful.

WHY DO PEOPLE USE COMPLEMENTARY MEDICINE?

In one sense this question is as easy to answer as the question 'why do people seek the services of plumbers or accountants?' They engage the services of plumbers in order to repair their household water systems and they engage accountants to do their accounts. Similarly they consult non-orthodox practitioners because they are ill and want to be cured of their illnesses. But the question 'why do people use non-orthodox medicine?' generally implies the unspoken subordinate clause 'when they could use the services of an orthodox doctor for nothing'. The question of whether people turn to non-orthodox medicine out of dissatisfaction with orthodox medicine is an important one, which I shall discuss in Chapter 3.

For the present I will deal with the question of patient motivation only in its naive sense; for what kinds of illness do people consult a non-orthodox practitioner? A very cursory glance at the evidence shows quite clearly that it is chiefly for conditions which can be described as chronic rather than acute, disruptive of normal life rather than life-threatening. Fulder suggests that we should expect people to use non-orthodox medicine for problems which orthodox medicine currently finds it difficult to cure, such as musculo-skeletal disorders, chronic pain, allergic conditions, stress-related and psychosomatic problems, etc. This is certainly borne out by available research data.

A study of sixty-five patients using a centre for complementary medicine in Southampton shows that 'pain' and 'allergies' were the two largest categories of presenting problem, although each of these comprised a variety of specific complaints (Moore, Phipps and Marcer 1985: 28). A poll of readers of the consumer magazine *Which* carried out in 1985 showed that the most common problem taken to non-orthodox practitioners was 'pain or a joint problem' (71 per cent of those who claimed to have used non-orthodox medicine), the next most common category being 'some sort of psychological problem' (15 per cent) (*Which* 1986: 443).

Problems of comparability bedevil any attempt to summarise the findings of different studies on this point. Most research uses patients' own descriptions of their presenting symptoms, which may or may not coincide with the nosological categories used by practitioners. Non-orthodox therapies may differ from each other in the way they classify symptoms or diseases quite as markedly as any of them differ from orthodox medicine. Practitioners of some systems may be unwilling to categorise patients by their symptoms at all, as they claim to 'treat people, not diseases' or 'not... the symptoms but the patients' (Davies 1984: 29).

What comes across very clearly is that in Britain the largest single group of problems taken to non-orthodox practitioners are disorders of the musculo-skeletal system, especially back pain. What is much less clear is whether this is a product of the specific pattern of non-orthodox healthcare provision in this country (osteopathy and chiropractic, commonly perceived as being specially competent in the cure of musculo-skeletal problems, are among the most widespread therapies) or of specific patterns of morbidity (there are a lot of bad backs around and some of them are bound to be taken to complementary practitioners).

Attempts to relate therapies to presenting problems suggest that patients are influenced by their perceptions of which kind of medicine can best treat a particular complaint. Fulder has summarised data from an Australian study which shows that musculo-skeletal problems feature strongly in the list of illnesses taken to each of three different kinds of practitioner. Chiropractic, however, attracted more cases of musculo-skeletal disorder while psychological problems were more likely to be taken to an acupuncturist (Fulder 1988: 34). Aslam found that hakims in Britain are consulted most often for the psycho-sexual problems of men and for digestive disorders (Aslam 1979: 73). Practitioners who advertise quite often specify disorders in which they specialise, as is evident from the pages of a journal such as *Here's Health*, but many of the practitioners whom I interviewed in my local study complained that the public were not fully aware of the range of diseases their particular therapy could treat. A hypnotherapist expressed disappointment that most of the people who came to see him came simply because they wanted to stop smoking; he felt that hypnotherapy could deal with many other behavioural and medical conditions, but this was not sufficiently widely known. Similarly an osteopath lamented the number of bad backs he saw – osteopathy could deal with such problems very successfully, he said, but people did not realise its potential for treating many other kinds of disorder, consequently his case load was not as varied as it might be. Much still depends on popular conceptions of each discipline's special competence.

CONCLUSION

In this chapter I have discussed quantitative data about the level of usage of complementary medicine, the characteristics of the users and what they use it for. Clearly a substantial and almost certainly growing minority of people consult complementary practitioners in Britain and other industrial countries. By the end of this century usage of non-orthodox medicine of some kind may well be a majority experience. The implication of this is that if orthodox medicine retains its status as the form of medicine authorised by the state in most western countries, it will continue to be 'orthodox' in the narrow political sense but may no longer be 'orthodox' in the cultural sense of being the form in which the public at large has the most confidence and regards as the most legitimate.

We should be cautious about making further generalisations when non-orthodox medicine itself is so diverse. Nor do users themselves form a discrete and homogeneous group. However, there is no reason to suppose that they are in any way marginal in cultural or structural terms. If it ever was justifiable to describe complementary medicine as 'fringe' medicine, this is the case no longer and, as I hope to show, the political and social issues which it raises are central ones.

2   Decisions about treatment
Some useful concepts

In the last chapter I discussed those aspects of the usage of non-orthodox medicine which can be quantified, drawing mainly on large-scale surveys conducted by social scientists. But if we want to understand *why* people use non-orthodox medicine, then we must turn from numbers to process. When a person decides to consult a complementary practitioner this cannot be treated as a simple 'one-off' occurrence which can be studied in isolation; it should be understood in the context of antecedent and subsequent events and conditions. What brings a particular individual to consider using non-orthodox medicine in the first place, and on the basis of what information or advice? How does the initial experience of complementary medicine affect subsequent decisions about healthcare? Surveys such as those which I reviewed in the last chapter can tell us a great deal about broad patterns of usage but are not particularly suitable for the study of decision making (which presents notoriously difficult problems for social scientists in general and not just in relation to healthcare decisions).

Fortunately there is a considerable sociological and anthropological literature on 'illness behaviour' or, as many prefer to term it, 'health seeking behaviour', which attends to what happens at the point when someone decides that they are ill. I propose to raid this literature for concepts which will help us to understand the decisions which people make when they begin (or continue) to use non-orthodox medicine and I shall use these concepts when I analyse data from my own study in the next chapter and subsequently.

According to Parsons's classic sociological analysis, the adoption of the sick role involves a remission of some or all of the individual's social reponsibilities, other than the duty to seek appropriate medical help in order to get well (Parsons 1951: 439ff). Although Parsons writes about the (active and conscious?) adoption of the sick role and although he uses the terms 'individual' and 'sick person' quite as often as he uses the term 'patient', his account has often been regarded as emphasising the passivity of the sufferer, implicitly accepting the model of the compliant patient assumed by much orthodox medical practice. The medical use of the term 'patient' certainly suggests *passive* suffering, obedience to what the physician prescribes or advises. Since Parsons wrote there have been a number of studies which have rehabilitated the active sufferer, the patient who makes choices, negotiates decisions with doctors or others, solves problems, accepts or rejects advice or treatment (Stacey 1988: 196,203ff).

If anything, long-term conditions such as those which are commonly taken to complementary practitioners should offer greater scope for patient initiative. The chronically sick person has time to find out about his/her illness, to discover and make decisions about available options, to explore the ways in which the illness can be accommodated in ordinary life. Yet the concepts which have dominated the study of chronic illness seem to be notions such as 'coping', 'strategies', 'management', 'adaptation' (Anderson and Bury 1988). These terms seem to imply the presence of the disease itself as chief actor on the social scene, which the sufferer responds to in some way, attempting variously to dominate, accommodate, accept, etc. This is probably quite a realistic way of representing the processes involved in dealing with chronic illness, yet in my view it is not the literature on chronic illness which yields the most useful concepts for our purpose but the literature on medical systems in developing countries where choices between systems of curative practice are commonplace.

The term *medical pluralism* has been used to describe the situation where the system of medicine which I have called orthodox medicine in the context of modern Britain, but which in the world context is more appropriately termed cosmopolitan medicine or biomedicine, exists alongside other systems of medicine or folk healing. For example, in India biomedicine is available in both the public and the private sector: homoeopathy (of western origin) and (indigenous) Ayurvedic medicine are well represented in the market place and even receive some government support; there is a great variety of other curative practices – both systematised and non-systematised, technical and ritual – which are available to the sick person who can afford them. In a few countries attempts have been made to incorporate the resources or personnel of traditional systems of medicine within the services provided by the state. For instance, in a number of countries efforts have been made to train traditional birth attendants in some of the techniques of western midwifery (Leslie 1980: 192). However, biomedicine commonly enjoys a privileged status vis-à-vis other systems, just as it does in the West, being the form of medicine recognised, funded and given priority by the state. In many post-colonial societies the hospitals and primary healthcare system are inadequate to the needs of the population, but nevertheless the biomedical doctor has access to resources and privileges which are denied to the village herbalist or spiritual healer.

On the other hand, the cultural ascendancy which biomedicine has enjoyed for some time in the West cannot universally be assumed. Acceptance of the assumptions and practices characteristic of biomedicine may be patchy, either because people have been little exposed to them or because they actually conflict with local knowledge and practice. Another difference is that in the post-colonial state, biomedicine is frequently perceived as essentially western medicine, having its roots in an exogenous culture imposed from without, in contrast to indigenous or at any rate long-established forms of medicine, which may be dismissed by the élite as unsystematised superstition but have considerable local support. In many western societies, it could be argued, the reverse is true since orthodox biomedicine is but one manifestation of an indigenous tradition of scientific knowledge and enquiry. It is often (though not invariably) the non-orthodox forms of medicine, like acupuncture and reflexology, which are of exogenous origin or recent introduction.

But both kinds of pluralism invite the sick person to evaluate different, even diametrically opposed, systems of curative practice and to make choices among them. There is not space here to review the considerable anthropological literature on the question of how such choices are made except to note that the process is usually complex, involving multiple criteria. Nonetheless, straightforward accessibility is often found to be an important factor. Minocha concludes that Indian patients may prefer modern medicine, but what they actually use in the event of illness will depend chiefly on what is 'easily available' to them in terms of cost and location (Minocha 1980: 221). A similar view is taken by Judith Lasker in her study of illness behaviour in the Ivory Coast. While it was not the only factor which could be used to predict the type of medical system an individual would choose, location was paramount, far more significant than (for example) education (Lasker 1981). Lasker suggests that if patients are convinced that modern 'scientific' medicine is superior to African medicine it will be because they have had the opportunity to use it, i.e. they live near to where it is practised and can afford it, and not because of some prior ideological bias.

On the other hand, in a study of curative practices in Melanesia, Lola Romanucci-Schwartz finds that the Manus are more influenced in their choice by the kind of illness the patient is thought to suffer from. Certain problems are deemed to be best dealt with through indigenous curative practices ('sickness belong ground') while others are properly taken to the practitioner of 'European' medicine:

...sets of alternatives may be ordered in hierarchies of resort, where sequences of one, or usually more alternatives may be resorted to as the

illness passes from one phase to another when cure is not forthcoming....
A last resort is reached as earlier choices are exhausted.

(Romanucci-Schwartz 1969: 205)

Janzen has also shown how in Lower Zaire different kinds of therapy are used at different stages or episodes of illness. Patients and their kin re-evaluate the situation if the sick person fails to recover, exploring other options and revising original judgements about the cause of the illness (Janzen 1978: 221). In an Indian village, Beals found that pragmatic considerations such as cost and accessibility interacted with notions of appropriateness to produce a fairly eclectic usage of both biomedical and indigenous treatments (Beals 1976).

This literature suggests that we should be looking at both the ideological and the practical considerations which inform decisions about what sort of treatment to seek. (Most decisions seem to be made in the context of an unstable mix of the two.) Secondly, it suggests that patients, or those who make decisions on their behalf, are best seen as essentially pragmatic and rational actors, making choices in the light of the costs and benefits which are held to accrue from the use of particular medical or ritual options. Preferences may be ordered according to various criteria in a hierarchy of resort, so that the patient will turn to second and third choices (in an order that is far from random) if the cure of the first resort fails. Thirdly, the literature suggests a patient who is prepared to use new forms of medicine when they present perceived advantages. That is, whilst people may be conservative in terms of their perceptions of how disease is caused or how it should be classified, they are not necessarily conservative in the sense of being unprepared to use new forms of healing when these are made accessible to them and are seen to be effective.

The literature on medical pluralism also suggests that decisions about treatment are seldom taken alone. Janzen uses the term 'therapy managing group' to refer to the group of kin who undertake the responsibility of seeing that a sick person gets appropriate treatment (Janzen 1978). Beals emphasises that identifying the appropriate healer in a particular case of illness involves a process of consultation with a range of friends and relatives so that the actual outcome will be very much influenced by the structure of the sick person's social networks (Beals 1976: 194). Studies of illness behaviour in industrial societies indicate that comparable processes of consultation take place. Freidson developed the notion of *lay referral* to describe the process by which a sick person consults family and friends, which tends to occur at some point between simple self-treatment and consultation with a professional practitioner. He pairs this concept with that of *professional referral systems* in which practitioners pass patients on to more specialised services or consultants to which they have access by virtue of their professional networks or structures (Freidson 1961: 146ff, Freidson 1960).

Freidson stresses that an important aspect of the way in which referral systems work is the extent to which those who refer and those who receive referrals share the same medical culture and reference groups. As the patient cedes the initiative to the professional s/he also cedes control of the curative process, for medical professionals are ruled by their colleagues' rather than by their patients' perceptions of what is proper treatment. However, just how much control is ceded depends on the kind of practitioner resorted to. An independent practice, that is, one which 'can operate independently of colleagues, its existence predicated on attracting its own lay clientele', remains subject to client control to a greater degree than a dependent practice, one which 'serves the needs of other practices, individual or organizational' (Freidson 1960: 380). Freidson does not explicitly contrast orthodox medicine with non-orthodox medicine here; he seems to be constructing ideal types rather than making reference to specific systems. But inasmuch as orthodox medicine in Britain corresponds to his 'dependent' practice and non-orthodox medicine is a less 'dependent' form of practice we may bear his distinction in mind for future use.

Research into lay perceptions of health and illness tell us a good deal about how lay referral systems operate in British society and suggest that a number of persons besides the patient – 'significant others' to use the infelicitous term favoured by some sociologists – may be involved in decisions regarding treatment. This at least is true if we include every kind of involvement. Blaxter and Patterson's study of Scottish women suggests that only a rather restricted range of people are explicitly asked for advice (Blaxter and Patterson 1982: 155). McKinlay argues that the actual size and density of people's kin and friendship networks has a considerable effect on their utilisation of medical services (dense networks with high frequency of interaction among members being associated with low utilisation of medical services (McKinlay 1973). Most studies focus on the threshold at which the patient initially decides to seek treatment, with the consequence that the circumstances in which patients typically consult a non-orthodox practitioner (i.e. *after* they have already consulted an orthodox practitioner at least once) have received little attention. Stimson and Webb, to be sure, emphasise that the process of lay referral does not only take place prior to consultation of a professional; the advice or treatment which a doctor metes out is appraised in the light of other people's comments or experiences (Stimson and Webb 1975: 72ff).

Most of the studies which have used the concept of lay referral have tacitly assumed that the main choices open to the patient consist of consultation with a medical doctor, self-treatment or no action at all. However, there is no reason why we should not apply the concept to decisions about non-orthodox treatment, or indeed any other kind of healthcare option. On the basis of what advice or information do individuals resort to non-orthodox practitioners? What – or who – encourages them to sample complementary medicine or, on the other hand, to rule it out as an option?

In this chapter I have sought to anchor the study of how patients use complementary medicine to existing concerns in the sociology and anthropology of health and illness, concentrating on the literature which looks at medical systems from the point of view of the patient and the way in which sick people (and their friends and families) make decisions about treatment. I think that the concepts I have introduced will clarify my own data on the way in which people decide to use non-orthodox medicine, to which I turn in the next chapter.

3 Using complementary medicine
A local study

In the last chapter I argued that the decision to consult a complementary practitioner should be studied as part of a process and in the context of the entire range of resources which a user has at his/her disposal in making decisions about healthcare – the advice of friends and relatives, concepts about what promotes good health, experience and evaluation of other kinds of medical system, etc.

We should also interest ourselves in 'what happened next' – do patients continue to use the practitioner whom they first consult? Did they sample other types of non-orthodox medicine and do any of these experiences have enduring consequences for their own or their families' healthcare practices? Except in emergencies, decisions about healthcare are generally made over time (though not necessarily very long stretches of time) and are frequently the outcome of interaction among members of the same family, though others may be involved also. Surveys capture and categorise the accounts which individuals give of their opinions and activities at a given moment in time. They are not a particularly suitable instrument for studying the way in which decisions emerge from groups or networks over time.

In this chapter I shall use data from my own fieldwork which suggests some of the factors which influence decisions about using non-orthodox medicine in preference to orthodox medicine. By studying such individual decisions we can perhaps learn something about why complementary therapies seem to be growing so rapidly in popularity and about the cultural processes by which patterns of health-seeking behaviour are transformed.

Much of the material in this chapter is drawn from a small-scale study of users of non-orthodox medicine which I conducted in the Stoke-on-Trent area between May 1986 and December 1987. It was supported by a grant from the Nuffield Foundation and was the first stage in what became a long-term project to study the use and practice of complementary medicine. Most of the fieldwork for this long-term project was conducted in the Midlands; the majority of studies of complementary medicine in Britain published to date have been conducted in the southeast of England, which is something of a special case since the provision of complementary medicine is particularly abundant there. It seemed useful to focus on a non-metropolitan locality where there is a fair representation (but not a super-abundance) of most kinds of complementary medicine. The northwestern Midlands region (besides being convenient for me to study in terms of my own job and living arrangements) conformed to these requirements.

The study of users did not escape entirely from the limitations I described as characteristic of surveys; like most of the research I referred to in Chapter 1, it was based on 'one-off' interviews with individual members of the public. However, within a broad framework devised to allow comparisons, interviewees were encouraged to construct their own accounts of the process by which they had come to use complementary medicine, and of what had happened subsequently. I interviewed thirty people who had used non-orthodox medicine at least once within the previous six months. I shall make extensive use of these interview data, employing pseudonyms to protect the anonymity of the individuals who so kindly gave their time to the research.

This was a self-selected group in that the interviewees were mostly people who had contacted me after a short article appeared in a local newspaper in which readers were invited to tell me about their experiences of non-orthodox therapies. I would surmise that people motivated to take this step and to submit to a fairly lengthy and probing interview would be those whose experience of complementary medicine had been substantial and fairly successful, rather than those whose experience had been cursory or, from their point of view, a waste of time. Bearing this likely bias in mind, I shall not attempt to draw any conclusions about rates of patient satisfaction from these data. We ought in any case to be cautious about the kind of generalisations which can be made on the basis of such a small number of subjects. Yet it is very difficult to devise methodologies where the details of process and personal experience can be captured without some sacrifice of scale. I feel that the quality of the data I obtained was good and that I have identified some patterns which are almost certainly not peculiar to my group of interviewees, being positively confirmed by much that I heard therapists say in my later study of practitioners.

In terms of socio-economic characteristics this group was predominantly middle class. Classifying the interviewees according to the occupation of the main breadwinner in the household to which they belonged, 50 per cent were from the professional and managerial class, with the rest divided equally among routine white-collar, manual working class and unwaged (students, pensioners, unemployed). There were far more women than men (the sex and marital status of the interviewees are summarised in Table 4) and while the age range was wide (the youngest was twenty-three and the oldest was over eighty), the majority of the respondents were between forty and sixty years old. This probably tells us as much about the kind of person who is motivated to write to newspapers about their experiences and volunteer for interview as it does about the 'typical' user of complementary medicine, but the group would seem to be not totally unrepresentative in the light of the population-based studies mentioned in Chapter 1.

Table 4 Sex and marital status of interviewees (user study)

	Female	Male	Total
Married	17	4	21
Unmarried	0	5	5
Divorced/widowed	4	0	4
Total	21	9	30

In addition to interviewing these volunteers I tried to find out as much as I could about local sources of information on complementary practitioners. To this end I contacted patients' associations and other organisations or agencies which might possibly act as channels for information about non-orthodox forms of treatment. Further interviews were conducted with key individuals who were known to be confirmed users of complementary medicine or to have been instrumental in disseminating information about it to others (e.g. through giving talks, teaching adult education or evening classes).

One of the questions I asked myself when designing the study was whether the individual was really the appropriate unit of study. If lay referral systems are important in decisions about non-orthodox as well as orthodox treatment, then the individual who has decided to use, say, the services of a chiropractor will probably have done so in consultation with others. And such a person may pass this experience of chiropractic (whether good or ill) on to others in turn. If parents, especially mothers, take decisions about diet and healthcare on behalf of their children, then their exposure to complementary medicine is likely to have especially marked effects within the household group. In the interviews I questioned respondents extensively about the healthcare practices of their families and friends with this problem in mind. In some cases the interviewee's spouse was present at the interview and provided additional comments after the main interview was concluded. This still yields no more than a partial account of 'what happened' and 'what happened next', but it does give us a window onto the interviewee's social networks as these are relevant to decisions about health and illness.

In some cases it was very difficult for me to establish the original diagnosis of the illness which had first motivated the interviewee to seek non-orthodox treatment (roughly classified in Table 5). Sometimes this seems to have been because the condition itself was obscure and may have foxed the orthodox practitioner. We must also allow for the possibility that doctors had not explained clearly enough to patients what they thought was wrong with them or that such explanations had been misremembered or misunderstood. In what follows I use the interviewees' own descriptions of their symptoms and of their doctors' diagnoses because my main concern here is with the patients' own understanding of the situation. There is, of course, no guarantee that their classifications tally with the nosologies used by the healthcare professionals (orthodox or otherwise) who attended them.

DECIDING TO USE COMPLEMENTARY MEDICINE FOR THE FIRST TIME

Most of the interviewees had first encountered non-orthodox medicine within the past ten years, but there were three people in the study who had been using it for much longer. These included a man of seventy-five and a woman of over eighty who had become interested in naturopathy and homoeopathy respectively before the Second World War. They had used these systems consistently since that time. Another woman in her forties, Anne Griffiths, had been brought up on naturopathy as her mother had been a pioneer of this method of healthcare as well as an enterprising organic farmer long before the current wave of interest in environmental issues. Anne continued to use naturopathy for her own children, although not as consistently or exclusively as her mother had done. These cases should remind us that embedded in large-scale statistics on the present day usage of complementary medicine there is a small but probably quite important cohort of people whose patterns of healthcare are the product of an earlier wave of interest in non-orthodox medicine.

All the interviewees, save Anne Griffiths, said that they had used non-orthodox medicine for the first time in order to cure some condition for which orthodox medicine had been either unable to offer any relief at all, or unable to offer a cure which was deemed satisfactory by the patient. Table 5 shows the nature of these problems as reported by interviewees, data which are fairly consistent with the findings of large-scale surveys that people generally use non-orthodox medicine to deal with chronic troubles rather than acute or life-threatening illnesses.

In all these cases the sufferer had followed the treatment of an orthodox doctor in the first place, indeed some had been receiving such treatment for years before resorting to a complementary practitioner. Maureen Pratt, a secretary with a grown family, had suffered from back trouble for fifteen

Table 5 Conditions for which complementary treatment was first sought (user study)

Illness/condition	No. of respondents
Musculo-skeletal (mainly back pain)	8
Allergies	2
Skin conditions	2
Asthma	2
'Stress'	2
Depression	1
Migraine	2
'Low vitality'	2
'Chest problems'	2
Other	7
Total	30

years and from migraines since an early and troublesome menopause five years ago. She went to see a chiropractor for the former because she was 'really desperate, nothing the GP gave me worked'. Sally Burnett, a saleswoman in her forties, had suffered from psoriasis since she was a teenager and had gradually lost hope of finding a cure from orthodox medicine before she turned to a herbalist. Some sufferers had not only been unable to obtain relief from orthodox medicine, but had become sceptical about their GPs' diagnoses. Jan Mason, an actress, described her fruitless visits to her doctor during the past year to treat extreme lassitude and depression.

> Before, I was a very fit person. I could swim, play squash, run, and suddenly I just keeled over. I went to the doctor but nobody could tell me what it was. My GP said it was glandular fever and gave me anti-biotics which gave me terrible thrush. Then he kept saying that he did not know what it was either.... I went through all the tests. I was really very poorly. It went on for six months. I was still ill and they still did not know what it was.

The GP then decided that Jan's tiredness was due to stress, she said, and offered anti-depressants. She did not agree with this diagnosis, although she was indeed feeling stressed by now since she was very worried as to whether she would be able to continue working. After listening to a radio programme on myalgic encephalitis she came to the conclusion that she was suffering from post-viral fatigue syndrome, a condition whose existence is more readily recognised by doctors now than it was at that time. A friend recommended homoeopathy and although it took her a little while to find a homoeopath whose approach she found sympathetic (the first one she visited expressed disapproval of her lesbian relationship) she was very satisfied with the treatment she was now receiving.

Another recurrent theme in the interviews was the complaint that orthodox medicine treats symptoms rather than causes. Dan Turner, a trainee youth leader, explained that conventional drug treatment prescribed by a psychiatrist had certainly had some effect on his chronic depression, but that when he discontinued the drugs the depression just returned.

> It did not work, it was just a sort of slow death, because the treatment did not get to the root cause of the depression.

A course of treatment with an acupuncturist had, Dan said, been very beneficial. He could not claim to have said goodbye to his depression entirely as it returned from time to time, but he felt much more relaxed and positive. He had gained the confidence to apply for a full-time job and was considering the possibility of training as an acupuncturist himself, for he felt that this system of treatment worked at a deeper level than orthodox medicine.

A very common concern was the side effects of drugs. A substantial group of interviewees described the treatment they had received from orthodox medicine as effective but only at the cost of unpleasant side effects. Doreen Peake, whose story I analyse in detail in the next chapter, had received drugs for high blood pressure which had controlled this condition quite successfully but which made her feel exhausted and breathless. Eileen Morcott, a housewife in her forties married to a police officer, had begun to suffer from depression about fifteen years before after a series of miscarriages. While the drugs her doctor gave her did control the depression they had other unacceptable side effects. Her GP told her that she must be exceptionally sensitive to this drug and prescribed another, but she had by this time discovered a local herbalist:

> The things he uses – I have no idea at all. I am no wiser now than I was when I first started going to him all those years ago. But I have been able to work all those years and kept going. I still have bouts of depression, it's a psychological thing with me, but I get through it with his help.

Both this patient and a number of others expressed generalised concern about what they saw as the over-liberal dispensation of drugs on the part of orthodox doctors without apparent thought for their long-term consequences. Lynne Rawlins, a cookery instructor who had first consulted a herbalist in connection with her son's allergies and childhood ailments, was very critical of her local GP:

> The kids in our street are always being given anti-biotics. I think it must lower the body's resistance, its ability to fight infection.

She felt confident that the herbal preparations prescribed for her son were likely to strengthen rather than undermine his immune system.

Sue and Mike Sullivan had been worried that the only orthodox treatment offered for their son's severe eczema had been cortisone ointment, which they regarded as too 'strong' and as dealing with the symptoms rather than the causes of the problem. They consulted several non-orthodox practitioners with varying degrees of success before working out for themselves that the child was allergic to a wide range of ordinary foods and commercial additives. Eileen Morcott went even further in her distrust of 'unnatural' chemical interventions:

> I think I have always tended to go for the wholesome things. I have never really liked the fact that they have spread DDT or inorganic fertilisers on the fields and so on. Time is proving me right.

Nell Bradbury, a lively octogenarian, had used naturopathy since before the Second World War and had great faith in curing illness through correct diet. She regretted that really 'healthy' food was hard to come by and gave an animated account of the time when she had complained to the manager of the local supermarket that the store's tinned tomatoes all contained additives:

> There was water, salt, citric acid. He came back joyfully and he said, you know, there is citric acid in all fruit. I said, yes, but that is natural. This is a chemical. The chemical isn't the same as the natural. I mean, they are making it out of powders and things. A lot of the things they do are quite unnecessary, they are just to make the food look attractive. Some things have got umpteen chemicals in them.

Some interviewees had been offered orthodox treatments which they regarded as too drastic or invasive to be acceptable. Beryl Hemmings, a middle-aged housewife, had been offered an operation for a spinal condition which had troubled her for several years. She was uneasy about undergoing a serious operation which in the event, she had been told, might not even be effective. She had tried a course of treatment with a chiropractor which had brought about considerable improvement, she said, to the extent that she felt confident that an operation was now unnecessary. Nicola Goodwin, wife of a lecturer, had also had back trouble for years. She had been offered various forms of treatment, including being encased in a plaster cast which had caused further complications, she said, since it affected her breathing. Unwilling to undergo treatment which she had found drastic and distressing, she had preferred to use the services of a chiropractor, as well as taking lessons in Alexander Technique from time to time. Her back trouble still recurred sometimes, but she felt that it was no longer intolerable.

Time had been another important factor to some interviewees. Individual sufferers have their own conceptions as to how long they are prepared to wait for a course of treatment (whether orthodox or non-orthodox) to work. This degree of tolerance is bound to be related to the amount of discomfort they are experiencing, whether this is caused by the condition itself or by the treatment provided. Doreen Peake was not prepared to wait while her GP ran through the gamut of available drugs until he found one which could control her high blood pressure without making her feel dizzy and exhausted, hence her resort to a herbalist. In several cases sufferers from back pain had first been motivated to consult a non-orthodox practitioner by the fact that although they had been offered hospital treatment they found that waiting lists were so long that they were unlikely to be treated within a year.

This is not simply a matter of individual fortitude, the personal capacity to 'grin and bear it' while waiting for treatment or waiting for treatment to take effect. In many of the cases I studied, the major factor affecting the sufferer's 'time tolerance' was work. Some sociologists have found that many sick people initially seek medical help at the point when their illness or condition is beginning to interfere with their ability to fulfil their normal social obligations (Zola 1978:127). One might add that the decision to seek further (non-orthodox) treatment often takes place at the point where this interference with the sufferer's ability to hold down a job or perform ordinary household duties is experienced as critical. Shirley Browne worked in an old people's home, a job which she found very satisfying but which was strenuous since it involved lifting disabled residents. She undertook a course of chiropractic treatment because her back pain was so severe that she had been obliged to contemplate giving up her job. Jan Mason's post-viral fatigue was so enervating that she had had to take on less and less acting work to the detriment of both her finances and her career. An exhausted actress, a depressed youth leader, a saleswoman with psoriasis – for these people actual or impending failure to meet the quotidian demands of a job prompted the move from orthodox to non-orthodox treatment when the pace of progress was felt to be unsatisfactory.

Non-orthodox treatments do not necessarily work any faster; indeed many (like homoeopathy) explicitly reject the 'magic bullet' approach and claim to coax the body's own healing system into more robust action. Some of these interviewees had arrived at a juncture where they feared so much for their ability to go on working that they resolved to cut their losses so far as orthodox treatment was concerned, decided that it was time to try another approach. Medical science seeks generalised 'cures' for cancer, the common cold, etc. Individual patients have particular priorities and limiting circumstances against which they judge what they are prescribed. They seek forms of treatment which are right for them in terms of the demands of the jobs they do, their own preferences and fears, or the kinds of discomfort they are prepared to tolerate.

Although all the people whom I interviewed claimed to have received orthodox treatment originally for the condition which first motivated them to try non-orthodox medicine, some had persisted longer with this treatment than others and their experiences of orthodox medicine had not all been the same. Twelve of the interviewees had either been referred to a consultant or hospitalised for this problem, the other eighteen having seen no-one beyond their own GP. Of the twelve who had used the services of a consultant, four had obtained these privately, and it is perhaps worth considering why this figure was not higher. If sufferers are radically dissatisfied with the kind of treatment that orthodox medicine has to offer (it has inacceptable costs in terms of side effects, invasiveness, etc.) then they may not wish to throw good resources after bad by seeking more expensive versions of the same unsatisfactory treatment. Complementary medicine is private medicine also, but it is still usually cheaper than private orthodox medicine in the locality which I studied. On the other hand if, as recent research has suggested, private patients of orthodox medical consultants are motivated by the perception that they are getting more of the doctor's time and attention and that the patient has greater control over the timing of treatment (Higgins 1988: 172, Horne 1984: 71), then the motivation may not be so different. Consider what one interviewee (middle-class and educated, but by no means wealthy) had to say:

> The attention you get is important. Going private (for an earlier skin condition) I did get a chat and an explanation. I was treated as an intelligent person. It is worth paying for that, although you should not have to. Jenny (the herbalist whom she was currently consulting about her child's allergy) does explain what she is doing and I feel more active in the treatment.

There are good grounds for suggesting that people who use non-orthodox medicine have tried orthodox medicine for their particular problems and found it wanting. Yet the criticisms made by the people I interviewed were fairly familiar ones – orthodox medicine has too little time for the patient, is invasive, relies overmuch on drugs and technology, addresses symptoms rather than causes. All these complaints have been made by others and some (such as the issue of the use of technology in childbirth) have been the subject of much public debate. Users of non-orthodox medicine become aware of these faults in the pressing circumstances of a troublesome illness, but unlike the woman in labour with a foetal monitor attached to her abdomen who has little power to resist medical decisions about the 'management' of her labour, they are in a position to walk out and choose something else. How do they become aware of this 'something else' as a realistic possibility for themselves?

FINDING OUT ABOUT COMPLEMENTARY MEDICINE

Now let us turn to the processes by which knowledge about complementary medicine is transmitted and spreads. How do people inform themselves about non-orthodox medicine, and how do they choose a particular practitioner? My interviews suggest that people usually consult a complementary practitioner for the first time as a consequence of a personal recommendation from a friend or acquaintance. Impersonal sources of information are unimportant compared to local lay referral systems. Sarah Elton, a teacher, had heard about the virtues of acupuncture from a close friend who had decided to train as an acupuncturist herself. Geoff Allen, a music teacher who suffered from repeated and painful ear infections, consulted a herbalist known to another lecturer in the same college. Lizzie Rayner had suffered for many years from back pain in spite of the best efforts of her GP and a hospital consultant, and had soldiered on with her job as a school caretaker. At last she visited an osteopath at the suggestion of her son who had had very successful treatment from the same man after an accident at work.

Table 6 How respondents heard about the complementary practitioner they used first (user study)

Source of information	No. of respondents
'Public' sources:	
Advertisements/Yellow pages	3
GP's recommendation	1
Local association/organisation	1
'Private' sources:	
Friends/acquaintances/colleagues	23
Relatives	2
Total	30

Table 6 summarises data about the way in which interviewees came to hear of the first non-orthodox practitioner they had used. The importance of personal recommendation as a pathway into complementary medicine confirms what other researchers have found. For example, the Dutch NIPG survey found that 71 per cent of respondents claimed that they had arrived at the idea of trying complementary medicine through suggestions made by friends, acquaintances or family members. When questioned in more detail about their reasons for choosing it, 31 per cent named the positive experience of non-orthodox medicine on the part of someone they had known as their most important consideration, and another 15 per cent gave this as their second most important reason (Ooijendijk, Mackenbach and Limberger 1981: 43,41. See also Parker and Tupling 1976: 374, Boven *et al.* 1977: 319, Christie n. d: 4). Reviewing such studies, Fulder concludes that

> These figures demonstrate that patients arrive largely as a result of a groundswell of opinion and shared experience. The flight to alternatives is a grass roots phenomenon, solidly based on personal experience. It is not a temporary media-enhanced fashion.
>
> (Fulder 1988: 30)

Evidently lay referral systems can be busy channels of information about non-orthodox medicine, but how do people evaluate the information they come by in this way? How much information about non-orthodox medicine obtained through local networks is discarded without being acted upon? And do people use recommendations received through their lay referral networks because they give positive weight to the experiences of friends and kin or, *faute de mieux*, because other sources of information are lacking or inaccessible? In the locality I studied, publicly available information about local practitioners of complementary medicine certainly seemed sparse. I could only locate these public sources of information:

Telephone Directory (Yellow Pages)
Citizen's Advice Bureau: would provide addresses of main national organisations, but not names of local practitioners
Book shops: a local radical book store made available a broadsheet which contained the names of several established practitioners (helpful but far from exhaustive)
Health food stores: some displayed notices put up by local practitioners, or assistants could give some information informally if asked
Public Libraries: some had notice boards on which local practitioners placed cards or announcements
Local newspapers: there were two, both of which carried advertisements from several practitioners from time to time.

None of these information sources was complete and the reasons for this are not hard to find. With so many new practitioners setting up business any list would need constant revision to remain up-to-date. Also many practitioners are bound by the codes of practice of the professional organisations to which they belong which forbid or limit direct advertisement. Established practitioners often do not feel the need for advertisement if they receive as many patients as they can handle through informal information networks.

Whilst it is true that the individuals whom I interviewed had almost always heard about the practitioner whom they first consulted through personal networks, I think that Fulder is incorrect to dismiss the role of the media in creating, or at any rate sustaining, a demand for non-orthodox therapies. Many of the interviewees, and not merely the educated middle-class patients who might be expected to be well-informed, had done 'homework' on their illness and some were in the habit of doing such 'homework' on any persistent health problem in the family. By 'doing their homework' I mean that they made a positive effort to inform themselves about the possible causes of and treatments for the condition from which they supposed they suffered. This included scanning popular magazines and newspapers, noting information disseminated through television or radio broadcasts, as well as using the resources of the public library or high street book store.

The more chronic the problem, the greater the effort invested in this kind of 'homework'. Mike Sullivan, a community worker whose son had suffered from mysterious allergic symptoms for some years, had taken his child to a homoeopath. This treatment had brought about some improvement, though not a complete cure.

> We have worked hard to try to identify what Colin is allergic to. We have identified some things like some food colourings, but his diet is clear of these anyway now. We will probably try this rotation diet. We read about it in a book which I just bought off the shelf. The case histories in this book are very similar to Colin's. It seems as likely as anything to succeed.

Lynne Rawlins, the parent of another allergic child, told me:

> I was interested in wholefoods and took a journal in connection with this, which had a lot of information about alternative medicine. At that time I got to know quite a lot about the theory of alternative medicine, but not much about the practice. I started going to Mary (a local herbalist) after I attended a talk she gave to the Soil Association which we belong to, and I thought she sounded good.

There is no reason to suppose that this process of self-information is peculiar to the patients of non-orthodox practitioners; it appears to be the product of a high level of public interest in matters of health and illness in general. Scanning the media is unlikely to provide information about specific practitioners; this is better sought from local social networks. Its significance lies in the fact that in the course of doing this 'homework', the individual may come across the kind of information which predisposes him or her to give non-orthodox therapies a try, as in the case of Lynne Rawlins.

How far is an interest in 'alternative' medicine related to participation in an 'alternative' culture? Of the thirty people whom I interviewed, only four could, in my view, be described as having a long-standing and consistent interest in 'alternative' life styles or politics. A judgement like this can only be crude and arbitrary – what counts as 'alternative' in Huddersfield may be quite conventional in Hampstead or Hove (and vice versa). I base it on interviewees' self-assessments, considered in conjunction with whatever they told me or whatever evidence I could observe in their homes of their cultural and political tastes (active participation in feminist or gay politics or the peace movement, rejection of aspects of the consumer culture, etc.). A number of interviewees were at pains to stress their own view of themelves as essentially conventional people, more than a little cautious at first of trying anything associated in their minds with eccentric or disreputable life styles. Several described themselves as 'initially sceptical' about non-orthodox medicine, pressed into using it only by a desperate need to remedy a particular health problem or by the convincing testimony of friends or kin. One interviewee rather endearingly described herself and her family as 'short back and sides people' and suspected that she might not have a lot in common with other people who used the form of complementary medicine she favoured.

Yet cultural and political pre-occupations are not irrelevant to choices of healthcare. We have already noted that the local Soil Association was instrumental in disseminating a good deal of information about non-orthodox therapies through a series of talks given to its members. Several interviewees mentioned an interest in plants and horticulture as a stimulus to find out more about herbalism or homoeopathy. Edith Glazier, the wife of an industrial chemist, had always loved gardening and was well-read on the subject of plants and their properties. She bought herbs from a local nurseryman, Lionel Edge, who had been much influenced by the ideas of Rudolf Steiner on the subject of farming and cultivation and who was well-known locally as an enthusiastic advocate of homoeopathic medicine. At his suggestion she had consulted a local homoeopath. Several interviewees who had taken part in yoga classes cited yoga teachers as sources of information or suggestions about non-orthodox therapies. A few mentioned an interest in sport and fitness as having stimulated their first forays into non-orthodox medicine; some osteopaths and masseurs specialise in dealing with sports injuries.

Using 'alternative' medicine, then, is not necessarily associated with adherence to an 'alternative' culture or life style, but some cultural and recreational activities are more likely than others to channel information about non-orthodox medicine. Therapists who are starting up in practice and have the time and need to do such 'public relations' work seem to know the kind of associations which welcome talks on the therapies they practice.

As well as the 'met' demand which social scientists study when they question samples of users of non-orthodox medicine, my own study suggests that there is also a considerable 'unmet' demand. There are those who would like to use some form of complementary medicine, but who have been unable to locate a suitable practitioner. For almost every person who contacted me volunteering to be interviewed, another contacted me seeking information about therapists in the locality. I responded to these enquiries by sending details of national professional bodies who could supply lists of registered practitioners in their own field. But I am not sure how helpful this will have been to such enquirers. Most of the people whom I interviewed had evidently not felt happy about approaching a practitioner without assurance from someone personally known to them that the practitioner in question was reputable and effective.

Personal recommendation is, of course, important in the choice of orthodox treatment as well as non-orthodox treatment. Many people select their GP on the basis of a combination of personal recommendation and proximity. In a major study of GPs and their patients, 22 per cent of the respondents said that they chose their GP primarily on the basis of personal recommendation and 6 per cent registered with their spouse's GP on marriage (Cartwright and Anderson 1981: 27. See also Ritchie, Jacoby and Bone 1981: 54). The testimony of known persons would seem to be an important element in many decisions about treatment, even when plenty of information is publicly available. Possibly this is because the services rendered by healthcare professionals are regarded as being of an extremely personal nature, for which formal qualifications alone are regarded as insufficient assurance. As one respondent in a general survey of the consumer demand for health information services said (though not in connection with non-orthodox medicine):

> It's no good putting up an address somewhere, because people might be terrified of going to a national place, or phoning someone in London.... It's got to be a personal thing, somebody who's coming to your house or who you are having contact with and to mushroom out from there.
>
> (Kempson 1987: 27)

Or, as one of my interviewees described the search for information:

> You need to go to someone whom you trust. You tend to have to dig around amongst friends. It's not like... well, I suppose it is like having to get yourself a GP. You do tend to talk to people locally and hear all their tales. They say, this one is terrible because you can't get an appointment, this one is good. It is very similar to getting a GP, but (complementary practitioners) are further apart and harder to find, so it takes longer.

If the area I studied is at all typical then there is evidently a need for more public information about the non-orthodox treatments locally available. Bodies such as Community Health Councils might be well placed to meet this need were they prepared to take the responsibility for telling the public about non-orthodox medical systems. The Association of Community Health

Councils for England and Wales has produced a very thoughtful report on complementary medicine (Association of CHCs for England and Wales 1988), and several local CHCs have run information days on complementary therapy (Institute of Complementary Medicine *Newsletter* July 1988: 4) but CHCs do not, as far as I know, undertake to inform the public about individual practitioners. The authorisation of orthodox medicine by the state makes it difficult for agencies which are themselves set up or funded by the state to take responsibility for any move which might appear to validate the claims of non-orthodox medicine. The Institute of Complementary Medicine, an independent national organisation with a concern for standards of training and practice among complementary practitioners, has set up Public Information Points in some parts the country where the enquirer may find out the names of local practitioners whose qualifications meet the Institute's standards. But even if this kind of information were universally accessible through well advertised sources, prospective patients might hesitate to use it without checking it against the reports of their own acquaintance and the judgement of the local 'grapevine'.

AFTER THE FIRST CONSULTATION: PATTERNS OF USAGE

Does exposure to non-orthodox medicine bring about long-term changes in people's health-seeking behaviour? For most of the people in my study, the first time they used complementary medicine was by no means the last time. Table 7 shows that the majority of the interviewees could remember having used more than one form of non-orthodox medicine in their life and several explicitly stated that they intended to continue to sample different forms of non-orthodox medicine for one purpose or another. Is this a sign of the failure of non-orthodox medicine (none of the therapies work, so patients do not stick with them) or of its very success (the therapies are so effective that people are not content to use one system alone)? Judging from my interview material, one could generalise much less about users' second or subsequent experiences of non-orthodox treatment than one could about initial experiences. Nevertheless certain patterns of usage can be discerned.

Firstly there are those whom I have called the 'earnest seekers' (five

Table 7 Number of types of complementary medicine used either serially or simultaneously (user study)

Types of complementary medicine ever used	1	2	3	4	4+	
No. of respondents	9	8	4	7	2	(Total 30)

interviewees). These are sufferers who are desperately casting about for a remedy for a specific illness but who seem neither to have settled down with any one system of therapy nor to have abandoned the search as a bad job and accepted their condition as incurable.

Two interviewees, both young men in their twenties, had used non-ortho-dox medicine for a specific condition with little or no success, but intended to go on searching for a cure among the non-orthodox therapies, convinced that orthodox medicine had little to offer them. One of these was Roger Avery, who had been diagnosed by a dermatologist four years before as suffering from seborrhoeic eczema. Finding that the drugs and ointments prescribed for him had no effect, he had consulted spiritual healers, a reflexologist and an acupuncturist and was currently undergoing homoeo-pathic treatment. Although he did not feel that his condition had improved very much as a result of all this effort, he appreciated certain features of the non-orthodox therapies he had used, especially the time given by practitio-ners to diagnosis and their preparedness to discuss treatment with the patient. He was determined to find a cure somehow:

> I have got very high standards for health. This skin condition is not very pleasant, it makes my skin sting. But I'm healthy in the larger sense. I enjoy very good health and I'm not prepared to put up with it. I never drank, I've always taken exercise and I don't intend to let matters ride.

Another young man, Dave Purchase, had been a very active sportsman until a football injury had laid him low with severe back problems. He had tried osteopathy on the suggestion of a sporting friend, but this had not effected any permanent difference. With a kind of dogged optimism he stated that he intended to work through all the non-orthodox options that he could afford to pay for until he found one which could restore his former fitness.

Others rated their initial experiences of non-orthodox medicine more favourably than Roger Avery or Dave Purchase. They had not been totally 'cured', but had been pleased enough with specific aspects of the treatment they had received and intended to continue with that treatment or to try others. Sarah Elton, a teacher, had consulted an acupuncturist who practiced in a town some thirty miles away about her son's susceptibility to colds and other infections.

> It was very effective in the early stages. But I don't know that he got the diagnosis quite right. We got on quite quickly at first, but then it got to the stage where we were going monthly and after the treatment he (the child) would have some reaction. I asked him about this and he said that he thought Peter was basically all right now, so it seemed he did not have any long-term plan. I felt that there were still one or two things to be sorted

out, but Peter's health was much better. Probably those first sessions had sort of broken the depression and lowness he had suffered from.

This interviewee had discontinued the acupuncture treatment, feeling that the benefits of the treatment were not great enough to justify the long journeys involved, and was now consulting a homoeopath about her son's health.

Sometimes the positive (if incomplete) results of non-orthodox treatment were such that the patient proposed to continue to use the practitioner, feeling optimistic about the eventual outcome. Geoff Allen, a music teacher in a local college, had suffered from ear and throat infections which were jeopardising his ability to play his instrument, but these had improved when he began a course of treatment from a local herbalist. He had still to complete the treatment and was not completely cured, but felt that his general sense of wellbeing had increased enormously:

> I felt that I trusted her. If I had gone to the doctor he would have just said, right, take this anti-biotic. I was convinced that the use of anti-biotics would damage my system. Jenny's (the herbalist's) treatment was not an instant panacea, but still quite dramatic. She convinced me that I had to treat the whole of my body. The diet she gave me seemed barmy at the time, but I had been so bad that I was considering giving up teaching music altogether and I was prepared to pay any money to prevent this.

The next category of interviewees (fourteen in all) I have termed 'stable users'. These had had a favourable initial experience of non-orthodox medicine and in the course of time achieved a fairly regular relationship with a particular practitioner in whom they had great confidence, or made regular use of a particular system of treatment in which they had faith. We might call these people 'converts' although I would not like to press the comparison with religion too far. Lionel Edge, whom I have already mentioned in connection with the case of Edith Glazier (see above), had started to use homoeopathy before the war as a result of his experience with a very severe ear infection. On the advice of a friend he had consulted a homoeopath in London and had become very interested in both the theory and practice of this system of medicine. For many years now, both he and his wife had used it for most health problems. They had not used the same homoeopath all this time, having lived in various different parts of the country. In fact, Lionel felt that he knew enough about homoeopathy to treat himself for routine ailments as well as using it preventively, and would only need to consult a professional homoeopath in the case of a serious problem. Homoeopathy generally seemed to be the system of non-orthodox medicine most likely to attract the stable 'convert'. This may be simply the consequence of its having been accessible for longer in the district I studied than more recent arrivals such as acupuncture or reflexology. Also the fact that homoeopathic remedies are available to the public over the counter in many local shops and can be administered as home first aid may also help to account for its adoption as a regular 'household therapy'.

The third group (ten interviewees) were best described as 'eclectic'. Whilst the 'earnest seekers' were looking for a cure for a single specific problem, and did not express any particular intention to continue to use non-orthodox medicine once this was achieved, the 'eclectic' users were those who, after an initial experience of non-orthodox medicine, had decided that it was a good thing and tended to 'shop around' for what they felt was the best form of treatment (orthodox or non-orthodox) for any particular problem. Some of these expressed an explicitly 'consumerist' approach to healthcare. Joy Sayers, married to a teacher and a former teacher herself, had used both homoeopathy and osteopathy for her family and herself and said:

> We don't talk about health a lot, but I think there is this thing... you go to the doctor and if you think the treatment is a bit much, or does not work, you look around for the right kind of alternative. I tend to try things, and if they work – great!

Another woman, who could remember using as many as seven different kinds of non-orthodox treatment for herself and her children during the past ten years, had been initially convinced of its potential when she had used chiropractic for what a consultant had diagnosed as an arthritic neck. Her attitude was now exuberantly eclectic:

> I am not criticising people, but very often they just go and accept what the doctor says. Perhaps there are some who can't afford it, but they will happily spend £15 on a meal when for the same money you could have alternative medicine as a second opinion. I am far more healthy than I was twenty years ago. I would advise anybody, yes, go to the doctor and get the best you can from there, but you can always get a second opinion from alternative medicine.

Kevin Singer, a factory safety officer, had used herbalism to treat the chest infections which prevented him from enjoying his chosen sport (cycling) to the full. He had, he claimed, changed his attitude to healthcare in general as a result of his experiences. He might go back to the herbalist who had treated him if he had other problems, but equally he was prepared to look at other systems:

> If we need to, we do go to our GP. We are not totally dedicated to one system. We aim to get the best out of all systems.

Note that Kevin Singer like Joy Sayers and most of the other interviewees, was by no means proposing to abandon the use of orthodox medicine, but was looking on it as one useful system among others. The patient/consumer reviews the treatments available and chooses the one which s/he judges appropriate for the problem, rather than relying on medical authority (whether orthodox or non-orthodox).

Members of both the 'eclectic' and the 'stable' categories were likely to express a sense of greater control over their lives as a result of using non-orthodox medicine. This may simply have been a consequence of having achieved confident good health, but several interviewees described immense satisfaction in this new self-reliance:

> I make my own mind up now about these things. Before, I just accepted it (the discomfort of chronic rhinitis). Now I feel that I am in control of my life.

Another interviewee felt that it was the attitude of the practitioner which had given him confidence to make choices and strength of will to carry them through:

> When I saw her I thought, she is of my intelligence, she treats me as an equal... the herbal treatment meant that I had to take the medicine very frequently. It needed confidence to stop a meeting and say, I have got to take my medicine.... You used to have to put your body into the hands of the doctor without questioning, but Mary (the herbalist) encouraged me to look at my own body and monitor what was going on. I have always wanted the kind of honesty she offers.

It is possible that the choices of the 'earnest seekers' and the 'eclectic' users are less random and more structured than I have implied here. Psychologists David Canter and Kerry Booker studied the patterns in consultation of 202 patients and found, as I did, that multiple consultation for a particular illness or health problem was common. Those patients who had used complementary medicine at all had visited an average of 5.4 practitioners each. But although choices appeared more arbitrary within the non-orthodox than the orthodox category, Canter and Booker did find some regularities. For instance, resort to a homoeopath was more likely to be associated with resort to a medical herbalist than with use of a chiropractor or a psychotherapist. These associations did not always bear an obvious relationship to the patients' presenting symptoms, and may reflect patterns of mutual referral among non-orthodox practitioners as much as patients' own judgements (Canter and Booker 1987).

I have summarised the patterns of usage of non-orthodox medicine which I have identified, in Figure 1. This classification is bound to be rather rough and ready – I have had to categorise individuals' usage as 'stable' or

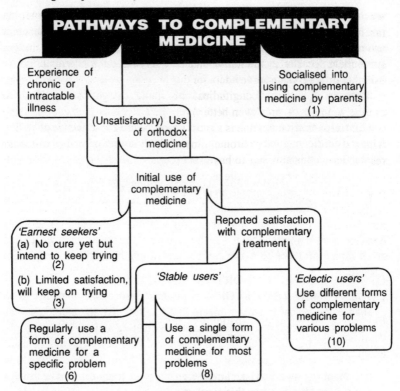

Figure 1 How people use complementary medicine: patterns of practice

'unstable' on the basis of what they told me about what they had done or intended to do, rather than on the basis of long-term observation. Some were clearly in the process of changing their 'health-seeking behaviour' and there could be no easy prediction of when and where this process of change might halt. Also there is no knowing how such patterns may be distributed in the wider community of users of non-orthodox medicine. This selection of this group of interviewees was probably biassed in favour of those whose experience of it is prolonged and conclusive and who therefore have more of a 'story' to tell. A large random sample might well net a number of transient 'one-off' users and would probably include more of the 'earnest seekers' as well. There may even be other patterns of usage which were not represented in my relatively small group, and others may emerge in future; this typology is no more than a summary of what I found at a particular time.

What this research does show very clearly, however, is that if we want a full answer to the question 'why do people use non-orthodox medicine?' then we must be prepared to study not isolated decisions, but chains of decisions taken over quite a long period. The considerations that prompted the initial use may not be the same as those which contribute to the second, third or subsequent occasions. Qualitative data such as I collected is probably more useful than large-scale survey data for this purpose, since it is better adapted to the study of process. (Longitudinal interview data gathered over a period of time would have been even better.)

Complementary medicine is almost always used in the first place to deal with a specific, generally chronic, illness which orthodox medicine has not resolved satisfactorily, but to have said this is not to have said very much, for 'what happens next' is quite as interesting as 'what happened in the first place'. Evidently many people are in the process of changing their approach to medical authority and to family healthcare, and the decision to consult a non-orthodox practitioner may represent only one moment in a series of connected shifts in practice.

ORTHODOX AND NON-ORTHODOX MEDICINE: COMPLEMENTARY USAGE

Reviewing survey data on patients of non-orthodox medicine in various countries, Fulder notes that few claim to have abandoned orthodox medicine altogether:

> The majority appear to be... attempting to get the best out of both systems. Time will tell whether this represents an end point, or a transitional moment, catching in mid-stream a major shift in health care systems.
>
> (Fulder 1988: 38–9)

The people whom I interviewed reported varying degrees of confidence in their GPs, but all could think of occasions on which they had consulted them during the past twelve months or could easily envisage situations where they might do so in the future. Two interviewees had very poor relationships with their GPs and said that they consulted them as little as possible. But one of these remembered seeing her doctor recently when she fell and injured her shoulder and the other said that she would visit her GP if she needed a blood test or inoculation. The rest described positive relationships with their family doctors notwithstanding doubts about particular aspects of orthodox health-care. Almost all of these could cite an occasion during the past twelve months when they had consulted their GP, either on their own behalf or on some other family member's account. Even the 'stable users' claimed that they would call their GP in the case of acute illness or an accident:

> I suppose that it would have to be an emergency situation, someone rolling

around the floor in agony or something like that, and things like breaks and stitches. But if it was something like a nagging pain, for instance, then I would consult the homoeopath first.

Even Lionel Edge, the local evangelist for homoeopathy, could remember calling the doctor when his wife fell and broke her hip, and again when she had a stroke while they were away on holiday.

A number of interviewees said that they might use their GP to obtain a diagnosis of any unfamiliar symptoms, keeping their options open as to whether or not they complied with the treatment recommended. Others felt that they knew from experience which problems their GP could deal with effectively and which were better taken to a non-orthodox practitioner. One 'eclectic' user said:

> We would go to the GP for infections and things like that. I try to resist anti-biotics unless I think they are essential. I don't go to the doctor anyway unless it is something I can't deal with myself. I have not seen a doctor in years about my back because I know I can cope with it outside. I just know that conventional medicine will say go to bed, or wear a corset.

This interviewee had taken lessons in Alexander Technique and had consulted a chiropractor to alleviate chronic back pain, which is what she was referring to when she spoke of 'coping with it outside'. She was fairly typical of a group of interviewees with musculo-skeletal problems who perceived manipulative therapies such as osteopathy and chiropractic as the first resort for these conditions but would take most other problems to their GPs.

A 'stable' user of herbalism who had first consulted the herbalist in connection with persistent eye infections said:

> I would go to my GP first for other things, not connected with my eye, anything that was beyond my ken, anything that was completely new to me. I would probably go to the herbalist first for routine things, but I would not be averse to going to the GP for something really strange.

His attitude reflected a very general view, that non-orthodox and orthodox medicine are complementary systems. As another 'stable' user said:

> We do use our GP for some things. When I had my last baby, for instance. There are things for which the GP has the best view and things for which the homoeopath has the best view. Neither has the whole view, but you can use each correctly.

These interviewees were behaving in a manner not unlike that of the Melanesian people studied by Romanucci-Schwartz (see above) who felt quite competent to judge for themselves which illnesses were appropriately taken to the practitioner of 'western' medicine and which were best treated by local remedies. Individuals and families are devising their own classifications of disease and calculating for themselves which sorts of disease are best treated by which sorts of practitioner. At present, conventional medicine comes first in the hierarchy of resort for most people, with complementary medicine only resorted to later if the treatment administered by the GP is judged unsatisfactory. This had certainly been the order of priority for the 'earnest seekers' in my study. Exposure to non-orthodox medicine, however, can change this order of precedence if it is thought to be successful; for many of the 'stable' and 'eclectic' users, the hierarchy of resort depended on the patient's assessment of symptoms. Most interviewees employed their own practical classifications of disease based on an opposition between 'routine' and 'strange/unusual' symptoms, or between 'acute/surgical' and 'chronic/nagging' conditions. Others relied on their GPs to provide a diagnosis of new symptoms, but having ascertained that they were not suffering from a serious illness would go to a non-orthodox practitioner for actual treatment.

There is certainly little evidence that those who consult non-orthodox practitioners have lost all faith in orthodox medicine or have ceased entirely to use the services available to them under the NHS. If, as I have suggested, many turn to non-orthodox medicine as a result of dissatisfaction with orthodox medicine, this dissatisfaction is not total. Many are warmly appreciative of services like screening for cervical cancer, childhood inoculation and diagnostic testing which are still free under the NHS. It could even be the case that those who resort to non-orthodox practitioners make more use of orthodox medicine than those who do not. The Dutch NIPG study found that recent users of non-orthodox medicine were more likely to have visited their GP eight or more times in the previous year than those who had never used non-orthodox medicine (Ooijendijk, Mackenbach and Limberger 1981: 12). This paradox may simply be a product of the fact that users of non-orthodox medicine are often chronically ill or at any rate have good reason to worry about their health.

What I find perturbing is that only a minority (30 per cent) of my interviewees had told their GPs that they were using non-orthodox medicine. Sometimes this was because the sufferer had consulted the complementary practitioner about a very specific problem (e.g. back pain) which the GP had already been unable to treat and which the patient regarded as having no bearing on any other problem subsequently presented to the GP. The patient simply found no occasion to mention the non-orthodox treatment. More frequently, interviewees expressed a positive concern that their GP should not find out about it, fearing ridicule or disapproval. May Howard, an elderly cancer patient who had used spiritual healing to cope with pain, said that she had never discussed this with either her GP or her consultant because she did not think that they would either understand it or sympathise.

> I think the hospital doctor is such a pragmatic person, he would regard it as a lot of mumbo-jumbo. I don't discuss it at all except with people I think will be receptive to it. There is no point if it is going to cause dissension. There are those sort of minds, doctors with totally closed minds. It would be useless discussing it with them.

And Rose Buckley, who had consulted a homoeopath for both back problems and 'nerves', said that while she had more faith in her present GP than in others who had treated her, she had never confided in him about her consultations with the homoeopath:

> My doctor doesn't know. It is something you have done on your own. All he said to me when I went to him is that I had lost a lot of weight. Let's face it, ten years ago if you went to a GP and told him about that (i.e. consulting a non-orthodox practitioner) he would be ready to throw you out of the door because they didn't want to know. And even now they are not keen.

A general fear was that the doctor would regard resort to a non-orthodox practitioner as a flouting of his/her medical authority, a breach of the rules governing proper patient behaviour which would disturb an otherwise harmonious relationship. Whilst, as I described in the previous section, the experience of using complementary medicine had sometimes stimulated an exhilarating sense of control over one's own treatment, there was continued recognition of the practical need to recognise the hierarchical assumptions on which orthodox medical practice is based if one is to continue to benefit from the services it can offer. Those who had discussed their use of non-orthodox medicine with their GPs were mainly articulate and highly educated people with a good deal of confidence in their ability to convince the doctors that their resort to a 'rival' was justifiable, or at any rate in their own capacity to withstand his or her disapproval. Actually, GPs' attitudes as reported by interviewees who had confided in their doctors were not always negative. Roger Avery had told his GP that he intended to seek non-orthodox treatment for his seborrhoeic eczema:

> He said he wouldn't use them himself, but if I thought they might help I should have a go. Well, if he could not help, then he hadn't really got a leg to stand on!

Joy Sayers told her doctor that she had consulted an osteopath and said:

I think she sort of tolerated it. She said, you know that you will keep having to go back to the osteopath for treatment. That was her comment. But of course she herself has not seen me for the past year as I have not had to get pain killers from her any more.

If these GPs were unlikely to give an official blessing to patients' experiments with non-orthodox treatment they did not feel able to condemn them when they were unable to cure the condition themselves.

I will discuss what is known about about GPs' attitudes to non-orthodox medicine in Chapter 5 and will show that there is a high degree of interest in non-orthodox medicine among some doctors. In the area where the research was conducted there are not a few GPs who take an interest in complementary medicine and who even co-operate actively with local non-orthodox practitioners. On the other hand, there are many in the orthodox medical profession who are worried that patients will receive inappropriate or even dangerous treatment from non-orthodox practitioners, especially from those who do not also have a conventional medical training (BMA 1986: 4, Stalker and Glymour 1989: 27). To what extent are such fears well grounded? From one point of view the medical profession might take comfort from the fact that when people first resort to a complementary practitioner it is usually only after they have already undergone lengthy (if from their point of view unsuccessful) treatment from orthodox doctors. Orthodox medicine has already had the opportunity to scrutinise the symptoms and identify any serious or life-threatening condition. Since few complementary practitioners do home visits, patients who are prostrate or severely injured will not normally be attended by such therapists anyway.

On the other hand, we have seen that there is a group of users of non-orthodox medicine who resort to it regularly for some conditions. These habitual users tend to judge for themselves which problems are best presented to the GP and which to a complementary practitioner. One might argue that if patients insist on taking the responsibility for making such decisions then they must take the consequences of their actions. If it turns out that a complementary practitioner has failed to diagnose a serious disease or has prescribed inappropriate treatment, then such patients have only themselves to blame. Yet, as we have seen, some of them have taken the matter into their own hands precisely because they feel that it is orthodox medicine which too often delivers dangerous or inappropriate treatment, and non-orthodox medicine which offers a 'safer' alternative. Some protagonists of non-orthodox medicine have pointed out that far more proven instances of damage to health and wellbeing resulting from use of orthodox medicine have hit the headlines than cases of dangerous incompetence on the part of non-orthodox practitioners. Inadequately tested drugs have led to children being born with major deformities, mistakes on the part of anaesthetists have resulted in brain damage to patients, and many hospital patients are cured of their original illness only to contract infections on the wards.

A less polemical view, and one held by several professional organisations of complementary practitioners, is that no danger to the patient can arise if non-orthodox therapists are well trained in all aspects of diagnosis and are prepared to refer patients back to orthodox doctors if they encounter conditions which they cannot treat themselves. Many complementary practitioners whom I interviewed claimed to do just that (see Chapter 7) and if this happens at all frequently, then the complementary practitioner may actually save rather than endanger the lives of patients, being in a position to identify symptoms which, for one reason or another, will not be presented to GPs.

This fear that serious conditions will be overlooked as a consequence of using non-orthodox medicine should not be dismissed out of hand as professional paranoia on the part of orthodox doctors. Many people are demanding more responsibility for their own healthcare, more say in decisions about what treatment they receive and wider options for treatment. If they go about making such decisions armed with adequate information about the strengths and weaknesses of the different kinds of therapy available to them (including orthodox medicine) and knowledgeable about screening facilities for serious illnesses, then taking reponsibility for their own choice of healthcare should expose them to few risks. To the extent that they feel actively involved in their treatment, this may promote a confident sense of control which could be beneficial to healing. Their safety will also depend on the orthodox and the non-orthodox practitioner each being well informed about the other's modes of diagnosis and treatment and their preparedness to communicate with each other quickly and amicably where there is cause for concern.

It has been pointed out to me that the demand that the patient evince loyalty to the practitioner's system is not exclusive to orthodox doctors; some homoeopaths, and possibly practitioners of other systems of non-orthodox medicine, occasionally tend to adopt an attitude of high-minded disapproval towards some orthodox treatments and this may communicate itself to the patient. Certainly many homoeopaths will put it to patients that they should attempt to wean themselves from reliance on allopathic drugs. While the emphasis is on coming off the drugs with the patient's agreement and at the pace which the patient feels able to cope with, it is possible that patients could be deterred from confiding in them about allopathic drugs which they are taking concurrently with non-orthodox treatment.

The likelihood that orthodox and non-orthodox treatments will actively conflict or interfere with each other in a way that is hazardous to the patient is probably remote in the majority of cases, but this does not dispose of the general problem of therapeutic responsibility. Formerly the individual who fell sick had a very limited number of options to choose from (self-treatment, consulting an orthodox practitioner, no action at all). A much wider range of possibilities is now available to many people. If the shift from medical monism to medical pluralism continues, then the rights and responsibilities of those involved in healthcare (and this includes patients themselves) will need to be re-thought and perhaps re-distributed. For the orthodox medical profession the problem is how to modify a conception of the doctor/patient relationship which assumes that it is the doctor who has control over and responsibility for the therapeutic process, while the patient merely 'complies'. This is particularly difficult for the doctor to do as long as s/he occupies a position within the bureaucratic organisation of state medicine. For the non-orthodox professions the problem is how to deal with the contradiction between a Hippocratic commitment to the patient's wellbeing and eventual cure with an ideological commitment to the principles of patient responsibility and patient choice, which surely carry the implication that the patient may choose to reject the therapist's advice at any time, or may simply choose another therapy.

COMPLEMENTARY MEDICINE, THE HOUSEHOLD AND CHANGES IN HEALTH-SEEKING BEHAVIOUR

So far, I have been discussing the decision to use complementary medicine as though it were a purely individual step. Most non-orthodox medical practice, like orthodox medical practice, is individualistic in the sense that whilst the practitioner may well take into account the patient's social roles and responsibilities in devising a plan of treatment, s/he nevertheless expects to deal with the adult patient personally and alone, in a dyadic relationship which is bounded by notions of privacy and confidentiality (see Janzen 1978: 224). Yet if we wish to study the process by which patterns of healthcare change, we may have to abandon or suspend this focus on the individual. We have already seen that membership of local networks affects access to information about new healthcare options. Medical sociology also tells us that the healthcare practices of the individual will probably be influenced by what other members of the household do. For example, studies of lay health practices in Britain have shown that women take major responsibility for the healthcare administered informally through the household. Their multifarious duties include ensuring smooth relationships among household members so as to reduce stress and anxiety; providing a healthy diet for the family; supervising the regimes of young children so that they get adequate rest, food and exercise; nursing members of the family who are sick; making decisions about when to consult the doctor on behalf of children. As carers of the elderly, handicapped or chronically ill it may fall to them to make decisions on behalf of adult members of the family as well.

> Their caring role places them at the interface between the family and the state, as the go-betweens linking the informal health-care system with the formal apparatus of the welfare state.
>
> (Graham 1985: 26)

When non-orthodox medicine is used, it seems just as likely to be women who have this mediating role where young children are concerned. Eight of my interviewees had children under the age of fifteen and in all but one of these families it appeared to be the mother who made decisions about whether children should visit practitioners (orthodox or non-orthodox) and who accompanied them to consultations. In families with older children this had usually been the practice in the past.

Adult men seem to have fewer responsibilities of this kind. Yet there is also a body of sociological literature on gender roles and the household which distinguishes domestic *responsibility* from domestic *power*; women have domestic responsibility but their exercise of this is constrained by the way in which men exercise domestic power. For instance, a wife takes responsibility for planning and serving the household's meals, but the kind of food she buys and cooks may be dictated by her husband's preference to a large extent (Charles and Kerr 1988: 63ff). Women are responsible for nursing sick members of the family, but a wife will have to co-operate with her husband's perceptions of illness; he may expect to be nursed at home when she does not regard the ailment as justifying this extra demand on her time (Cornwell 1984: 139). Whether this compliance is exacted through women's material dependence on men or whether it is the product of ideological conceptions of manly or womanly behaviour is a large issue which we cannot hope to resolve here, but it is not difficult to see that gender roles are relevant to understanding the household dimension of non-orthodox medicine.

If the healthcare practices of both adult men and women are tied in with a gendered system of domestic privileges and reponsibilities, then perhaps the household is a more appropriate unit of study than the individual. Many interviewees reported that since starting to use non-orthodox medicine themselves they had also used it for their children, or that other members of the household or close family had used it for themselves at their recommendation. We have already seen how users discover practitioners through lay referral networks. Table 8 (see p.67) shows us how these networks operate when we consider the interviewee as initiator rather than as recipient of advice or information about complementary medicine. In some cases the interviewee's spouse or other adult relative has simply made a 'one-off' trial of non-orthodox medicine for a specific illness, but in others one spouse has effectively 'converted' the other to his/her preferred system or pattern of usage.

Kevin Singer, for instance, is a young factory inspector who first became interested in non-orthodox medicine when a herbalist successfully treated the chest infections which were interfering with his sporting activities. This delighted him and he suggested to his wife Joy that she see the same practitioner for a troublesome condition of the scalp which was causing her hair to fall out. She too liked the herbalist's approach and they both became what I have termed 'stable' users of this system of medicine, though they also continued to use their GP for some purposes. On the advice of the herbalist they have changed their diet considerably, from a fairly conventional 'meat and two veg.' regime to one which includes more wholefoods and some purely vegetarian meals. As yet, Joy said, they had made only slight modifications to the children's diet, as they did not feel that such young children would take easily to the kind of food they were beginning to relish themselves, but she expected that they would introduce more changes as the children grew older and went to school.

I interviewed more women than men in this study, and it was very obvious from what they said that it would be difficult for a wife to introduce radical changes in her own or the household's health regime without, at the very least, the friendly co-operation of her husband. Jan Mason, a divorced actress, had used homoeopathy for some years, having first encountered it when she was still married. Her husband had vehemently opposed her using it for their sons:

> My beliefs went one way and his went another. It was incredibly difficult. The kids had sort of asthma and eczema. I was interested in treating things through diet and that was relatively prior to my interest in homoeopathy. But it was hard to introduce new treatment in the household or new diets either, because the two tend to go together.

Whilst this was not the only bone of contention between herself and her former husband, she felt that dissension over the children's healthcare had embittered their relationship further. She now lives happily with a lesbian partner who shares her interest in non-orthodox medicine. Both women consult a homoeopath for themselves and for their children, and both have become complete vegetarians.

In some families the husband could not share the wife's enthusiasm for non-orthodox medicine but was content that she use it for herself and their children. Anne Griffiths, who had been brought up to use naturopathy by her mother, told me that her husband had never consulted a naturopath himself:

> My husband goes to our GP on his own behalf. He comes from a family

where they tended to reach for a pill box for any little thing and he still is a bit like that. It goes by your family. But he always backed me up when I tried to nurse the children through illnesses the naturopathic way.

The husband appears to have treated the children's healthcare as a matter which was well within the wife's province and therefore one in which she had discretion to do as she pleased so long as the children thrived, and so long as the breadwinner was not required to change his own habits.

Other women described much more positive attitudes; in some cases the encouragement of other members of the family had helped them to persevere with demanding regimes prescribed by non-orthodox practitioners. Maureen Pratt, a middle-aged clerical worker, found her husband and children very supportive when, at the suggestion of a herbalist, she undertook a rigorous diet in order to control severe migraine.

My family reacted very well, really. Actually my son did the fasting with me, he was absolutely wonderful. He did three days fasting and two on fruit juice only, just to keep me company, nothing else. He didn't cheat. Later my daughter went to Mary (the herbalist) too, also my husband for his blood pressure. It taught us a lot about eating sensibly.

She then went on to describe further dietary changes which she had felt might be beneficial for the whole family:

I went through a spell of not eating anything with additives. Then I thought, this is stupid, it is a matter of finding out which additives are bad and which are good. I don't eat so much tinned stuff now... my husband does agree with all this, but you do tend to go back to old habits and he does like his steak sometimes. But he is still interested.

This case is a good example of the way in which the wife's experiments with non-orthodox medicine and her exploration of new ideas on health and nutrition, encountered in the course of what I have called 'homework', have had an effect on the healthcare culture of the whole family. Most of the married women emphasised without my prompting them that whilst it was obviously simpler for them to undertake dietary changes themselves if the whole family were agreeable, obviating the necessity to cook two quite different meals all the time, they could not introduce their own dietary ideas to the rest of the household if the husband was not supportive or at least tolerant. Husbands seemed to be more active and vocal in choices involving family diet than in choices about children's treatment, where they seemed more ready to leave the initiative to their wives. A larger and more randomly selected sample would tell us more about how common these attitudes are; how many women, like Jan Mason during her marriage, are prevented from introducing changes which they believe in by the antagonism of husbands, and how many, like Maureen Pratt, meet with co-operation and even constructive interest.

Women, especially where children are concerned, seem to be the most active channels of new ideas about healthcare into the family, but men are not without influence. There were only four married men in my sample, but in each case the wife had used her husband's preferred form of non-orthodox medicine at least once, either for herself or for her children. Unmarried adults, however, seem less likely to have a very marked input into family patterns of healthcare, even if they still live with their parents.

Households with young children tend to develop their own 'sub-cultures' where healthcare is concerned. The parents create an ethos in which certain health choices are approved or disapproved, certain ways of dealing with ill health will be regarded as appropriate or inappropriate, certain dietary habits will be favoured or frowned on. These cultures tend to persist over time, but they can change quite sharply if either partner can persuade the other that things should be done differently. In some of the cases I have described the cultural 'micro-climate' of the household had been altered either as a direct result of a member's exposure to non-orthodox medicine, or as a result of a more eclectic exploration of new ideas about diet and wellbeing.

In the course of the research I became interested in the question of whether the younger generation in such households will perpetuate their parents' healthcare practices, especially their usage of non-orthodox medicine. Unfortunately very few of the people interviewed had adult children who had grown up and left home since the interviewee had begun to use non-orthodox medicine. However, some of the data do throw light on the process by which young people take over responsibility for their own healthcare. Some were obviously very receptive to their parents' ideas. Yvonne Mullineux, a farmer, said:

> Both my sons take an interest, but the younger one in particular. He has tried umpteen things for his acne. I got him some ointment from the homoeopath and he was very willing to try.

In this family, the younger son was actually considering taking up osteopathy as a career at the time of the interview.

Jill Kinsey, a teacher's wife with a large family, found that her younger teenage children co-operated fairly readily with her ideas about healthcare. Her twelve-year-old son had expressed grudging appreciation of the slow but effective homoeopathic treatment of his eczema provided by the practitioner to whom his mother had taken him. The eldest daughter, however, was seventeen and was very sceptical. She has more or less taken over her own healthcare. She has gone off homoeopathic remedies lately. She is very adult. Mothers aren't anything to do with where she is at. All her friends at college seem to have their aspirin bottle handy and you tend to throw over family habits at that age.

Possibly adult children who have actually left home or are about to do so are more receptive to new ideas about healthcare introduced by their parents, having less need to assert their independent judgement. Sally Burnett, whose recent exposure to herbalism had led her to become very cautious in her use of conventional drugs, had daughters who were in their early twenties, and she found that

> They are like me. I am probably more interested in herbalism than they are but I can see the influence is growing on them. They have seen my experience and now they have to be desperate to visit a doctor.

Most of the interviewees who claimed that members of the family outside the immediate household had tried non-orthodox medicine on their recommendation or suggestion were referring to grown sons and daughters who had left home, as in the case of Joy Sayers' adult daughter, who tried osteopathy after her mother had received treatment for back pain, even though the other members of the Sayers family tended to regard Joy's experiments with complementary medicine with amused tolerance.

Possibly there is more continuity with daughters than sons. If it is women who have the greater hand in shaping the healthcare 'micro-climate' of the household, then much will depend on the women whom sons marry. Nell Bradbury, widow of an engineer, had used naturopathy for many years, had strong ideas about healthy diet and had brought up her two sons as vegetarians. Her story says much about the ways in which new family health cultures are created and maintained:

> The children were brought up the same. I dealt with Tony when he had diphtheria and with the health of all the family. I was very worried doing it on my own. It's one thing doing it for yourself or your husband, but it is far different risking a child. I felt it was right, you know, but I would have liked the backing of somebody very experienced behind me. I did go to this naturopath in Leeds, you know, and he said you are doing the right thing, keep on doing the right thing, and that was a relief. But I would have liked to have had somebody near who would have just come to see the kid, you know. My eldest son would certainly use these ideas now, but it's wives, you know, that don't.... Jessica, my elder daughter-in-law, had to show me that she could do what I could do, but she doesn't do so much of it now. And Tony, my youngest son – his wife has never gone

along with it. You know, the men have to accept what the women provide. But the grandchildren enjoy the vegetarian meals I cook when they come here.

A few interviewees had tried to persuade older members of their families to use non-orthodox medicine, with occasional success. Mike Sullivan's wife Sue had urged her mother to visit the homoeopath which Mike and Sue had used for themselves and their children and she had been pleased with the treatment. But most interviewees thought that any such attempt to persuade their parents would be ill judged and a waste of time. Mike Sullivan thought his own parents would

> go back and back to their GP even when he could not diagnose a problem. They wanted re-assurance. They would be contemptuous of things like homoeopathy, they would think it nonsense.

Sociologists who have studied attitudes to family healthcare have sometimes noticed that generational differences are fairly common. Blaxter and Patterson note that while a range of attitudes was found in all three generations of the Scottish families they studied, a 'passive dissatisfied' attitude was relatively more common among the young mothers, while compliance and deference was more common among the older women (Blaxter and Patterson 1982). Other sociologists have noted that older people often subscribe to a more moralistic view of illness, while younger people are more likely to see illness as a product of social and environmental factors (Stacey 1988: 150). If this is the case, one might expect that it would be younger people who would be more dependent on professional advice and treatment. Margaret Stacey argues that it may be the experience of free treatment that is the crucial factor here, rather than age as such. The whole post-war cohort in Britain have learnt to take for granted the free medical treatment available under the NHS (Stacey 1988: 151). If they demand more professional attention it is because they have grown up to expect it and cannot conceive of things otherwise.

Most of the people I interviewed were between thirty and fifty years old and would have been children in the immediate post-war decades. Their own mothers' experience of healthcare would certainly have been dominated by the rapid growth of the NHS during this period. If there is a reluctance to contest the word of the GP, which many interviewees attributed to their spouses or siblings, it could be the product of this generation's perception that there can really be no 'alternative' to orthodox medicine. Yet an older group of interviewees could often identify aspects of their mothers' practice which they regarded as having predisposed them to use some kind of non-orthodox medicine. In Stoke-on-Trent, as in many other predominantly working-class areas, many families before the Second World War relied very largely on home remedies for their healthcare, being unable to afford the doctor. Herbal preparations or the unprocessed herbs themselves could be bought cheaply across the counters at a number of herbal stores, some of which still flourish today. A professional herbalist, who still practises in the city, described those days as follows:

> It was a very poor area, where women always had to work, where kids were sent out with a penny and out of that they had to buy chips and a round of bread and fat. They still come to me, those old ones. They couldn't afford the doctor when they were young, so they had to use the herbalist.

An elderly working-class woman actually described her parents as being 'herbalists'.

> They were all for herbs, were Mum and Dad. And they treated themselves. They didn't bother with the doctor much at all, they had got to be very ill before they had the doctor. When you got a cold an onion was sprinkled with sugar and you would have the juice. My father used to buy his own herbs, put them in pans and boil them up, make the liquid and drink it that way.

If some young women are disposed to be more questioning of the orthodox doctor's advice, more ready to explore and accept alternative viewpoints, they may be practising from choice the medical self-reliance which some of their grandmothers had to practise from necessity.

I have concentrated on the household and family as channels for the spread of new ideas about healthcare, but plenty of interviewees could give instances of how unrelated friends or colleagues had tried complementary medicine at their suggestion. Jessica Moore, a retired teacher who was a thoroughly eclectic user of non-orthodox medicine, gave a good account of how lay referral works through neighbourhood networks:

> I would never push it down anyone's throat but if it crops up then I would always mention it because I feel, I would always say, why don't you try it? I wouldn't try to persuade them because I don't believe in that but I would always give them my experience. I have told lots of people about little things like the yoga exercise for sore throats which works. I have given that to lots of people at school. One or two have tried the homoeopath.

The waves that begin when a household experiments with new forms of healthcare ripple outwards into the community through all kinds of social networks (see Table 8 for a summary of categories of people who had used complementary medicine at the recommendation of interviewees).

Table 8 Individuals cited in interviews as having consulted a complementary practitioner on the recommendation of one of the interviewees (user study)

Friends or acquaintances of interviewees	8
Kin (members of immediate household)	12
Kin (outside immediate household)	5
Total	25

USING COMPLEMENTARY MEDICINE: AGNOSTIC DESPERATION OR CULTURAL CHANGE?

The use of non-orthodox medicine can be treated as the product of individual decisions for the purposes of research, but we have seen that often these decisions are not made alone, nor are they always without consequences for others in the patient's family or social circle. If complementary medicine is used more widely that it was, say, twenty years ago, then the dynamics of the household and of local networks are crucial for an understanding of this kind of cultural change at the 'micro' level.

But perhaps we should not use terms like 'cultural change' too eagerly. If some people are initially turning to complementary medicine chiefly because they have illnesses which orthodox medicine cannot cure, as the first part of this chapter suggests, is this not simply a situational response to particular problems? The eclectic usage of assorted curative systems characteristic of some of my interviewees suggests a kind of medical agnosticism, an absence of commitment to any system of medical knowledge, decisions made on purely pragmatic grounds. As Morgan, Calnan and Manning have pointed out, it is always difficult to judge how far a decision about healthcare, studied in retrospect, was guided by particular beliefs about the causation of disease:

> In the case of studies of illness behaviour, respondents' accounts of their behaviour may be coloured by their experience since the decision to seek medical care was made, and particularly through the knowledge gained from visiting the health service.... Since data on health beliefs are collected at the same time as statements of retrospective behaviour, it is difficult to identify whether beliefs determine behaviour or vice versa.
>
> (Morgan, Calnan and Manning 1985: 88)

This was equally true of my own study inasmuch as the people I interviewed had already visited at least one complementary practitioner and had been exposed to his/her practices and ideas. Using this methodology it would be difficult to identify prior mental dispositions such as might have made, say, homoeopathy or acupuncture more acceptable alternatives to a particular patient. Several interviewees remarked that in deciding to consult a non-orthodox practitioner for the first time they had had to overcome doubts of a more or less intellectual nature, and that they did not go to the practitioner initially with any great faith in the validity of this system of medicine:

> Iridology is to me a questionable, contentious issue, but it works. I found it incredible, but I was so pissed off with the doctors, I thought this is not going to be a cure at all, but I will give it a try.

> I was cynical at first when I went to the homoeopath for the first time, for the same reason that I am cynical of conventional medicine... I don't accept authority easily.

Not all interviewees claimed this degree of scepticism, but desperation generally dominated conviction in their accounts, a readiness to 'try anything', however contrary to 'common sense'.

Studies which have compared the attitudes of users with non-users of complementary medicine, such as the Dutch NIPG study, have generally concentrated on situational judgements about the efficacy and delivery of different systems, rather than explored underlying cognitive predispositions (Ooijendijk, Mackenbach and Limberger 1981: 26ff). A study by two British psychologists (Furnham and Smith 1988) which did try to discover whether people choose non-orthodox medicine on the basis of theories about the cause and cure of illness, compared samples of patients from a homoeopathic and a GP practice. The samples did not differ significantly in respect of broad demographic characteristics, but did exhibit some differences in attitude. The homoeopathic patients were more inclined to believe that the body can heal itself and less inclined to endorse a passive attitude to treatment. However, the researchers found that in many respects the beliefs of the two groups were fundamentally similar and that such differences as existed could easily be accounted for by the patients' experiences of illness. If homoeopathic patients have negative attitudes towards orthodox medicine, this may simply be because they have tried it and found it useless in respect of some major health problems. An Australian study found that while patients of naturopaths usually held beliefs about the importance of diet which were consistent with those of their therapists, patients of chiropractors often appreciated the results of treatment without any particular commitment to the theory behind it (James, Fox and Taheri 1983: 384). Furnham and Smith are probably right when they state that treating consumers of complementary medicine as an undifferentiated category may be misleading – there is no reason to suppose that they all have the same motives (Furnham and Smith 1988: 688).

To distentangle entirely the effect of recent experience from enduring belief may be impossible, but the task is the harder if we do not distinguish between first-time resort to non-orthodox medicine and subsequent usage. My interviewees' accounts of their experiences over time suggest that the initial visit to a complementary practitioner is almost always motivated by a straightforward and pragmatic desire to cure some intractable problem. Subsequent decisions will be influenced by the outcome of the first encounter, by interaction with practitioners' ideas and methods, perhaps also by the degree of encouragement they receive from family members. It would make cultural belief systems easier for social scientists to study if they were always stable and orderly, but in the area of health and illness – as in most others – ideas and values are constantly being re-worked in the light of personal experience, interaction with others, exposure to the media and a myriad other influences.

SUMMARY

The general conclusions we can draw from a small-scale study like the one described here must be limited, but my data confirm what large-scale studies also have found, i.e. that initial resort to non-orthodox medicine is usually motivated by the need to cure a particular health problem (usually chronic). This problem will be one which orthodox medicine has not been able to cure, or has not been able to cure on terms which the patient accepts. Users generally find out about particular practitioners through informal sources, but have usually tried to inform themselves about their disease and about possible cures. The structure of local networks and the organisation of the household have a lot to do with the way in which use of non-orthodox therapies spreads. Dissatisfaction with orthodox medicine is seldom total, and users of non-orthodox medicine will generally continue to use orthodox medicine for some purposes. We cannot generalise from such a small group of subjects about how many people who use complementary medicine continue to use it subsequently, but the data suggest a variety of orientation and degree of commitment. From the data I have presented we can deduce a good deal about the way in which the use of complementary medicine is disseminated, especially the role of the household and of local social and cultural networks. These 'micro' changes are now quite widespread and so we need to consider how far they add up to a larger shift in patterns of healthcare, and the broader import of such change. I continue this theme in the next chapter.

4 Satisfactions and dissatisfactions
Consumers and patients

In this chapter I continue the theme of whether the popularity of complementary medicine is evidence of a change in the way in which people perceive and evaluate healthcare. Does it imply new criteria of efficacy or different perceptions of the patient role? How far does it imply a rejection of or dissatisfaction with orthodox medical care?

RATING SATISFACTION

Studying the people who use complementary medicine tells us a great deal about the way in which particular therapies or practitioners are chosen; it should also tell us something about how people perceive the treatment they are given and how they rate its success. In this chapter I draw some general conclusions about how complementary medicine is perceived by those who use it and the implications of these perceptions for future demand.

Everyone who has an open mind on the subject would like an answer to the question 'does complementary medicine work?'. Unfortunately the social scientist is not qualified to answer this question in a clinical sense. Indeed, the issue of who precisely is qualified to answer it is a contentious one. So long as the orthodox medical establishment insists that double blind trials are the only scientific way to test the efficacy of any system of treatment, many therapies will remain untested because they do not lend themselves to this kind of trial. Where clinical trials have been carried out, there has not always been agreement as to how the results should be interpreted.

Meredith McGuire cautions social scientists against an unthinking acceptance of medical definitions of the problem. She suggests that

> A quite radical approach to the problem is to set aside... the assumption that the medical reality, as promulgated by the dominant health specialists in this culture, is necessarily the 'true' reality. From a sociological perspective, the medical definition of reality must be seen as one among

many competing conceptions of illness, its causes, and treatment. Medical reality, too, is socially constructed.

(McGuire 1988: 5)

Writing on ritual healing groups in the United States of America, she states that

Nonscientific medical systems 'work' because they provide meaning and empirical proofs in support of their explanations. The quality of such proofs is that the sickness episode is consistent with the expectations of the participants. There is a sense of reassurance in knowing what to expect to experience – such as feeling pain when one is supposed to feel pain. Therapy consists of not only the various means for healing illness but also the means by which an illness is named and given cultural form.

(McGuire 1988: 235)

and that

Much alternative healing works in all of these meaning-providing senses of the word. Indeed, part of the appeal of these medical systems is their lack of sharp dichotomies between the meaning-providing elements and the healing practices, in contrast with 'scientific' medicine.

(McGuire 1988: 6)

This, she admits, is more characteristic of some therapies than others.

McGuire's research concentrated largely on groups which do not fall within the definition of non-orthodox medicine which I have used in this book. She is concerned primarily with non-medical systems of healing such as Christian science, spiritual healing, occult and metaphysical groups and is only secondarily interested in the kinds of curative practice which I have researched (which she terms the 'manipulative and technique practitioners'). But I find very useful her suggestion that it is possible to see some forms of healing not merely as systems of therapy but also as systems of knowledge which address themselves to the nature of the human individual and which attach new symbolic interpretations to the sick person's symptoms and suffering. In the last chapter we saw that the patient does not always or even usually arrive at the practitioner's consulting room with any prior knowledge of how the therapy is supposed to work, nor any special commitment to its theories. To the extent that the practitioner's discourse replaces orthodox explanations with meanings and interpretations which are more satisfactory to the patient, and provides evidence consistent with those meanings, then they may be said to 'work', although not in any clinical sense.

Let us take the hypothetical case of a person who consults a homoeopath for asthma. Suppose that after some initial treatment the patient feels that the asthma is improved but not eradicated. The homoeopath sees the problem as deep-seated and explains this to the patient. It might be that the homoeopath sees the problem as stemming from the inappropriate treatment of chest infections in childhood, some chronic weakening of the system, or as related to stressful episodes in the patient's recent past. The patient is assured that the asthma can be cured if s/he will adhere to the regime suggested by the homoeopath, although it may not be a speedy process and a temporary return of symptoms in the course of treatment may be regarded as normal. The asthma is still there to some extent but the patient has been provided with a new context of explanation for his or her suffering. Insofar as this new interpretation is found acceptable and creates positive feelings of comfort and confidence on the part of the patient, then there is a sense in which it has 'worked'. This, at least, is how I understand McGuire's suggestion, and the joy expressed by some of the interviewees at having been offered a new way of looking at their illnesses, that sense of a more relevant order being imposed on problematic experiences, certainly gives support to her view.

Consider, for instance, Geoff Allen's delight when an iridologist gave him an explanation for his chronic ear infections. She related this illness to bad dietary habits and long-standing digestive problems:

> What got me was that she said that from a holistic point of view, if you cannot eliminate in the normal way where does the residual muck go? It can go into your eyes, your breath and your ears. And lo and behold, I realised it. She said I was excreting rubbish through my ears and this of course fitted into place, because the wax was black and sticky. No-one ever told me that, they just said 'you're producing too much wax'. And again I discovered to my astonishment.... I said what about all this BO I used to have? She said 'well, if you don't excrete in the normal way then you exude it in another way' and this struck me as so patently obvious.

In the interview Geoff expressed a lot of anger that these connections had not been made by the various doctors who had treated him throughout his life, thereby (as he saw it) prolonging his suffering so that he was near to giving up his teaching job on account of ill health. His delight with Mary's treatment was not simply a matter of relief from discomfort, but came from being offered a view of his body and person which made sense of a lot of diverse experiences (poor digestion, nervous tension, ear problems, bad breath) by linking them within a holistic framework and assuring him that improvement in all these things was possible, although it might take time and dietary discipline on his part.

If this constitutes efficacy then it is not the kind of efficacy which will satisfy the medical scientist who would be more interested in the nature of the substances administered in the course of Geoff's treatment, the precise kind of dietary regime which was followed and how these might be considered to have affected the ear symptoms first presented. In any case, we cannot assume that all patients are as open to new interpretations of their symptoms as Geoff Allen and his like. But if complementary therapists are offering what patients feel to be more plausible accounts of chronic or intractable suffering, then this is an aspect of their appeal which orthodox medicine cannot ignore.

Another more conventional approach open to the social scientist is simply to measure patients' expressed satisfaction with the treatments offered by complementary practitioners, leaving it to the respondent to decide what counts as 'satisfaction'. Researchers who have used this method have generally reported high levels of expressed satisfaction with non-orthodox treatments. The survey of readers carried out by the consumer magazine *Which* showed that 82 per cent of respondents who claimed to have used complementary medicine said that they had been cured or that their condition had improved, and about three-quarters of the respondents said that they would use this form of medicine again (*Which* 1986). The MORI poll found that 81 per cent of the respondents who had used complementary medicine claimed some degree of satisfaction with the treatment (MORI 1989) and several smaller studies show similar results.

But simply asking about general satisfaction with a system of treatment is a very blunt research instrument; it does not, for instance, tell us whether patients have the same expectations of complementary medicine as they do of orthodox medicine, nor whether they judge different kinds of medicine by the same criteria. Donnelly, Spykerboer and Thong carried out a study of asthmatic and non-asthmatic hospital patients in Australia and found high levels of expressed satisfaction with both orthodox and 'alternative' medicine among respondents (Donnelly, Spykerboer and Thong 1985: 540). When they disaggregated the responses of those who had used non-orthodox therapies they found that chiropractic elicited more expressed satisfaction than homoeopathy or acupuncture. Similar findings are reported in another Australian study (Parker and Tupling 1976: 607). I agree with Taylor that attempts to measure or explain satisfaction with complementary medicine when it is treated as an undifferentiated category may not be useful:

> Different therapies may have gained adherents for different reasons, not all of which may be expected to relate to developments within modern medicine.
>
> (Taylor 1984: 204)

We learn much more about the therapeutic process when questions about satisfaction are refined or when responses are related to other data. A study of fifty-six patients at an alternative healthcare centre in Southampton found that after eight weeks thirty-three of the patients who were interviewed felt much better, although only nineteen had completed their treatment at the time. This subjective improvement was associated with decreases in scores for depression and pain. But the researchers also noted that most of the patients were well informed about complementary medicine and had high expectations of treatment:

> Expectations appeared to be correlated with outcome: if people expected to get better treatment was more likely to be effective.
>
> (Moore, Phipps and Marcer 1985: 28)

In an Australian study, chiropractic patients were administered a questionnaire around ten weeks after the initial treatment, the result being that 37 per cent reported 'total' improvement, 32 per cent reported 'considerable' improvement, 19 per cent 'some' improvement and 11 per cent no improvement at all. The authors note that at the start of treatment most patients were 'confidently reassured' that they would get better, which 'resulted in a rapid relief of symptoms and a considerable reduction in the expectation of serious morbidity' (Parker and Tupling 1976: 375). This raises the possibility that what we are seeing here is the placebo effect – the patient is distressed and in pain, the therapist confidently suggests that they will be better before long (i.e. s/he cheers them up) and consequently they do indeed begin to feel relief from their symptoms.

At first glance this seems to confirm a view of non-orthodox medicine widely held among the protagonists of orthodox medicine, i.e. that if it works at all it can only be because of the placebo effect. This in itself is not implausible. After all, many orthodox medical practitioners use placebo treatments, that is, they use treatments which the doctor does not regard as having any proven medical effect on the symptoms in question but believes will make the patient feel that something is being done. This, Jean Comaroff finds in a study of GPs in South Wales, enables the physician 'to treat psycho-social symptoms in the idiom of organic illness' (Comaroff 1976: 88). I am not very enthusiastic about the use of the term 'placebo effect' as an explanatory concept since I believe that it conflates all those symbolic aspects of the healing process which medical sociologists and anthropologists (and many holistic practitioners) regard as important. The problem for both orthodox and non-orthodox medicine is to identify precisely which factors in the treatment process contribute to the placebo effect in any particular kind of case – is it the fact of having been given something to take or do? Is it the confidence inspired by the practitioner's manner or personality? These may be very difficult to disentangle from the more concrete aspects of the treatment (the substances administered, the manipulation or massage, the insertion of needles, the dietary changes recommended).

It is possible, however, to identify those aspects of the healer–patient interaction which engender the greatest satisfactions and dissatisfactions among patients of different kinds. In the last chapter I cited a number of concerns about the way in which orthodox medicine is delivered (rushed consultations, lack of individual attention, failure on the part of doctors to explain treatments to patients). There is no shortage of supporting evidence from other studies to substantiate the idea that users of complementary medicine have found orthodox medicine unsatisfactory in respect of the way it is delivered. Vigdis Christie's Norwegian study asked respondents to compare the treatment they had received from orthodox physicians with that received from non-orthodox practitioners. Respondents often mentioned what they disliked about the form of consultation used by the orthodox physician (not enough time for the patient, unprepared to explain things, treatment of symptoms rather than cause). On the count of personal behaviour more positive comments were made about non-orthodox practitioners, interviewees appreciating the kind of relationship they tried to establish with the patient and contrasting it with what they perceived as the formal and even arrogant behaviour of doctors. On technical matters, however, the respondents made more positive comments about orthodox medicine; they appreciated the opportunities for blood testing, X-rays, etc. and rated the diagnostic capacity of orthodox medicine highly. Christie, however, recognises that people who are using non-orthodox medicine are probably doing so because they have recently experienced orthodox medicine's failure in respect of a particular illness, and therefore may have a more jaundiced view of the orthodox medical profession than others (Christie n.d: 7).

This methodological difficulty can be resolved by comparing what people who have used non-orthodox medicine have to say about orthodox medicine with the responses of people who have only ever used the services of the orthodox physician. This approach was used in the NIPG study carried out in the Netherlands. The two groups were asked to give their opinion of their GP by responding to a number of statements such as 'My GP spends a lot of time with you', 'My GP has special gifts'. While those respondents who had not used non-orthodox medicine endorsed positive statements more often, the two groups did not differ enormously. Twenty per cent of the users of non-orthodox medicine agreed that their GP had special gifts compared with 23 per cent of the non-users, 61 per cent of users agreed that their GP 'finds out what is wrong with you quickly' compared with 66 per cent of the non-users. The widest differences were in respect of the statement 'My GP prescribes medicines which are not harmful in any event' (only 47 per cent of users of complementary medicine agreed compared with 65 per cent of non-users), and 'My GP thinks as I do about the causes and treatments of disease' (48 per cent of users agreed compared with 64 per cent of non-users)

(Ooijendijk, Mackenbach and Limberger 1981: 26). McGuire's American study also finds that users of non-orthodox medicine do not differ so sharply from non-users in their approach to orthodox medicine as we might expect. The users of ritual and other non-orthodox healing methods were compared with a control group who had never used such therapies. Members of both groups 'shopped around' for the best medical care they could afford, were sometimes critical of the passive attitudes orthodox medicine seemed to pre-suppose on the part of the patient (McGuire 1988: 200).

A FLIGHT FROM ORTHODOX MEDICINE?

On the face of it, the evidence of my own study supports Fulder's contention that patients of complementary practitioners are in one sense or another 'mostly refugees from conventional medicine' (Fulder 1988: 30) and confirms Christie's view that

> Alternative medicine can... only be understood as an answer to the basic features of modern medicine [so that the] rising popularity of non-ortho-dox medicine has to be related to the backlash created by inflated expectations of allopathic medicine and weaknesses in the form of de-livery of that type of medicine.
>
> (Christie n.d.: 1–2)

It may well be the case that, as Rosemary Taylor argues, dissatisfaction with the kind of patient–doctor relationship assumed by orthodox medicine is by far the most important element in this rise in popularity, related to the failure of modern medicine to effect improvements in this relationship in spite of its impressive advances in the technical aspects of medicine. Pressures on the NHS have cancelled out any improvement derived from more enlightened attitudes to GP training, resulting in a very general discontent with the quality of the 'medical encounter' (Taylor 1984). Yet most of the dissatisfactions with orthodox medicine expressed by individual patients of non-orthodox medicine in studies like my own are generalised from problems experienced in relation to a particular unsatisfactory treatment (worries about invasive treatments, side effects of drugs, etc.). If there is a general discontent it must, at the present time at least, be made up of many little discontents since (as we have seen) users of non-orthodox medicine do not in fact abandon orthodox medicine entirely.

But these discontents are by no means confined to users of complementary medicine. Cartwright and Anderson, in their 1977 study of general practice, make special note of the more critical attitude expressed by respondents compared which the findings of an earlier study in 1964, explaining this as a manifestation of higher expectations on the part of patients and a 'greater willingness to express criticisms of a service which the great majority value highly' (Cartwright and Anderson 1981: 9). Interestingly, second to the issue of home visiting, some of the biggest changes in rating of the GP's services related to such matters as the time spent by the doctor on consultation, whether or not s/he explained things fully, i.e. to aspects of delivery rather than technique. Important weaknesses in the mode of delivery of orthodox medicine have been the object of campaigning organisations representing groups of highly dissatisfied clients of conventional medicine with no collectively declared bias towards non-orthodox medicine, for instance the Association for the Improvement of the Maternity Services, or the Society for the Welfare of Children in Hospital. If, as the BMA report (in a rare moment of humility) suggests, the use of non-orthodox medicine implies a criticism of some aspects of the practice and delivery of modern medicine (BMA 1986: 78), then many of these dissatisfactions are not new ones, nor are they peculiar to users of complementary medicine. In this book we are not dealing with an eccentric group of people with deviant criteria for medical efficacy and satisfactory care; they are voicing fairly general discontents, but voicing them in the context of a particular kind of suffering and through a particular course of action.

CONSUMERS OR PATIENTS?

In the previous chapter I used the term 'consumerism' to describe the behaviour of some of the interviewees. Insofar as consumerism represents an individual attitude of mind it implies an alertness to the opportunities for intelligent choice between products, an active insistence on value for money. Considered as a social movement, consumerism has stressed the need for protection of the purchaser, but also for information. As one commentator puts it

> I do not think that merely providing more products is the answer. I, too have looked through the hi-fi markets and I am bewildered by the number of products available. There are hundreds of speakers, hundreds of amplifiers, hundreds of turntables. There is no way I can rank or compare them. So merely offering me dozens does not help me make a choice. I have to have some additional information to make those choices intelligently. I would really endorse the suggestion that much can be accomplished simply by giving consumers information to make intelligent choices.
>
> (Comment on a paper by Richard D. Murphy in
> Jones and Gardner 1976: 150–1)

Recently many formal health information services have been developed and there has been much discussion of the form they should properly take. For the most part this discussion is based on the assumption that health information means information about services which are available under the NHS and that it should be part of the patient care provided by the NHS (see for example Kempson 1987: 88). On the other hand, the College of Health, established in 1983 under the aegis of the Consumers' Association, has been very aware of the need for information about complementary medicine and provides information about both orthodox and non-orthodox treatments. Popular journals have probably always fulfilled an important 'consumer' function so far as health is concerned and some, such as the long-established *Here's Health*, regularly carry references to non-orthodox therapies.

But is not the consumer of a public utility in a different position from the consumer of a product which is offered in a competitive market place? Public discourse tends to refer to 'users' rather than 'consumers' of public services such as electricity or railways. Sometimes discontent with such services generates consumer associations dedicated to securing improvements in the services in question (e.g. railway commuters' associations). From the point of view of the providers of public services the user is likely to be 'represented' on advisory panels (such as the National Gas Consumer Council or the Post Office Users' National Council) rather than 'consulted' through market research. In the sphere of healthcare this 'representation' has taken the form of participation in the politically weak Community Health Councils.

The privatisation of some public utilities to which the present government is committed will probably not change this situation very much, to the extent that the providers of such services will still have a monopoly of provision in a given area. The consumer will not be in the position of choosing between products and so, in terms of this discourse, remains a 'user'. In the current situation of the NHS – of a hard-pressed and under-funded public utility existing alongside a proliferation of private and non-orthodox practice and dominated by a government which has a track record of taking very selective notice of professional protest – the patients, managers and doctors compete for control of the rhetoric by which the user/consumer/patient role is constructed.

Margaret Stacey has pointed out that all this discourse overlooks the fact that it is not only the medical profession that produces healthcare, but ordinary people themselves. Through their own (non-professional) practices they produce good health and prevent bad health (Stacey 1976, 1988: 6). However, the 'producer' construction of the lay person's role is at even greater odds than the 'user' and the 'consumer' construction with the role implied in the day-to-day practice of conventional medicine. In public healthcare, the patient is a 'work object', for 'this is a service industry which does things *to* people rather than *for* people' (Stacey 1976: 195).

The medical profession cannot claim authority in healthcare unless it can assert the dominance of its understanding of medicine over lay under-standings. A sensitive doctor will be aware of patients' conceptions of what they need and what constitutes appropriate treatment for a particular problem, but professional interest dictates that the doctor's view must prevail or at any rate be seen to prevail. If a patient comes to the doctor suggesting that s/he be prescribed a drug s/he has heard is good for the complaint in question, some doctors will not openly concede to the request, even if they think the suggestion an excellent one. They will prescribe either nothing at all or a drug with a similar medical effect but a different name, deceiving the patient in order to maintain the impression of exclusive professional control of knowl-edge (Comaroff 1976: 90). Yet the modern patient may be very well informed indeed. Media reporting of medical advances and the availability of clear accessible accounts of common diseases and their newest treatments ensure that many patients arrive at the doctor's surgery with an active and informed interest in their problem and its diagnosis. They expect the doctor to share knowledge as well as dispense treatment and this raises new questions for the doctors, who are not trained to expect such participation. Should patients have access to their notes? Should the doctors have training in how to impart medical information themselves? (Blair 1985).

Yet there are enormous institutional obstacles to Blair's recommendation that doctors actively participate in rather than resist this empowerment of the patient, if only the limited time that doctors and consultants have available for patients under the NHS. Freidson has pointed out that while doctors may prefer euphemisms such as 'management' and 'compliance', the profession 'must in some way manipulate or exercise control over the patients' (Freidson 1975: 308). A profession which feels beleaguered, whether because of pressure from government to demonstrate greater 'cost effectiveness' or from patients who expect to exercise greater choice and control over their treat-ment, is unlikely to relinquish this control willingly. Despite the rhetoric of patient choice which the present government likes to use, it is improbable that changes in the organisation of the NHS will really shift power to the patient. Major choices about treatment will continue to be necessary – should this person have dialysis? Where will this patient get the best orthopaedic treatment? – but it is likely that these choices will continue to be controlled primarily by the medical profession.

This construction of the role of patient on the part of the medical profes-sion is of course quite at odds with the role of consumer as constructed by the consumer movement – the individual purchaser of services who is well informed, capable of weighing the advantages and disadvantages of a par-ticular choice, actively intelligent rather than passively compliant. Users of complementary medicine often avoid overt confrontation with this contra-diction by concealing the fact that they have visited non-orthodox practitioners from GPs who they feel would be unsympathetic to this exercise of consumer choice. As I have argued already (see p.58), this is unlikely to imperil the patient, but it does rule out the fruitful communication and even co-operation between the complementary practitioner and GP which some members of both professions would like to see.

When describing the behaviour of some users of complementary medicine as 'consumerist' I am referring to what happens at the point of choice, the decision to use complementary medicine rather than orthodox medicine and to use one form of complementary medicine rather than another. I do not mean to imply that sick people may not display conventional 'patient' behaviour towards their non-orthodox therapist. Some of the people I interviewed clearly valued the therapist whom they consulted precisely because they felt that the relationship between practitioner and client was more egalitarian and that they were being encouraged to take more active responsibility for their own health. On the other hand if (as McGuire suggests – see above) the non-orthodox healer's treatment operates at a moral and intellectual level as well as a physical level, must this not involve a suspension of personal judgement, a preparedness to accept the healer's definition of the problem unreservedly if it is to work? There is very little empirical data on this point and the impression I gain from my own study is that there is much variation in the way the patient role is interpreted both among patients and among healers. I discuss in Chapter 7 some of the ways in which non-orthodox therapists define what they require of their clients.

THE RATIONAL PATIENT AGAIN

In Chapter 2 I referred to sociologists' and anthropologists' view of the patient as a maker of rational choices. Sick people (or those reponsible for their recovery) consult kin and acquaintance whose opinion or knowledge they value and then choose a course of action which they believe will produce the best outcome with the minimum outlay of resources. A 'rational' choice may not necessarily be a 'good' choice of treatment from the point of view of the independent observer as the information available may be limited and the patient's judgement of the outcome of a particular course of action inaccurate or misguided; it is rational in the formal and calculative sense. Sick people or their relatives make these choices within the framework of established systems of cultural belief about the body, health and illness, but the rapid uptake of 'foreign' treatments indicates that patients are not totally culture-bound. Americans will use Chinese acupuncture and Papua New Guineans will use western medicine if they think these treatments constitute the best option in a particular situation.

Both my own and other studies of users of non-orthodox medicine confirm the notion of the rational rather than the culture-bound patient. Choosing to consult a non-orthodox practitioner does not in itself mean rejection of orthodox medicine as a total cultural system (nor total acceptance of an 'alternative' system). Sick people weigh up the advantages and disadvantages of a particular form of non-orthodox treatment in relation to a particular illness or condition. But their judgement of what constitutes either a cost or a benefit will depend on their own priorities and cirumstances.

This idea is by no means a totally new one. In his book *The Process of Becoming Ill* Robinson suggests that sick people (or their relatives) choose among courses of action in terms of the consequences which they believe will follow from them. They will consider both the physiological and the social, both the long-term and the short-term implications. In the example Robinson gives, the case of Mr M. who had injured his knee shortly before he is about to begin a new job, the short-term cost of accepting a treatment which will involve immobilising his knee will be that he will not be able to do his work and may even face some loss of prestige from not turning up on the first day of a new job in a workplace where he can count on no accumulated store of goodwill. At a physiological level the treatment will be uncomfortable, though it may relieve the worst of the pain. But provided it is successful, the treatment may be expected to yield long-term physiological benefits in avoiding disability from compound injury, which would probably entail the social cost of giving up the job anyway (Robinson 1971: 33ff).

A number of interviewees gave me accounts of their decision to use non-orthodox medicine which implied exactly the same kind of rationality at work. This is best illustrated by taking a single example and analysing it at length and I will quote from an interview with Mrs Doreen Peake. She and her husband come from local mining families but her husband started his own small business some years ago. This had not been an easy transition but the business was now prospering and the couple were comfortably off, though still living in the traditional terraced house they had occupied since their marriage. Doreen has three children, now in their late teens and early twenties and has not had paid employment since the birth of the eldest. According to her account, five years ago an illness episode led to her doctor diagnosing high blood pressure:

> I had had pyelitis as a young woman which is inflammation round the kidneys so they more or less put it down to the fact that in later life it is giving me high blood pressure. So he started me off on tablets but I was just no-how on those. I couldn't even walk out at all – if I went upstairs I had to sit on the bed before I could do anything. The doctor gave me another drug. Well, I took it and after an hour I could hardly breathe so I got on the phone to the surgery and told them what had happened. The

receptionist went in to see the doctor and he said 'Take no more and come and see me again'. Well, when I go back there is another tablet there – he says 'we've got hundreds of tablets, it is just a matter of going through the range until we get one that suits you' so I was no-how on doctors' tablets. It was the side effects. It was bringing the blood pressure down... but it had slowed me down to such an extent that I felt like an old woman.

As a result of a recommendation from the owner of the caravan site where she and her husband spent holidays in Wales, she went to see a herbalist who lived in a small town in central Wales, about a hundred miles from her own home.

I didn't really trust alternative medicine, put it like that – I wasn't very sure about it.... My husband was all for it because he thinks if you're not getting any help you go where you can. I told my doctor right from the beginning. He is a Pakistani, he was very nice, I couldn't fault him in any way. He said, 'Well, my dear, I can't tell you to go ahead just like that because I am your doctor, but let me put it like this. If you were in my country you would be treated with herbs in the first place for what you have got.'

Mrs Peake made an appointment and travelled all the way to the herbalist's practice the next week. Mr Evans' treatment, she said, had kept her blood pressure down for the past five years and relieved the unpleasant kidney symptoms. She did, however, have to go into hospital once during that time owing to acute pain from a kidney stone which in the event she passed in her urine without the need for surgery:

I was at home a good week before I gave in to the pain and went into hospital. The thing is about herbalism you cannot do without your doctor and your hospitals. It's a thing you can combine because if you want quick pain relief you can't get it from herbs but for such things like high blood pressure or stress then it is very good.

Mrs Peake stated that she paid about £8.50 (in 1986) for a monthly consultation, not including the cost of the medicines, blood tests and other specific treatments. But she felt that the help she was getting was worth this outlay as she valued her new sense of wellbeing and ability to enjoy life. She was critical of neighbours who, she claimed, thought she was odd to pay for private medicine when treatment on the NHS was free, but concluded that different people had different priorities when it came to household budgeting. To her it was a question of whether you 'put your health before the money in your pocket. If it was double I would still pay it'. Her husband, who usually drives her to her appointments is now also consulting Mr Evans for 'stress' and finding the treatment very satisfactory.

If we examine Doreen Peake's account of how she came to consult a herbalist it is clear that it was not the *ineffectiveness* of treatment under the NHS but its *cost* in terms of side effects to which she objected. Although the doctor promised her that a suitable drug with no side effects could be found, this sounded to her like a lengthy process of trial and error which she was not prepared to undertake. The time and money which she and and her husband spend travelling to Wales every month is worthwhile from her point of view, although she is quite prepared to use the services of her doctor as well in the case of an acute episode or excessive pain.

The structure of her decision to use non-orthodox medicine could be represented as follows, using Robinson's distinction between physiological and social costs and gains:

Herbalist	*NHS treatment*
Physiological gains:	
blood pressure drops;	blood pressure drops
feels energetic	
Physiological costs:	
none perceived	unpleasant side effects, tiredness. She finds these intolerable. Prospect of long wait before suitable drug is found
Social gains:	
she can do her work and enjoy going out with her husband; other kin use same healer; approval of husband	none perceived, as she still feels tired
Social costs:	
expenditure of time and money on travel	few: the treatment is free and near at hand, and she likes her GP

It occurred to me that it was not really necessary for Mrs Peake to travel so far to find a qualified herbalist as I knew there to be several practising in the city. But her own information networks seem to have been defective in this respect. She knew of no other local complementary practitioners except one herbalist, but had not considered consulting him. This practitioner had treated her brother for a short time many years ago and Doreen had accompanied him one day. But she noted that

He put me off herbalists because he never took any note of anything he had done – to me it wasn't done right and he just went behind a screen and brought out a bottle. With Mr Evans, he keeps notes. He's got a file there just like a doctor and everything is put down. If I wanted to look at the file in five years' time, there is every mortal thing I said to him, it's all down there.

Frequent visits to Wales were not experienced as a problem; she and her husband often went there for weekends and her condition was not such that travelling represented an additional strain. (Would Mr Peake have been so willing to find time and money for these expeditions if he had not also benefited from Mr Evans treatment?) She contrasted her own situation with that of her sister Margaret who had also consulted Mr Evans at her suggestion about a very painful back problem. But Margaret had to wear a support collar and found the long journey very unpleasant in her condition, so she had only consulted Mr Evans a few times. The herbal treatment had not diminished the pain in her back but she claimed, according to Doreen, that it had helped her with the depression she had experienced as a result of her constant pain and disability. Doreen would occasionally fetch herbal remedies for Margaret when she visited Mr Evans herself.

I have recounted this case in some detail because it illustrates very appropriately the nature of the 'patient rationality' at work in decisions about non-orthodox medical treatment. Doreen conveys quite clearly what constitutes a cost and a gain from her point of view and indicates the range of people whose interests or opinions might be considered relevant to her decision to start (and subsequently continue with) the treatment. By her own account, Doreen was fairly sceptical about complementary medicine in the first place and still insisted that no person should consult a practitioner who was not properly qualified. She had by no means abandoned using conventional medicine altogether although disturbed by the common reliance on drugs which had unpleasant or dangerous side effects, and spoke warmly of her own GP as well as the treatment she had had in hospital. If she is to be considered as a 'refugee from orthodox medicine' and as 'satisfied' with non-orthodox medicine then it must be in terms of her own criteria for judging the costs and benefits of either system. Satisfaction with a form of treatment is not always generalised to whole systems of medicine. Patients will experience 'satisfaction' or 'dissatisfaction' in terms of their personal criteria, depending upon their particular priorities and circumstances. These may be defined by all kinds of factors – the nature of the disease, the patient's temperament, occupation or domestic circumstances. 'Being cured' or 'relief from symptoms' need not be the only criteria for satisfaction, nor inability to produce a cure or relief from symptoms the only kind of failure.

This point may seem trivial or even obvious, but it is nonetheless an important one; even if the clinical trials of non-orthodox remedies which the medical profession (and numerous non-orthodox professionals) would like to see conducted were to prove conclusively that orthodox medicine 'works' best in a strictly clinical sense, then this will not change the judgement of a substantial category of people whose choice is based not just on the merits of complementary medicine in general but on the perceived costs of specific orthodox treatments for particular diseases. Bearing this in mind, it need not surprise us that individuals may prefer orthodox medicine for one purpose, homoeopathy or herbalism for another. The eclecticism which I noted in the last chapter is in some cases a rather random, even desperate, sampling of treatments for recalcitrant ailments; in other cases it could represent a quite calculated estimation of the costs and gains to be derived from different treatments for different complaints.

CONSUMER RATIONALITY AND CULTURE CHANGE

In focussing on decisions about treatment one tends to view the use of non-orthodox medicine in terms of the behaviour of individuals or very small social groups. Is the growth of complementary medicine in the past decade just the sum of thousands of such consumer choices on the part of individuals or households? Or should we not see it as symptomatic of some broad cultural change, some radical shift in values? Rosemary Taylor sees the present popularity of complementary medicine as a product of the 'participation revolution' of the sixties which challenged many forms of authority, including those of the medical profession. But while this revolution yielded some attempts to involve the public in the planning and review of health services, it did not bring about any fundamental change in the relationship between doctor and patient. The latter had no more reponsibility or control than before. In effect 'medicine shrugged off the demands of the sixties' and the market orientation of the eighties obliged patients to express their new definition of themselves as reponsible partners in the business of healthcare in terms of the 'exit option', the choice to opt out of this relationship by resorting to other kinds of practitioner (Taylor 1984: 205ff).

It is possible to relate the popularity of non-orthodox medicine to even broader cultural changes. Rosalind Coward describes alternative medicine as part of a cultural current which also embraces 'New Age' therapies, holistic health, the wholefood movement, the quest for the 'natural' in therapy, childbirth, food and a dozen other areas of life. This new view of the person interprets the human individual as essentially capable of perfect health and mental adjustment if only s/he is prepared to take responsibility for her/his own health. This is a moral and spiritual quest as well as having implications for the routine care of the body:

Sharing the views and aspirations of the alternative health movement is very often considerably more than sharing a critique of orthodox medicine. More often than not it is to share this commitment to the natural, to the involvement of the individual in well-being and to sense that the spiritual side of human kind has been badly neglected.

(Coward 1989: 11)

Complementary medicine, Coward argues, expresses changes in attitude which are not confined to its patients and proponents. Alternative therapies have become popular

not just because they offer a more caring approach to health than orthodox medicine but also because they correspond to, perhaps even spearhead, these changed views. Clearly people's expectations of health, and their sense of personal involvement in it have changed. So too have beliefs about how much they can exercise conscious 'choice' over health and disease.... Interest in alternative therapies rarely stops at using one particular therapy to deal with an ailment when allopathic medicine has failed. The interest invariably extends into a wholehearted adoption of these philosophical concepts.

(Coward 1989: 196)

Both Taylor and Coward draw our attention to the fact that this cultural shift in understandings of health and illness and consequently what healthcare should be expected to deliver is related to a general increase in the symbolic load which medical care of the body is obliged to carry:

medicine has acquired an enormous political and cultural significance as its jurisdiction over social life has been extended. Birth and death are defined as medical events. Problems which used to be the sole responsibility of the church or the courts – juvenile delinquency, divorce, crimes of passion – now fall in part to medicine for resolution.

(Taylor 1984: 217)

Coward goes even further:

alternative therapies make explicit – and give a theory to – the absolute centrality which the body and health have acquired in our consciousness. Attending to health and well-being has become a major cultural obsession and alternative therapies satisfy something of the sense that we should be 'committed' to our bodies and our health.

(Coward 1989: 197)

Treating the body as the site of personal concerns, Coward points out, is not new in the West. But while in the Victorian age it was expressed through an obsession with self-determination through control over the body's sexual urges, the present emphasis is on positively choosing to be natural and healthy.

One cannot but agree that insofar as there is such a thing as an alternative healthcare 'movement', it consists of more than just techniques or practices which can be used in preference to orthodox medicine but which are based on essentially the same model of what constitutes 'medicine'. Many of the ideas which Coward attributes to this movement we shall certainly hear articulated in a later chapter by some of the practitioners I interviewed. The idea that the individual can choose to be healthy, that some are ill because at some deeper level of the self they 'need' to be ill, that perfect health is attainable if one but overcomes the obstacles, both in oneself and in one's (increasingly unnatural) environment – these are certainly very common among practitioners of some complementary therapies. They are also, if my own interview data is anything to go by, familiar to a certain section of their clientele, mainly members of the intelligentsia who have had fairly long experience of non-orthodox medicine or 'New Age' therapies.

But Coward is jumping rather too far ahead when, without any empirical evidence, she attributes these new cultural definitions of the body and health to all users of complementary medicine. People like Mrs Peake appear relatively unacquainted with the discourse Coward describes, at any rate as expressed in their interviews. If their own accounts are anything to go by, most patients are simply using complementary medicine as a way of dealing with an intractable condition which orthodox medicine cannot cure to their satisfaction. Perhaps Coward has been listening more closely to the purveyors of alternative therapies than their patients? On the other hand, much of the evidence I have reviewed in this chapter (both from my own study and those of others) does suggest certain broad patient attitudes. There is a more critical attitude to orthodox medicine (especially its iatrogenic aspects), an active search for information relevant to one's own health problems and a more positive confidence in their ability to make choices for their own healthcare. At the 'micro' level of the individual patient this just presents itself as greater pragmatism or a form of consumerism. But at the collective level it could be regarded as adding up to a real change in lay health culture and one which is by no means confined to users of complementary medicine.

Patients may start out using non-orthodox treatment holding health beliefs which are no different from non-users, but their very exposure to the ideas of their therapists may effect such a change over time. If, as we have also seen, people who have used one type of non-orthodox medicine for a specific problem are quite likely to experiment with other kinds of therapy, then the scope for such exposure is increased. There were plenty of examples in my own research of patients experiencing changes in their own attitudes to healthcare related to their use of non-orthodox medicine.

My own view is that whilst Coward has correctly linked the rise of non-orthodox medicine to some wider cultural changes, she nonetheless overgeneralises from the 'supply' side. In doing so she overestimates the extent to which new ideas have penetrated all the levels of society from which users of non-orthodox medicine are drawn, i.e. the 'demand' side. There is no reason to suppose that therapist and patient always share beliefs about health and illness, but equally there is no reason to suppose that the one may not influence the other as they interact. So the cultural conceptions about the body and its care which she describes may well become more widespread in future, proving her premature rather than incorrect.

I have contrasted action based on pragmatism and action based on conformity to cultural beliefs as though they were two discrete modes of behaviour. But this is something of an artificial opposition. Culture is not a set of rigid prescriptions which individuals conform to willy-nilly – what I call the 'autopilot' view of culture. It represents the range of options which a community of people regard as legitimate or thinkable at a particular time. And if sufferers from chronic and intractable diseases regard the choice of non-orthodox treatment thinkable now (even if rather reluctantly, like Mrs Peake) when they would not have done so a decade ago, then this shift in the range of options in itself represents some kind of cultural change. Culture is a practical process of choice and activity.

This discussion suggests that it is not very sensible to think of the popularity of complementary medicine as being the result of a single cause or set of circumstances. Pressure on the NHS, the over-technological nature of modern medicine and the demand for a more person-centred therapy, the rise of informed consumer consciousness, the participation revolution – all these have certainly contributed to the demand for non-orthodox medical services. But complementary medicine is not their only child. All these currents have other manifestations. Therefore, whatever we may think of the particular arguments of such commentators as Coward or Taylor, they are indubitably right in asserting that the popularity of complementary medicine has to do with very fundamental changes in society and that its causes are entangled deep within the cultural and institutional foundations of the modern polity.

Part II

Practising complementary medicine

5   The national context

The total number of people practising complementary medicine in Britain today has increased greatly during the past decade and, given the very rapid expansion in opportunities for training in non-orthodox therapies, we can predict that it will continue to increase for some time.

The most extensive study of non-orthodox practitioners published to date was carried out in 1981 by S. Fulder and R. Munro for the Threshold Foundation. Using information provided by professional organisations the investigators estimated that 2209 medically qualified therapists and a further 11,184 therapists without orthodox medical qualifications were in active practice. They calculated that there might be a further 16,980 therapists who were in practice but who did not belong to any professional organisation or official register. This total of 30,373 practitioners is based on a slightly broader definition of non-orthodox medicine than the one which I have been using in this book, since it includes Alexander Technique teachers, music therapists and masseurs. If we eliminate these therapies, we arrive at an estimated total of 26,483 active practitioners, still an impressive figure. According to the Threshold Foundation study, the best represented therapies were healing, hypnotherapy, osteopathy, acupuncture and homoeopathy (Fulder and Munro 1982: 42). When we consider that there may be a number of people who provide treatment without taking money (especially among spiritual healers) the total provision of complementary medicine may be even greater than these estimates suggest.

Whatever the numbers might have been in 1981, they are certain to be much greater today, a decade later. Fulder and Munro also analysed trends in the numbers of practitioners, using the registers of professional organisations as the basis for their calculations, and found that between the years 1978 and 1981 there had been substantial increases in practitioners of all forms of non-orthodox medicine except herbalism, the greatest being found in acupuncture, hypnotherapy and homoeopathy. They point out that the mean increase in registered therapists over the three-year period studied was 11.5

per cent per year – 'nearly 6 times the annual increase in the total number of doctors in the UK' (Fulder and Munro 1982: 37).

These practitioners are far from being evenly distributed around the country. In a study conducted for the Institute of Complementary Medicine, Peter Davies took a random sample of practitioners from the registers of ten professional associations and found that about 32 per cent of his respondents came from the south central region, 17 per cent from the Midlands, 15 per cent from the southeast and 11 per cent from the southwest. Complementary medicine seems to be poorly represented in Scotland, Northern Ireland, the north of England and Wales (Davies 1984: 13).

Many practising therapists offer (and are trained in) more than one therapy. In Davies's sample of 411 practitioners, around half practised two different therapies and about a quarter offered a third therapy (Davies 1984: 14). In the Threshold Foundation study, a sample of 137 practitioners yielded a total of fifty-eight who used more than one therapy (Fulder and Munro 1982: 38). A common combination is osteopathy with naturopathy, mainly because naturopathy is taught alongside osteopathy at a major training school. Naturopathy may also be combined with herbalism and homoeopathy, and homoeopathy and Bach Flower Remedies may be used as an adjunct to acupuncture or a manipulative therapy. Radionics is often associated with homoeopathy.

Levels of training vary, but there seems little foundation for the fear that large numbers of untrained people are practising non-orthodox medicine on a vulnerable public. Fulder and Munro found that half of the practitioners in their sample had attended a training college for a full-time or part-time course, whilst the remainder had learned by apprenticeship, group work, or correspondence course (Fulder and Munro 1985: 543). Davies found that of his sample of 411 practitioners, approximately 53 per cent had had full-time training for their main therapy, 44 per cent had trained part-time and only 3 per cent through correspondence courses, although with respect to second and third therapies there was a much higher proportion of practitioners who had trained by correspondence course (Davies 1984: 15). The length and standard of course is far from uniform – an issue which is much debated in the complementary medicine movement at present. Instruction in a long-established therapy such as osteopathy is generally formal and lengthy, but there are few opportunities for full-time training in therapies such as radionics or reflexology as yet. Even where training is known to be long and rigorous, experience is often limited. Fulder and Munro found that the average number of years in practice for their sample was 7.5. This merely reflects the relative novelty of complementary medicine as a career, but it means that where training has been brief it is unlikely (at the present time) to be compensated by long years of practical experience.

THE AVAILABILITY OF COMPLEMENTARY MEDICINE

Most people who use non-orthodox medicine consult one of the growing number of private practitioners. But these vary greatly in the scale of their practice and clientele. At one extreme there are celebrated therapists who attract a national or even international clientele, charge fees nearer to those charged by orthodox medical consultants and operate from consulting rooms in prestigious (often metropolitan) locations – the 'Harley Street' of the non-orthodox medical world. At the other end of the spectrum there are modest practitioners who serve very localised clienteles, often from their own homes; their fees will vary according to the area they work in, but are usually nearer to those charged by, say, qualified piano teachers or evening class instructors than to those of orthodox medical consultants. Lay enthusiasts or students who have not yet completed their training may offer their services free of charge to family, friends and acquaintances, sometimes as a kind of 'trial run' before setting up a professional practice. Many (probably most) spiritual healers offer their services free of charge and some operate on a very limited scale. Practitioners who treat patients without payment do not come within the scope of this study, but we should not overlook their existence as they probably constitute a significant, though unadvertised, sector of complementary medical services in some localities, and may do much to stimulate interest in and demand for non-orthodox therapies.

A substantial number of practitioners work only part-time. About a quarter of the practitioners in Davies's sample did not work full-time, mainly acupuncturists, homoeopaths, herbalists and naturopaths. My own data suggest that there may be various reasons for this. Some work part-time because they are recently established and have not yet built up an extensive clientele. Many have other activities, usually directly or indirectly related to their practice, which they choose to maintain (see p. 150). Both Davies's study and the Threshold Foundation data indicate that a number of non-orthodox practitioners see fewer than twenty patients per week (Fulder and Munro 1982: 38ff, Davies 1984: 18), although to some extent these apparently low levels of professional activity may be the consequence of long consultation times rather than short working hours.

Group practice is popular among complementary therapists, just as it is among orthodox GPs. Davies found that half of his sample were working in a group practice of some kind (Davies 1984: 17). However, my own data indicate that the term 'group practice' may be used to describe very diverse arrangements. It may refer merely to a situation where two or more practitioners work alongside each other from the same address, possibly sharing a receptionist or other facilities. At the other extreme, there are integrated natural health centres where the patient is counselled in order to make a choice among therapies offered by a co-operative team of practitioners. A number of such centres exist, especially in southern England, and an organisation (the Natural Health Network) has been established to encourage and link such groups.

It is not the case that complementary medicine is unavailable within the National Health Service. There is a high level of interest in complementary medicine among GPs, which I discuss later in this chapter, and many doctors have some knowledge of or training in one or more non-orthodox therapy. This interest and knowledge certainly generates referrals from GPs to complementary practitioners, but the number of patients treated by GPs themselves using these methods is hard to determine. In a study of GPs in Oxfordshire, Anderson and Anderson found that as many as thirty-five of a sample of 222 GPs practised some form of non-orthodox medicine. But the total number of patients with whom they had used non-orthodox therapy of any kind during the past year was 2056, representing no more than 5 per cent of the total number of patients consulting these doctors during that period (Anderson and Anderson 1987: 53). Again, this low rate of non-orthodox medical activity could be directly related to consultation time; among this sample the average consultation time for non-orthodox treatment was 21.9 minutes compared with 9.0 minutes for orthodox treatment. It could also be an indirect result of long consultation times; where professional associations forbid GP members to take fees for non-orthodox treatment from their NHS patients (as in the case of the British Medical Acupuncture Society, for instance) there can be little incentive to offer a treatment which requires at least twenty minutes while the queue of patients in the waiting room grows ever longer. A more recent study by Dr Jeremy Swayne, however, suggests much higher rates of NHS non-orthodox treatment among a group of homoeopathic doctors, although shorter consultation times are implied in his figures, so perhaps it would be unwise to generalise when so little research data is available (*Homoeopathy* February 1990: 15–16).

The interest which doctors take in non-orthodox medicine is significant from the political point of view, as I shall argue later, yet the scale of provision in general practice is still very limited. It appears that few GPs treat patients who are not registered with their own practice (Wharton and Lewith 1986: 1499), and of course they are prohibited from advertising such services to a wider clientele. Whether patients can obtain non-orthodox treatment from a general practitioner under the NHS depends entirely on whether they happen to be registered with one of those few GPs who not only know something about non-orthodox medicine but who actually offer it to patients on a regular basis. Otherwise, the most that can be hoped for is advice about non-orthodox treatment or (possibly) a referral to a local practitioner who is known to the GP. An interesting and constructive development has been the recent establishment of holistic health centres which offer a range of services, such as the St Marylebone Healing and Counselling Centre (see *Holistic Health*, Spring 1989: 5) or the Hoxton Health Group. But these services are available only to a limited number of NHS patients in metropolitan areas.

Non-orthodox treatment is provided in some hospitals, but here again the provision is patchy and depends much on the attitudes and initiatives of local NHS personnel and managers. Acupuncture and hypnosis are sometimes used in hospitals for pain relief, and manipulative therapies may be used in the treatment of back and neck problems (Fulder 1988: 67). Five homoeopathic hospitals are maintained under the NHS, but these have been especially vulnerable to the effects of the crisis in health service funding (see Fulder 1988: 77). On the other hand, there is an increasing tendency to use therapies like shiatsu, massage, reflexology and aromatherapy on hospital wards as part of a patient's integrated treatment plan, largely it would seem, as a result of initiatives on the part of nurses. The therapies used are those which can be most easily incorporated into a programme of treatment prescribed by an orthodox physician, and not those (such as herbalism or homoeopathy) where treatment may be very lengthy and diagnostic procedures may conflict.

Where medically unqualified professionals are employed on the wards it is strictly in a subordinate capacity. As one aromatherapist said:

We have elected to take on the role of a complementary service, treating the stress that surrounds illness rather than the illness itself. By relieving distress we believe we can help maximise the patient's recovery and help the physicians to do their work more potently.

(*Here's Health*, February 1990: 20)

To summarise, the provision of complementary medicine under the NHS is patchy and localised, being the historical result of local initiatives on the part of particular NHS personnel. Probably this provision will increase in the near future, but not as part of any concerted national plan. Where non-orthodox medicine is available under the NHS it is either provided as a sideline by registered doctors, whose training in complementary therapy is sometimes very limited compared with that of the best-qualified independent practitioners, or else by trained therapists who are not registered doctors and who provide treatment very much under the supervision of members of the orthodox medical profession. We are very far from a situation where the patient who desires, say, osteopathic treatment for back pain, or homoeopathic treatment for allergic symptoms, can opt for the treatment of his/her choice and have the full cost borne by the state.

THE STATUTORY SITUATION OF THE NON-ORTHODOX PRACTITIONER

Under the 1858 Medical Act, it became illegal for any person who had not been registered as a qualified medical practitioner to claim to be one, and the General Medical Council was given the task of defining medical qualifications and overseeing standards of education. This Act privileged the allopathic medical profession, at a time when homoeopathy still presented a popular alternative. Indeed, it hastened its unification and led to a general 'firming up' of its boundaries. The 'orthodox' medical profession was now empowered to specify the qualifications necessary for registration, and only registered practitioners could hold official medical positions under the state. There have been attempts on the part of non-orthodox medical groups to obtain registration on the same terms as orthodox doctors, but to date none has been successful. The National Health Insurance Act of 1911 and the National Health Service Act of 1948 fortified this partnership between the orthodox medical profession and the state by vastly increasing the scope of public medical services in whose organisation and administration doctors had a dominant role.

The 1858 Act did not prohibit non-orthodox or non-registered practitioners from treating patients provided they did not claim to be registered doctors, nor did the 1948 Act explicitly preclude the practice of non-orthodox medicine within the NHS. But with the state only prepared to employ registered practitioners directly, and with the qualifications necessary for registration defined exclusively by the orthodox medical profession, the marginalisation of non-orthodox medicine has been the inevitable (if indirect) consequence of modern legislation. The relationship between the state and the organised medical profession, which has only been sketched most crudely here (see Parry and Parry 1976 for a fuller account), has not been without its vicissitudes, but there is no reason to expect that it will be abandoned. The advantage to governments of being able to deal with a single more or less unified profession, and the advantages to that profession of the privileges of statutory recognition are self-evident.

The Professions Supplementary to Medicine Act (1960) regularised the position of a number of paramedical professions operating within the NHS, largely crystallising a division of labour which had been developing during the interwar years. While allowing some limited professional autonomy for groups like physiotherapists, radiographers or chiropodists, this legislation affirmed the dominant position of doctors in a state-approved hierarchy (Larkin 1987: 21) and ruled out any immediate prospect of registration for non-orthodox practitioners, in spite of interest on the part of osteopaths.

The secondary role to which the state has relegated complementary medicine is also evident in its lack of support for non-orthodox medical training and research. Whilst medical students are eligible for statutory awards, those who wish to pursue full-time courses in a branch of non-orthodox medicine can, at best, hope for a discretionary award from their Local Education Authority. Some LEAs seem to be more liberal in this respect than they used to be – the county in which I conducted my study of practitioners had made a few awards to students of osteopathy in the past five years – but the number of students of complementary medicine who can pay for their training in this way is very small indeed. The medical profession has set its face against the introduction of courses relating to non-orthodox treatment within the medical school, unlike the situation in France where diplomas in acupuncture and homoeopathy are issued by several medical faculties. Nor is there any system of state funding on which those who wish to conduct research in non-orthodox treatment can depend. To be sure, some clinical trials of non-orthodox treatments have been carried out in hospitals and orthodox research institutes and a few have even been funded by the Medical Research Council, but the disposal of research funds is, in practice, largely in the hands of people trained in or sympathetic to orthodox medicine. Researchers in non-orthodox medicine have had to compete for funds either from privately funded organisations, usually with relatively small budgets (such as the Koestler Foundation, the Healing Research Trust, or the Research Council for Complementary Medicine), or from charitable foundations which promote research into particular conditions or illnesses. The funding situation could best be described as one in which the state tolerates the orthodox medical profession's intolerance of non-orthodox medicine.

On the other hand, the alliance between the medical profession and the state has in no way precluded the legal practice of non-orthodox healthcare outside the NHS. There is no statutory obstacle to any person, trained or otherwise, offering their services on the market as healer or therapist. There are some restrictions which affect specific forms of treatment. For instance, the Herbal Remedies Order of 1977 defines the circumstances under which herbalists may supply certain herbs such as atropa belladonna, and no practitioner of any kind may advertise treatments for cancer. Some therapists fear that their considerable freedom to practise might in time be seriously eroded by the cumulative effect of piecemeal legislation designed to meet specific contingencies or resolve specific problems, but this seems rather a hypothetical danger at the present time. Non-orthodox medicine is 'non-orthodox' simply in the sense that it is not explicitly supported by the state. But the state does not explicitly oppose it either and in this limited legal space it has survived since 1858 and latterly flowered. This rather negative statutory position (non-orthodox medicine is permitted to exist by default and at the margins) is regarded by many practitioners as precarious, the more so as the coming of the the Single European Market in 1992 is perceived as likely to precipitate an unfavourable revision of the situation. What is the likelihood of this and what have governmental attitudes been in recent years?

GOVERNMENT AND POLICY

On the whole, governments since the last war have been unwilling to restrict the individual's right to choose private, including non-orthodox, forms of medical treatment or the liberty of the therapist to set up practice. Indeed the present Conservative government is well known for the fact that it looks with favour on the individual who takes out private health insurance and who does not rely solely on the provision of the state. A Thatcherite market-based economic policy ought surely to treat a form of medicine which can capture such a substantial share of consumer demand for healthcare with special kindness.

Complementary medicine has always had its influential friends, members of the élite and of both sides of the Houses of Parliament who have used it themselves and who have acted as its informal advocates in high places. In February 1989 an all-party alliance of parliamentarians was launched, the Parliamentary Alternative and Complementary Medicine Group, with a membership of thirty MPs, fifteen peers and a number of eminent non-orthodox practitioners. The predilection of certain members of the royal family for homoeopathy is well known and probably counts for more than the view of Professor Michael Baum (professor of surgery and leading member of the Campaign Against Health Fraud) that he would refer patients to the Queen's homoeopath 'only in very special circumstances' (*Journal of Alternative and Complementary Medicine* June 1989: 12). On what grounds have governments been so unwilling to do anything which would seriously erode the professional monopoly of orthodox medicine, in the face of complementary medicine's great popularity and in spite of considerable lobbying on occasion from the more established non-orthodox professions?

Attempts on the part of various complementary professional groups to obtain registration under the Medical Act of 1956 have met with the charge that they first prove their efficacy. Effectively this means proving their efficacy 'scientifically', i. e. on terms which the orthodox medical profession approves and understands. We might regard this (as many non-orthodox practitioners certainly do) as positive evidence of the overweening influence of orthodox doctors. The whole matter of efficacy is a much debated issue in the complementary medical movement. Many practitioners feel that where clinical trials of a 'scientific' kind can be carried out, such research should be given priority, in order that complementary medicine may have the public credibility they feel it deserves. Others point out that there are many forms of non-orthodox medicine where double blind trials would be inappropriate or irrelevant. Homoeopathy, for instance, is based on the idea that every individual has his/her own characteristic 'constitution'. Much prescribing will be according to constitutional type and not solely in response to presenting symptoms. No homoeopath would expect the same remedy administered to a sample of like cases to produce similar results, whether favourable or unfavourable. Denis MacEoin, questions the very dichotomy between 'scientific' and 'non-scientific' methods of proof which, he says, the medical profession favours in order to legitimate its claims (MacEoin 1990: 15–18). The medical profession is, however, supported by a state which demands publicly understood and bureaucratically acceptable procedures of proof and ratification in the interests of political and administrative convenience. (But how could non-orthodox medical researchers be expected to develop alternative procedures when there is such little funding available for their research?)

In the House of Lords debate on complementary medicine in 1987, Lord Skelmersdale, Under-Secretary of State, DHSS, expressed muted disappointment with the conservatism of the 1986 BMA report on alternative medicine but approved of its insistence that

> efficacy is at the centre of any considerations affecting health care: upon that there could be no compromise... increasingly natural therapy groups seem to recognise the need to demonstrate beyond reasonable doubt the efficacy of their procedures. That is essential if a general understanding is to develop between all those concerned with the provision of good health care.
>
> (*Hansard* 11.11.87, Columns 1414–15)

In respect of non-orthodox medicine, the political Right must juggle various potentially contradictory ideological and practical considerations – the desire to protect individual freedoms, the desire to restrict public expenditure and privilege private medicine, disinclination to disturb the *status quo* with respect to the position of the orthodox medical profession, unwillingness to embark upon a radical revision of the professional division of labour within the NHS. The net result has been what Lord Skelmersdale terms 'benign neutrality', i.e. governmental inertia.

The voices from the political Left express similar contradictions and tensions. To the extent that non-orthodox therapies are thought of as just another form of private medicine they are liable to be treated as suspect, and defending the right of therapists to practise is hardly likely to be seen as a pressing political issue. Socialist journalist Duncan Campbell defends his participation in the Campaign Against Health Fraud (lately re-named Health

Watch), protesting that he is not against alternative medicine as such, but regards it as under the obligation incumbent upon all forms of private medicine to demonstrate that commercialism does not conflict wih the interests of the patient:

> I would like all good medicine to be free. I want the public scrupulously protected from bad doctors and bad alternative practitioners alike... the old principle of 'caveat emptor' ('let the buyer beware') is completely unacceptable in any sort of health care, whether alternative or orthodox.
>
> (*JACM* November 1989: 13)

Campbell calls for more regulation of standards in alternative medicine, accepting that

> if self-regulation in alternative medicine means anything, it means that some people now have to be put out to grass.
>
> (*JACM* November 1989: 13)

As purveyors of private medicine, non-orthodox therapists can expect no special sympathy from those who are opposed to the creation of free markets in medicine: rescuing the beleaguered NHS from Thatcherite insistence that it mimic the market place is perceived as a much more urgent task.

On the other hand, a socialist commitment to providing the very best treatment for the patient, especially the patient who does not have the resources to buy expensive private medical care, could imply positive advocacy for the insertion of complementary therapies into the NHS. And to the extent that the use of non-orthodox medicine represents an implicit subversion of, or challenge to the authority of the powerful medical profession, it carries a potential political appeal to the radical. This has been very evident in the women's movement, where the use of natural therapies has often been commended as empowering; non-orthodox medicine generally encourages the patient to take control of her own health, and achieve a limited independence from the oppressive power of a highly masculine profession.

But this idea of personal control and responsibility carries problems for those who hold collectivist values. Taking individual responsibility for one's health must be valuable where it enables the individual to challenge professional control, but what if this empowerment has no wider consequences than individual independence? Rosalind Coward states this objection thus:

> the emphasis on personal responsibility rarely generates political empowerment. It may generate a sense of being able to accomplish things within the existing *status quo*, but it rarely promises the ability to transform social structures... alternative implies co-existing with existing structures not challenging them. And action simply becomes a matter of

personal choice between two routes, rather than a matter of creating a different society with different values.

(Coward 1989: 204–5)

The ambivalence of the Left towards non-orthodox medicine is apparent in the pages of *Health Matters*, journal of the Health Rights Campaign, dedicated to improving the NHS and securing equality in access and treatment. An editorial rejects the philosophy of consumerism and the market as a guiding principle in health policy just as firmly as Duncan Campbell, whom I quoted earlier (*Health Matters* April/May 1989). But in another issue of the same bulletin, Charles Brien points out that holistic and natural medicine should be taken seriously because they 'consider the person and take into account environmental factors' (*Health Matters* Winter 1988: 9). That is, they combine a concern both for the individual person and the wider social and physical context. This point is picked up by Nicholls, writing about the political message of homoeopathy:

> While on the one hand [holistic medicine's] emphasis on the importance of the unique experience of sickness produced a therapeutic individualism which may inhibit the development of collective awareness of the material circumstances which determine the health of nations, on the other, the metaphors of harmony and balance, of the human organism as a delicate self-sustaining and self-correcting vitalistic system in its own right, resonate strongly with ideas informing the ecological critique of industrialism.... Holistic therapy, then, possesses a philosophical structure whose terms, while primarily representing a critique of orthodox medicine, also provides a 'green' vocabulary in which an alternative, non-aggressive, harmonious mode of economic interaction with the environment can be envisaged.

(Nicholls 1988: 285)

Complementary medicine appeals to values which cannot easily be appropriated by any one political tendency to the exclusion of others. It raises questions which are complex, from whichever positions in the British political spectrum they are viewed, and which do not lend themselves to simplistic polemic. Although non-orthodox medicine may become a political issue, it is unlikely that it will become a straightforward *party* political issue in the foreseeable future.

So far as the present government is concerned, the ball is definitely in the court of the complementary therapists; if they wish for registration or any further strengthening of their statutory position it is their business to convince Parliament and the public that they deserve it. For some years, this was given to mean that the different professions would have to 'get their act together' and present a united front, especially with respect to the problem of defining and maintaining standards of training and practice. Lord Colwyn, known to be sympathetic to the cause of complementary medicine, wrote in the *Journal of Alternative and Complementary Medicine* in 1989 that

> Governments and agencies are busy people. They do not have time to bother with a group here and a group there. But they have every time for groups who have shown by their resolution, intelligence and wisdom that they are capable of forging a united and complete front to an issue. And you show you are capable of it by doing it.
>
> (*JACM* October 1989: 10)

Official insistence that the complementary therapists 'get their act together' was often interpreted as a convenient delaying tactic but helped to stimulate the growth of various pan-professional organisations which I shall refer to in more detail in a later chapter. On the other hand, if piecemeal legislation is to be avoided in future, this policy implied that groups who may have little in common other than their historical divergence from orthodox medicine must themselves see a political interest in unity, however difficult this is to achieve. Baroness Trumpington, Under-Secretary of State for Health at the time, was confident in 1985 that this would happen without government intervention. Meanwhile, she said, no government would ban complementary medicine, although measures to protect the public from harmful medicines or unsupported claims might be desirable (Trumpington 1988: 81).

Government insistence on pan-professional unity as a condition for any movement in the direction of legitimation of non-orthodox medicine by the state has recently been modified. In the House of Lords debate on 'Medicine: Complementary and Conventional Treatments' in May 1990, Baroness Hooper, Junior Minister for Health, explicitly stated that

> the government's stance on umbrella bodies has changed in recent years. There is little homogeneity among the various natural therapy groups... given the diversity, practice and aspirations of those professions – coupled perhaps with their increasing proliferation – we now believe very firmly that it must be for each therapy group to determine its own future development.
>
> (*Hansard*, 9 May 1990: 1432)

One interpretation of this about-turn, supported by approving remarks made by the Baroness in the rest of her speech, is that the government has been so impressed by the progress made by some individual professions towards unity and the regulation of standards of training (notably the osteopaths and chiropractors) that it has seen this as the best way forward for (and within the reach of) the other professions as well. A less charitable interpretation (and one for which there is also some evidence in the statement) is that the government is so alarmed by the rapid growth in the public utilisation of non-orthodox medicine, along with the proximity of 1992 and the Single European Market, that it has decided not to wait upon a political process of unification over which it has no control and which may still take many years.

It is interesting that Conservative policy makers have not used the impending re-organisation of the NHS as an opportunity to respond to consumer demand for complementary medicine. Certainly some sympathetic politicians have seen this period of upheaval and re-organisation as a good opportunity to bid for the explicit inclusion of non-orthodox therapies within NHS healthcare. Three attempts were made to introduce such amendments to the NHS and Community Care Bill in the House of Lords during 1990, the vote on the third occasion (12 June) being only seventy-seven to seventy-four votes against the amendment.

But whilst there is a whole section in the key policy document, the white paper *Working for Patients*, on patient choice, the choices in question seem largely to be choice of doctors and choice between the services offered by GPs, and not choice of therapy (*Working for Patients* 1989: 54–5). It is true, as more than one commentator has pointed out, that this Act could encourage non-orthodox medicine indirectly; if GPs and hospitals are to be given more responsibility to control their own budgets and are encouraged to give value for money, they might well decide to use natural medicines or to buy in the services of non-orthodox therapists (e.g. Huggon 1990b: 14, *JACM* May 1989: 10). A less optimistic view is that hospitals will concentrate on a high throughput of straightforward surgical cases at the expense of forms of treatment which are 'long-term, indefinable and difficult to cost', and that GPs will have less time for patients because they will have an accumulation of administrative work (Marcovitch 1989: 4–5, see also Stacey 1989a and b).

Conservative policy remains implicitly permissive, rather than explicitly prescriptive in this matter. It does seem, however, that explicit prohibition is not on the political agenda and persistent and well organised lobbying from the non-orthodox medical professions will ensure that any move affecting the freedom to practise receives very thorough public debate.

So far as the availability of 'natural' medicines is concerned, the situation is rather different. Here official attitudes have generally been more stringent:

> There is an essential difference between medicines which are regulated, and therapies which are not. Medicines are consumed and once consumed the arrangements for reversing the process if the product is unsafe can be very distressing for the patient – hence the licensing requirement. In the

case of most therapies the patient can withdraw and seek other advice if he is not satisfied. Usually no harm is done, but I recognize that this may not always be the case – especially if effective treatment is seriously delayed as a consequence.

(Trumpington 1988: 80)

But any regulation of natural medicines has a profound effect on the practice of those forms of complementary medicine which involve the administration of substances to the patient, chiefly homoeopathy and herbalism. It also affects practitioners who use the Bach Flower Remedies, biochemical tissue salts or anthroposophical medicines as a major part of their treatment. Therefore a severe curtailment of the freedom to supply or prescribe such remedies would effectively curtail the freedom of many therapists to practice at all. A DHSS review of natural medicines commenced in 1987, and in June 1989 Linda Anderson, pharmacologist and DHSS spokeswoman, revealed that only 1400 out of 3500 submissions for the licensing of herbal medicines had been granted to date. Presumably the medicines did not meet the requirements necessary for issue of a product licence (*NMS News*, No. 12, Winter 1989) but the high cost of licence fees probably deterred some small manufacturers from applying in the first place (*NMS News*, No. 11, Summer 1989). Manufacturers mobilised opposition to these moves, supported by many sympathetic users of natural medicines and by therapists who rely on them for their livelihood, but had only limited success, and the government reliance on the advice of the orthodox medical profession, rather than experts in the use of natural medicines, has always been an understandable grievance of the Natural Medicines Society, a pressure group established to preserve the availability of herbal and homoeopathic medicines. The motivation for all this governmental activity has largely been the need to bring British practice into line with EEC directives, with the creation of the Single European Market in late 1992 imminent (Huggon 1990a: 13). A draft directive on homoeopathic medicines is being considered as I write, and there is a risk that this may also result in the withdrawal of some remedies from the market. There is justifiable concern that appropriate criteria should be used to assess the safety and efficacy of these products (*NMS News*, No. 13, March 1990).

In the light of this experience it is perhaps not surprising that many complementary therapists regard the establishment of the Single European Market with trepidation, seeing it as certain to jeopardise freedoms which they regard as fragile. So far as the freedom to practise is concerned, this anxiety seems to stem chiefly from the knowledge that in many European countries the practice of non-orthodox medicine is forbidden to those who are not also qualified doctors. This does not mean to say that complementary medicine does not flourish on the continent, although there is much variation from country to country. The most restrictive legal situation is probably that which obtains in Belgium where the practice of non-orthodox medicine by those who are not qualified doctors is forbidden. Training in non-orthodox medicine is not available in medical schools, so that when doctors do practice it, it is a result of their own initiative and no doubt in response to the considerable demand for natural therapies which exists in spite of prohibitive legislation. In France the legal situation is rather similar, but homoeopathy and acupuncture are taught in some medical faculties and widely practised by registered doctors. Treatment under these systems can be reimbursed by the state. The most permissive situation must be that which exists in Holland, where legislation similar to that obtaining in France and Belgium has been superseded in practice by a government initiative to integrate orthodox and non-orthodox systems of medicine; a state Commission for Alternative Systems of Medicine was set up in 1977 to oversee this process, and the cost of non-orthodox treatment is generally recoverable from public and private insurance schemes (Aldridge 1989, Fulder 1988: 89ff, Sermeus 1987).

One strongly voiced fear is that there will be increasing pressure for uniformity within the EEC (probably powered by the energy of the French medical profession) and that the recommended policy will favour the restrictive French rather than the liberal Dutch model (e.g. *JACM* February 1990: 30). This is conceivable, yet there appears to be no such proposal under discussion at the present time. An informed commentator suggests that pressure for uniformity within the EEC is more likely to arise from discontinuities in consumer protection arrangements than from diversity in health policy, and urges that lobbying at the European level is required to forestall this (Huggon 1990a: 13, 1990b: 15).

THE VIEW FROM ORTHODOX MEDICINE

Orthodox medical attitudes are an important part of the context within which non-orthodox medicine is practised, if only because of the political power of the medical profession at the national level. What is striking here is the evident disjunction between most *ex cathedra* statements on behalf of orthodox medicine and the expressed views of many ordinary doctors.

An editorial in the *British Medical Journal* characterised the popularity of complementary medicine as symptomatic of a general 'flight from science'. The public has grown out of its enchantment with modern science and technology, it argued, but this critical attitude – fuelled by consumerism – leads them to underestimate the achievement of modern medical science and to be unwilling to accept its standards of proof or at any rate unwilling to apply them to non-orthodox medical techniques. This is seen essentially

as a flight from reason. Reason, however, demands that patients take seriously the scientific foundation of orthodox medicine:

> What is wrong is the refusal by the critics and the fringe practitioners to
> accept the standards of proof that medical scientists have developed in the
> past hundred years: not for nothing has the double-blind controlled trial
> been described as one of Britain's most important contributions to medi-
> cine since the war.... New ideas have to be set up as hypotheses, tested by
> experiment, and revised in the light of the results. The same standards
> should be adopted by the opponents of orthodox medicine – and by any
> group offering treatment based on alternative theories.
>
> (*BMJ* Editorial 5.1.80)

In 1986 the British Medical Association published a report on alternative
therapy which represented the findings of a working party set up in 1983 to
consider how alternative therapies might be assessed. This working party did
not include any doctors with a practising knowledge of non-orthodox
medicine and so it is probably not surprising that its findings were largely
negative. In explaining the appeal of complementary medicine this report
laid less emphasis on the essential irrationality of the patient/consumer and
more on the failure of many orthodox doctors to provide an empathic service
which was holistic and cognisant of the patient's psycho-social needs.
However, we find the same accusation of non-scientificity re-iterated. The
extent to which non-orthodox medicine could possibly offer anything which
the best orthodox medical practice did not already provide, the report argued,
was limited. The working party saw the possibility of conducting objective
and scientific trials for certain types of non-orthodox treatment (especially
some aspects of homoeopathy, acupuncture and chiropractic), but the
non-scientific nature of complementary therapies was seen as a major
obstacle to any kind of integration, and no concrete proposals were made for
any early rapprochement (BMA 1986). It seems, however, that there is now
some unease within the medical profession about this report because in
August 1990 the BMA's Annual Representative's Meeting called for a new
report on the subject with wider terms of reference. This new enquiry will be
headed by Professor James Payne who led the 1986 investigation, but will
be produced with the likely influence of the European Community in mind
and will pay special attention to training programmes and registration
facilities. Efficacy it would seem, is now not the only matter on the agenda.

Ordinary members of trades unions or professional associations do not
always, of course, concur with the political statements of their official
representatives. There always have been a number of orthodox doctors who
have practised or taken an interest in the more established disciplines like
homoeopathy or osteopathy, though they have not been very influential in

relation to the profession as a whole. Within the complementary medical movement there are even organisations like the British Medical Acupuncture Society which are exclusive to registered doctors. Their combined membership probably totals well over a thousand, and there may well be many registered doctors who practise some form of non-orthodox medicine but who do not belong to these associations.

In 1983 David Taylor Reilly conducted a survey designed to examine the attitudes of general practitioner trainees to complementary medicine and found that his eighty-six respondents showed a high level of interest. The established therapies such as acupuncture, hypnosis and homoeopathy were regarded as 'useful' by a majority. As many as seventy expressed a desire to train in one of the better-known non-orthodox therapies (hypnosis and manipulation being the most favoured). More than a third had actually referred patients for non-orthodox treatment and twenty-two had used such therapies themselves (Reilly 1983). Wharton and Lewith studied GPs in the Avon area and found that 38 per cent had actually had some training in non-orthodox medicine and a further 15 per cent would like to train. Fifty-nine per cent thought that such therapies might be useful to their patients – acupuncture, manipulation and hypnosis being the most positively regarded. The majority claimed to have referred patients to non-orthodox practitioners (Wharton and Lewith 1986). A study conducted in Oxfordshire by Eileen and Peter Anderson found similarly high rates of interest, knowledge and referral of patients (Anderson and Anderson 1987). All these writers conclude that proper and recognised training in non-orthodox therapies should be made available to doctors.

Possibly these studies do not represent the entire medical world; Avon and Oxfordshire are in the southern heartlands where non-orthodox medicine is most available; it is not surprising that in these areas we should find such large numbers of GPs knowledgeable about non-orthodox medicine and prepared to refer patients to its practitioners. Reilly's survey, however, was not based on a southern sample but on a random sample of students attending a conference in Scotland. A study of GPs in a Midlands town also reveals a high level of interest in and support for complementary medicine (Nicholls and Luton 1986). If we want to explain the discrepancy between these findings and the official stance of the BMA, the differences in perspective and experience between the GP and the hospital doctors may be more relevant than regional variations. Reilly points out that:

It is unlikely that general practitioner trainees are representative of the profession at large. A pilot study has shown much less interest among junior hospital doctors and less still in more senior doctors.

He suggests various reasons for this:

The relative lack of interest in junior hospital doctors may reflect the different roles of these techniques in the more technological and specialised hospital environment. It may also, however, show something of the different attitudes to medicine in these groups, with the primary care doctors more concerned with 'holism'.

(Reilly 1983: 339)

(Had the BMA Working Party which produced the 1986 report on Alternative Therapy been differently constituted – it did not include one representative of general practice – might its conclusions perhaps have been more positive?)

I have not had much to say about the considerable interest in complementary medicine on the part of nurses and the paramedical professions, mainly because there is little research data of the kind I have cited for GPs. The appearance of informative articles on particular non-orthodox therapies in professional journals such as the *Health Visitor* suggests a receptive attitude. Around 10 per cent of the membership of the British Holistic Medical Association consists of nurses and other paramedical professionals. One commentator has shrewdly observed that hospital nurses are often motivated by a concern to highlight the distinction between their approach and that of doctors because 'there is within nursing a strong need for a professional identity separate from that of medicine' (Stalker and Glymour 1989: 58) and this may certainly be an ingredient in the interest in some forms of complementary medicine shown by the nursing profession. Healthcare professionals such as health visitors, physiotherapists and district nurses, because of their training and the nature of their work, are also likely to see the patient in his/her social context and to be receptive to forms of medical care which are broader than the overly technological approach of much hospital medicine.

HOLISM

Holism is not in itself synonymous with the non-orthodox in medicine, although the word is sometimes used as though it were. The ideal of holistic healthcare is one which both orthodox and non-orthodox practitioner can share. In the medical context the term 'holism' is generally used to refer to the kind of care which treats the patient as a whole person. This has two implications. At the level of individual treatment it implies that the patient should not be dealt with simply as a mechanical body, but as a person inhabiting a social environment and having psycho-social, even spiritual needs as well as physical needs. At the level of professional organisation it implies the need to address the problem of over-specialisation in medicine. If the patient is a whole person, then does it make sense to have completely different teams of people dealing with his/her musculo-skeletal system, digestive tract, mental health, etc?

Most forms of non-orthodox medicine claim to be holistic in one sense or another, as judged both by the official pronouncements of their professional associations and by the ideals expressed by individual practitioners.

> Homoeopathy... recognises that all symptoms of ill health are expressions of disharmony within the whole person and that it is the patient who needs treatment not the disease.

> Herbalism treats the whole patient as a person, not as a collection of symptoms.

> Aromatherapy... is a holistic treatment which does not use toxic or violent remedies, and so the essential oils do not have unpleasant side effects. It is a caring, hands-on therapy...

> Chinese medicine takes into account not only the disease symptoms but also the age, habits, physical and emotional traits and all the other aspects of the individual, and attempts to put together an overall picture of the patient in order to evaluate any patterns of disharmony that have arisen.
>
> (Extracts from leaflets and publicity material used by practitioners)

Of course, whether practice can actually be holistic or not will partly depend on whether patients want or permit this. The data from my local study suggests that many do appreciate this kind of care. Yet, as one writer has pointed out, when patients 'shop around' they may well end up consulting different kinds of non-orthodox practitioner for different kinds of symptom. There is a danger that the osteopath will be resorted to for backache, whilst the herbalist prescribes medicine for digestive complaints and local pain is relieved through acupuncture (Reilly 1983: 339).

Probably few professionals who espouse the term holism would understand holism to mean that the patient should be treated by one practitioner alone, who deals with all his/her ills – bodily, spiritual, psychological and social. But it is not difficult to see why this broad interpretation of what health and healing mean has an especial appeal to GPs, and to those non-orthodox professionals who see their task as similar to that of the GP in respect to patients who choose their particular therapy. The concept of holism provides a rallying point for proponents of quite different therapeutic techniques who desire a more person-centred form of medical practice.

A major voice in the promotion of holistic healthcare is the British Holistic Medical Association, founded in 1983, which sees holism as resting on the following principles:

Firstly, responding to a person as a whole within the environment, seeing that person as mind, body and spirit

Secondly, to be willing to consider a wide range of interventions (including orthodox drugs and surgery, education and communication skills, self-help techniques and complementary therapies)

Thirdly, to modify the doctor/patient relationship so as to encourage patients' own self-regulation and responsibility

Fourthly, to realise the importance of the practitioner's own awareness and health.

(BHMA leaflet)

However, whilst espousing therapeutic open-mindedness (some might say eclecticism) and whilst sharing with many forms of non-orthodox medicine a humanistic concern with the nature of the therapeutic relationship, the BHMA is dominated by the orthodox medical profession. According to its constitution at least half of the trustees (including the chair) must be registered medical practitioners. In 1988 the secretary of the BHMA, Dr David Peters, stated:

The BHMA certainly wants to see a broad range of interventions available, but our main focus for developing health care in the 21st century is not about complementary medicine.

(*Holistic Health*, Winter 1988: 5)

Though friendly to many forms of non-orthodox medicine and having many members from the complementary medical professions, the association's priorities are mainly geared to transforming the kind of primary care available under the NHS.

I have examined the issue of holism at length in order to illustrate the fact (which we shall encounter again in a later chapter) that even where orthodox doctors favour non-orthodox medicine and wish to enter into dialogue with its practitioners, their different structural situations mean that political co-operation is difficult to achieve on an equal basis; in the most willing partnership divergent interests will surface and make themselves felt.

Non-orthodox professionals practise in a very curious context. They have widespread public and even medical acceptance, but this approval does not guarantee security and the continuation of present freedoms, for these freedoms are based on a negative right (the right to practise something which no-one has got round to prohibiting). It may be true, as Baroness Trumpington says, that no government would actually ban non-orthodox medicine. But rights can be eroded by action which is far short of an outright ban, by the chipping away of facilities and a gradual narrowing of the political and jural space within which non-orthodox medicine is practised. Complementary medical organisations are probably not being alarmist when they call for positive action to ensure their existing freedoms and in a later chapter I shall consider the kinds of practical politics which they have pursued.

These issues are not merely of narrow professional concern, for they affect the public. Whether or not the practice of non-orthodox medicine is restricted after 1992, whether registration is extended to non-orthodox practitioners, how training for practitioners should be regulated and standardised – these are matters which affect a very large number of people, given the popularity of non-orthodox medicine. It is easy enough to find out what homoeopathy ideally consists of, what acupuncture professes to be able to achieve, what procedures hypnotherapists claim to employ, etc. Debates about the future of non-orthodox medicine need to be informed by research on such topics as who actually becomes a homoeopath, how acupuncturists practise, what kind of relationships hypnotherapists aim to achieve with their patients. Such matters will form the content of the next two chapters.

6   Professions, power and the patient
Some more useful concepts

In Chapter 2 I raided the sociological and anthropological literature for concepts to help us understand the way in which people use non-orthodox medicine. In this chapter I conduct a similar exercise with respect to its delivery. Has social science identified questions and concepts which will help us to understand and analyse the rapid growth in the provision of complementary medicine?

The practice of non-orthodox medicine is a particular kind of work, with its own forms of training, organisation and typical practices. It seems appropriate therefore to examine it in the context of the sociology of occupations and the professions. I shall argue that the complementary therapies are endeavouring to conduct a process of professionalisation and that it is therefore pertinent to ask what kinds of control such professional groups might expect to exercise. I shall consider some of the different kinds of professional power which they might attempt – control over the market for their services, control over the patient, control over entry and standards of training. Knowledge can also be a source of power – some would argue the most important source of power in modern societies; does the kind of knowledge on which complementary medical practice is based lend itself to the exercise of professional control? What prestige can it command and what legitimacy can it claim in the wider society?

COMPLEMENTARY MEDICINE AS AN OCCUPATION: PROFESSIONS AND TRADES

Practitioners of non-orthodox medicine sell a service, for the most part in the private sector of the economy. Is there anything about the way in which it is organised, or indeed about its intrinsic nature, which distinguishes this service from others which are bought and sold, such as those of window cleaners, or automobile engineers? Both sociologists and the general public use the term 'profession' to distinguish certain kinds of occupational service from others, and it is a term which complementary therapists certainly apply to themselves. Medicine is definitely regarded as a profession, carpentry is not. Is this anything more than a re-inforcement of prevalent social snobberies, blessing those who practise certain non-manual skills with a fancier occupational title?

I shall not try to review the multifarious sociological definitions of the term 'profession' here since, as Larson points out, there is little disagreement as to its general dimensions:

> The cognitive dimension is centered on the body of knowledge and techniques which the professionals apply in their work, and on the training necessary to master such knowledge and skills; the normative dimension covers the service orientation of professionals, and their distinctive ethics, which justify the privilege of self-regulation granted them by society; the evaluative dimension implicitly compares professionals to other occupations, underscoring the professions' singular characteristics of autonomy and prestige.
>
> (Larson 1977: x)

In fact there is more than one comparison implied in the way in which social scientists (and frequently professionals themselves) characterise the professions. Professionalism is distinguished from manual craftsmanship (which may take just as long to learn), but professional activity is also contrasted with entrepreneurial activity or trade. Commercial knowledge cannot be transmitted entirely through formalised training – it is practical knowledge of people, things and markets. Trade is normative only to the extent that it is constrained by whatever principles of common decency individual business men and women subscribe to, and by the limits of the market and the law. Its evaluative dimension is characterised by an equation of success with profit; a business cannot be 'good' business if it is not profitable. An embodiment of these characteristics can be found in David Lodge's recent novel *Nice Work*. His sales manager Vic Wilcox, with his suspicion of formalised learning and his contempt for those who like to imagine themselves immune to market forces, is commercial activity personified.

Real life, as the characters in Lodge's novel find out for themselves, calls dichotomies like this into question. Some areas within the commercial firm (such as personnel) are open to professionalisation and some of the complementary practitioners whom I interviewed had taken courses in setting up a small business. Maybe the dichotomy is best understood not as an empirical classification, but as a moral construct used by the professions to justify their claims. Some have argued that the notion of a 'quack', practising a spurious medicine solely for the pursuit of profit, was necessary if doctors could claim to be 'professionals', practising genuine medicine for the benefit of the patient (see Beier 1981: 30). But it remains the fact that most complementary practitioners, in common with many other professionals (but not NHS doctors), are self-employed and rely for their livelihood on demand from patients expressed through direct appeals to their services. If they fail to understand this market they will not be in a position to pay for the outgoings involved in maintaining a practice, let alone make a satisfactory income for themselves. While those who practise non-orthodox medicine, as we shall see in the next chapter, stress their professionalism and dissociate themselves from the 'cowboy' who is out to make money rather than give a service, they must themselves have some commercial skills if they are to survive. The taking of payment is, after all, what distinguishes them from that other outsider category, the 'amateurs', from which several of my interviewees were equally anxious to dissociate themselves.

This tension between professional and commercial orientation is not peculiar to complementary medicine. One reaction evoked by recent government 'reforms' of the education system has been outrage over the fact that head teachers are being expected to take much more responsibility for school finances. The orthodox medical profession has responded in a similar way to government intentions to make GPs financial managers of their own 'budgets'. In both cases the unease is often expressed in terms of a fear that the management of resources (paperwork, doing accounts, fund raising) will compete for time with what is seen as 'real' professional work (treating patients, teaching pupils). I would not wish to argue that non-orthodox practitioners conceptualise professionalism in a way that is fundamentally different from the way in which the idea is used among orthodox doctors, only that the contradiction between professional (service) and commercial (market) considerations confronts them more immediately, since almost all of them operate in the private sector. In the next chapter I shall deal with the way in which they experience and handle this contradiction.

ALTRUISM AND THE RHETORIC OF PROFESSIONALISM

However, we do not need to assume in advance that this tension is an overwhelming pre-occupation. As several sociologists have pointed out, there is a danger in accepting too easily the professionals' own definitions of what distinguishes professions from other kinds of work:

> Professional rhetoric relating to community service and altruism may in
> many cases be a significant factor in moulding the practices of individual

professionals, but it also clearly functions as a legitimation of professional privilege.

(Johnson 1972: 25)

Reviewing research on the motivation of doctors in the United States, Freidson notes the increasingly scientific orientation of medical students, and suggests that there is

little evidence that those aspiring to medicine have a stronger service orientation than those aspiring to other occupations.

(Freidson 1975: 174)

Isobel Allen's recent study of three cohorts of British medical qualifiers shows that the desire to be of service is but one among a number of career motivations mentioned by doctors. Being good at science subjects (22 per cent), wanting an interesting career (17 per cent), always having wanted to be a doctor (15 per cent) and the influence of friends and relations (15 per cent) were more often cited as main reasons for choosing to be a doctor than wanting to help people (12 per cent) although, admittedly, financial rewards and job security scored even lower (Allen 1988: 49). The career motivation of complementary practitioners may be at least as complex, since many entrants to these professions are mature people who have switched from other work. I shall examine data on motivation with this issue in mind.

Professions lay claim not only to a special ethical orientation but to special expertise. In doing so, they run the risk that a gap may open between what the profession claims and what it can actually deliver. Medical professionals, orthodox and non-orthodox, cannot always cure their patients. An autonomous profession is expected to control and if necessary discipline its members in order that discrepancies are minimised. A profession may construct its own myths and ideologies (Arluke 1977: 108) and present these to the public in the hope that they will prove convincing, but how much purchase does it have over any gap that emerges between what the public expects and what the professional can actually provide? A fairly common view is that modern medical science is the victim of its own success. It has done so well in curing many acute and infectious conditions that people now expect doctors to be able to cure everything. When they find that this is not the case they may become impatient and turn (unreasonably, in the BMA's view) to non-orthodox medicine (BMA 1986: 4). Will the non-orthodox medical professions be any more successful in managing gaps between promise and performance? At present complementary medical organisations have few effective sanctions over their members (in the absence of any system of state registration such as doctors have, there is nothing to prevent a practitioner who is struck from his or her association's register from continuing to practise) and the problem is more often addressed in the form of a concern over standards of training and the content of qualifications.

PROFESSIONALISATION: PROCESS AND POWER

So far I have proceeded as though it were not in question that non-orthodox medical practitioners do indeed constitute a profession. They certainly approximate to the ideal type characterised above in important ways – more so than do, say hospital cleaners, medical secretaries or ambulance drivers. They are organised into a number of associations which subscribe to ideals of service to the patient, co-ordinate or oversee training in their respective systems of medicine and define codes of conduct for their members, some modelled very closely on the code of ethics to which doctors subscribe. However, sociologists have pointed out that the distinction between an occupation and a profession is not something that simply and naturally 'occurs'. The process by which professional status is successfully claimed by a group of workers is usually contentious. To the extent that a profession is a group with control over its members and a degree of autonomy in determining its own modes of training and criteria for membership, it claims a certain kind of power and that power may not be accorded easily. The orthodox medical profession emerged as a very powerful group in the nineteenth century, an alliance of physicians, surgeons and apothecaries. This alliance was not without its internal tensions, but the consolidation of medical education and the state recognition of orthodox medicine through the 1858 Medical Registration Act promoted the amalgamated power of qualified practitioners of this kind of medicine, both in relation to those who practised other forms of medicine (homoeopathy was a strong competitor in the first half of the nineteenth century) and in relation to groups who did not have formal qualifications but who performed work of a medical nature, e.g. midwives (Parry and Parry 1976). This profession now had a large measure of control over the medical division of labour.

The professionalisation of groups who perform work related to that of the hospital doctor or GP (such as nurses, health visitors, radiographers) has had to take place in the context of an existing division of labour and an existing division of power, ultimately sanctioned by the state. Most non-orthodox practitioners are outside this state-sanctioned division of medical labour altogether as things are at present. Yet the patients they treat also use the services of medical doctors within the NHS, and so any claims on their part to professional autonomy and competence in the management of treatment must bring them into a direct contest of power with the orthodox medical profession.

Although the different groups representing non-orthodox practitioners are fairly unanimous in claiming professional autonomy and status, they by no means speak with one voice on the question of how this power struggle is best resolved. Given that the state is the ultimate arbiter of the matter, can non-orthodox practitioners make any further advance in professionalisation without submitting to some kind of control by the state? Would not professional equality with medical doctors imply the right (or duty) to work within the NHS? Could the medical profession cede some ground to the complementary practitioners without the latter becoming simply another paramedical group, a 'paraprofession' to use Freidson's term (Freidson 1975: 75), fitting into a division of labour still dominated by the orthodox medical profession? Some practitioners whom I interviewed argued that the medical profession has paid for the high degree of professional autonomy which the state has conferred upon it by the fact that most of its members are obliged to work within what is essentially a state bureaucracy. This imposes many organisational constraints, even if it provides the doctor with secure employment and privileged control over the treatment of patients. Many non-orthodox practitioners, as we shall discover, can see their dilemma quite clearly; the professionalisation of complementary medicine probably cannot proceed much further than it has without action on the part of the medical profession (whose officially expressed attitude so far has been negative) and/or the state (hitherto otiose in this matter). In either case this might mean exchanging existing freedoms for future status.

One important point to remember, however, is that professionalisation is not a process with a stable and permanent end condition (Johnson 1972: 59). Professions mobilise different resources at different times to capture available markets (Larson 1977), and there is no guarantee that the market for a particular form of professional labour will remain constant. Professions have little control over the demand for their services, but they can assay control over the supply side through restricting access. Raising the level of educational qualification necessary for entry into training or prolonging the training itself are strategies which have the added advantage of enhancing the credibility of the group's claims to esteem and expertise, but plain discrimination is not uncommon. Orthodox medicine made entry harder for women until very recently and the Commission for Racial Equality found evidence that some medical schools have discriminated against black people (CRE 1988). In most of the non-orthodox medical disciplines training requirements are far from standardised, so that entry is open to people with quite varied educational backgrounds. On the other hand it is still quite difficult to get funding from the state for such training, so access is still largely dependent on the entrant's ability to fund him/herself. From what range of backgrounds do the non-orthodox medical professions recruit and will this range narrow if the process of professionalisation proceeds?

Does complementary medicine provide special opportunities for women? Women are certainly well represented in most of the non-orthodox forms of medicine, just as they are in the orthodox paramedical professions and the 'caring' professions in general. The 'feminisation' of an occupational group has generally been regarded with ambivalence by women themselves; if the group is able to capitalise on sexual solidarity and wrest some control over their conditions of work and training, then feminisation can be seen as a positive process. But women's wages still lag behind those of men in so many areas, and a predominantly female membership may make it easier for rates of pay to remain depressed. What consequences might a high proportion of female entrants have both for the non-orthodox medical professions generally and in terms of career opportunities for women? We should take seriously Witz's stricture that

> The generic concept of profession is also a gendered one as it takes what are in fact the successful professional projects of class-privileged, male actors at a particular point in history to be the paradigmatic case of profession.

Taking the example of nursing she demonstrates that

> women have engaged in professional projects, attempting to be mistresses of their own fates, rather than fatefully acquiescing to the role of 'handmaiden' to male professionals.

> (Witz 1990: 688)

Whilst there are few complementary therapies in which women are not well represented there are also very few in which they have an overwhelming majority, so that it might be argued that they have the worst of both worlds. They occupy a minority position in professions which are already weak in terms of public power and so are obliged to fall in with the professional projects of men, lacking the space to develop strategies of their own as women. Much more research needs to be done on the gendered organisation of complementary medicine, but I touch on this question at various points in the next two chapters.

Strategies of closure address the supply of professional labour; the demand side may be much harder to manipulate. But neither markets nor status can be captured easily without a stable form of organisation (Larson 1977: 14ff, 69ff). Complementary medicine is at present characterised by a plethora of organisations claiming to represent the interests of its practitioners. There are, for instance, at least three professional organisations among trained homoeopaths and at least five among acupuncturists. There is more than one umbrella organisation working to promote unity of interest among non-orthodox practitioners (see p. 192ff). This could be treated merely as a sign of the very recent emergence of the profession – after all, much non-orthodox medicine is relatively new in this country. Or it could be treated as indicative of the heterogeneity of its members – have we any business to assume that non-orthodox practitioners constitute or ought to constitute a single profession just because they occupy a common political status (i.e. not being directly sanctioned by the state)? The reasons for this organisational diversity will be discussed when we consider the politics of complementary medicine.

So far I have discussed the collectivity of non-orthodox practitioners in terms of whether or not they constitute a profession. But they do not stand alone in the challenge they pose to orthodox medicine. Complementary medicine enjoys the advocacy of various groups, some quite powerful. The Consumers' Association has done much to collect and disseminate information about complementary medicine and has a generally sympathetic attitude. Within the orthodox medical profession itself there are many who either practise some form of non-orthodox medicine themselves or who see its positive possibilities, and this has led to all kinds of co-operative alliances at the local level (see p. 156ff below) and at the national level through organisations like the British Holistic Medical Association (see previous chapter). Companies which manufacture herbal and other 'natural' remedies also have an interest in the issue. In the sphere of formal politics there is now an all-party Parliamentary Complementary and Alternative Medicine group. If we are to treat non-orthodox practitioners as a professional group, we cannot ignore their relationship with these allies outside the profession. To the extent that they actively co-operate with these various friends, practitioners can be seen as part of a social movement, a 'deliberate collective endeavour to promote change' (Wilkinson 1971: 27). In this case the desired change is, broadly speaking, a more secure future for non-orthodox medicine, although as we shall see, there is much debate as to how this security is best guaranteed.

In a modern industrial society it is ultimately the state which sanctions the degree of security and autonomy which a profession can enjoy. Monopolies of competence can scarcely be maintained without this consent, whether explicitly or merely tacitly given, especially where the state is expected to be the chief provider of important services such as health and education. In Britain we have a rather strange situation in that while the state has legitimated orthodox medicine – indeed it is only this legitimation which allows us to speak of 'orthodox' and 'non-orthodox medicine' – it has done little to control the growth of other forms of medicine. It could be argued that orthodox doctors pay for the power which the state has conferred upon them by the fact that most of them must practise within the bounds of the bureaucratic organisation of the NHS. Complementary medicine has lost out in terms of power but compensates in terms of freedom from bureaucratic constraint. The limits at present are only the market and the law, both of which are favourable to non-orthodox practitioners as things stand at present.

PROFESSIONAL POWER AND THE PATIENT

Professionals have power over their clients to the extent that they have expert knowledge which is not easily accessible to lay persons – though where health is concerned lay people may try hard to obtain it (see my discussion of 'homework' in Chapter 3). The state may also delegate to a profession the power to control clients' access to other facilities; thus GPs act as gatekeepers to hospital care, consultants' services, certain types of diagnostic screening, etc. The knowledge controlled by non-orthodox practitioners is not in itself less specialised than orthodox medical science, but they may have to be prepared to share some aspects of it if they are to convince users that it is worth paying for. They do not, however, act as gatekeepers to other services and it is impossible for them to sanction patients who are uncooperative. The fact that people tend to use complementary medicine for chronic conditions rather than in emergencies means that the dissatisfied patient usually has time to search for another practitioner. A profession has only as much control over clients as it is able to obtain and perhaps the professionalisation of non-orthodox medicine has not gone very far in this respect.

However, sociologists have recognised that the concept of professionalisation can embrace a number of types of relationship between practitioner and client, involving different configurations of power and control (Johnson 1972). With respect to medicine, Freidson distinguishes between medical practice in which the practitioner him/herself is subject to client control, and practice in which the practitioner has considerable control over clients but is subject to the control of professional colleagues (Freidson 1960, 1975). In an ideal typical 'dependent practice' clients arrive through institutionalised channels, rather than simply as a result of the operation of lay referral systems, or of an open market for medical services.

> dependent practice is *most* able to resist control by clients but *least* able to resist control by colleagues.
>
> (Freidson 1960: 381)

The service provided by hospital consultants under the NHS in Britain would be a good example of dependent practice. Independent practice, in its ideal typical form, relies entirely on lay referral as its source of clients and is not 'plugged into' any kind of professional referral network. The practitioner is relatively independent from the control of colleagues, but can exert little control over clients and will be subject to their control in the sense that if practice is not moulded to their demands and expectations they can desert it at any time. William Rothstein argues that homoeopathy and psychoanalysis in the United States of America constitute forms of independent practice, both of which have modified the forms of treatment they offer under pressure from client demand (Rothstein 1973).

Complementary medicine in Britain approximates closely to Freidson's 'independent' type. The patient may be unfamiliar with the techniques used by the non-orthodox practitioner and seldom arrives already socialised into thinking them superior. This being so, do practitioners attempt to manage client relations in such a way as to keep the patient satisfied without compromising their own concepts of what good treatment should be like? If, as Freidson implies, lack of control over clients is the price that has to be paid for freedom from pressure from professional peers, how do non-orthodox practitioners perceive this pay-off? It may be this very lack of hierarchical control over the patient which makes non-orthodox medicine attractive to some people who use it. How then (if at all) do they attempt to maximise their professional autonomy and control at the level of individual practitioner–client relations?

NON-ORTHODOX MEDICINE AS A FORM OF KNOWLEDGE

So far we have considered non-orthodox medicine as a form of practice. But, as Larson suggests, claims to professional status usually involve claims to special forms of knowledge and the training that is needed to acquire them. What is the cognitive base of complementary medicine?

Orthodox medicine has for long made natural science its cognitive base (Larson 1977: 165, Morgan, Calnan and Manning 1985: 116) and insofar as science is seen as successful and prestigious, this has helped to substantiate doctors' claims to professional status and authority. Doctors are socialised into a scientific culture which makes an absolute distinction between their own systematised knowledge and the medical knowledge of the 'lay' person. Arguing that this rigid dichotomy between 'science' and 'non-science' is no more than a myth (science being a human enterprise as permeable to the influence of interests, prejudices and moral values as any other), Denis MacEoin points out that there are, nonetheless, understandable reasons why doctors should have such an investment in this particular way of drawing boundaries around claims to truth and authority.

> Most medical students and many qualified doctors share with Muslims and Calvinists a deep need for their system to be the truth.
> Studying medicine is no fun. It is very hard work, with the terror of failure looming like hell itself round every corner. Nobody invests that much of themselves in something without needing very badly the conviction that

it is absolutely true and anything else a delusion, that it is a worthy
vocation and any other is a waste of one's best opportunities.

(MacEoin 1990:16)

But the knowledge of the non-orthodox practitioner is not intrinsically less
specialised and esoteric than orthodox medical science from the point of view
of the untrained lay person. Are we dealing with knowledge of a completely
different order – addressing the same phenomenon to be sure (human health
and sickness), but as different from medical science as the knowledge of the
witch doctor or spiritual healer? Or can we regard complementary medicine
as a group of systems which are recognisably of the same order as orthodox
medicine, in spite of their substantial differences?

According to Thomas Kuhn, 'normal' science consists of the solving of
puzzles within an accepted paradigm, i.e. a model or framework of ideas
which, among other things, defines in advance what sort of problem can
legitimately be formulated and by what rules such problems should be solved.
The advance of science is discontinuous and not unilinear; differences
between paradigms are never resolved intellectually because 'the proponents
of different paradigms practise their trade in different worlds' i.e. they look
at the same phenomenon from the point of view of radically different
conceptual frameworks (Kuhn 1962: 149). The difference between orthodox
medicine and most forms of non-orthodox medicine (in their 'pure' forms at
any rate) is certainly paradigmatic, although there has been convergence with
orthodox medicine within some disciplines, notably osteopathy, and there
are medical doctors who are very ready to accept the practices of some
systems even if they cannot endorse the theories.

Many orthodox doctors and medical scientists would, however, contest
whether non-orthodox systems constitute any kind of science at all. The
thrust of the 1986 BMA report on Alternative Therapy was that there can be
no incorporation of the latter unless it is prepared to provide *scientific*
evidence for the efficacy of its treatments (BMA 1986: 75). Stalker and
Glymour go even further and aver that

insofar as it extends beyond banality, the holistic medical movement
constitutes both a deliberate attempt to substitute a magical for an engin-
eering concept of the physician and an attack on scientific understanding
and reasoning.

(Stalker and Glymour 1989: 23)

But who decides what is genuinely scientific? As Barnes argues, the
demarcation between scientific and other forms of knowledge or procedure
is a matter of cultural practice; it is an actors' category and not a sociological
one (Barnes 1974: 100). Scientific evidence in the context of medicine

generally means evidence derived from double blind trials of drugs or forms of treatment. Considerable research effort is being devoted to devising trials which are appropriate to the nature of non-orthodox medicine but which also stand some chance of convincing medical scientists, whilst some complementary practitioners question whether doctors have the right to dictate the terms on which the contest takes place.

Whilst claims to scientificity may help a professional group to gain credibility they are not strictly necessary to the process of professionalisation as I have outlined it here. Codification is probably more important from this point of view. Professional knowledge needs to be recorded and transmitted in some kind of impersonal and systematic fashion so that it can be passed from the instructor to the student (as opposed to the unrecorded knowledge which is passed on through highly personal means from guru to disciple or from master to apprentice). It is difficult to see how the professionalisation of spiritual healing could proceed much further than it has done in the absence of such a codified body of theoretical knowledge, although public agreement on practical knowledge (how to communicate with patients, how to record their cases) can take such a group a good deal of the way. Orthodox medicine has the advantage of both a codified body of theoretical knowledge and agreed rules about how practical knowledge can be applied.

The contest between orthodox and unorthodox medicine may be between forms of knowledge, but the prize is, in the last analysis, the patient. If patients are not convinced that a form of treatment works, intellectual arguments about the validity of the knowledge on which it is based will be of little avail. Sociologists and anthropologists have interested themselves in the lay knowledge which the patient brings to the consultation, and the extent to which this knowledge may affect the way in which medical treatment is evaluated and medical advice complied with. If this research has produced a rather patchy picture, this may well be a result of the lack of structure in lay medical knowledge itself. Summarising a discussion of what is known about lay medical beliefs in Britain, Morgan, Calnan and Manning note that they are

difficult to pinpoint. The dominant scientific medical beliefs seem to have been accepted by many groups, with the germ theory of disease being one of the more commonly used. However, the scientific medical belief system does not appear to totally dominate the way lay people think about health and illness. Alternative theories sometimes reflect humoural notions of balance, or are products of a particular subculture, or may be created as a result of experience.

(Morgan, Calnan and Manning 1985: 97–8)

The evidence of Chapters 3 and 4 suggests that many patients who use complementary medicine are pragmatic and eclectic in outlook, more interested in efficacy than the theory behind the practice, but that they do appreciate explanations which order and make sense of previously unaccountable experiences or symptoms. What about those who do not use non-orthodox medicine? Do they eschew it because they uncritically accept the tenets, or at any rate the authority of medical science? I cite below evidence that many more people in Britain are prepared to use non-orthodox medicine than actually use it (see p. 210) which would suggest a certain open-mindedness about any exclusive claim to authority on behalf of medical science on the part of some who, at the moment, do not actually use any other system. Possibly lay convictions about causes of health and illness are relatively unstructured, and patients are prepared to try anything that seems to work, or has worked for people they know. Another possibility is that lay people do hold stable beliefs about health and illness but that these ideas are compatible with both orthodox and non-orthodox systems of treatment. One of the questions I shall ask of my data on practitioners is the extent to which they explicitly and consciously offer alternative explanations of health and illness to the patient; is the encounter between practitioner and patient used as an opportunity to socialise the patient into new ways of interpreting what happens to his/her body, or do practitioners treat their special knowledge as a source of dominance, a resource they are not prepared to share?

Freidson suggests that professionals transform the knowledge that academics and researchers produce, but also that client groups may have a strong effect on the kinds of knowledge which is preserved or is rejected as irrelevant (Freidson 1986: 220ff). In view of the strong degree of client control which might be supposed to exist in the case of complementary medicine (see p. 121) we should expect to find practitioners influenced to a high degree by patients' perceptions and expectations. On the other hand it is much harder in the case of complementary medicine to make a strict distinction between the 'producers' and the 'practitioners' of professional knowledge. There is less institutionalisation of research compared with orthodox medicine as yet (largely through lack of funds), and therapists are likely to develop their own ideas in the course of their practice. Indeed this intellectual autonomy bedevils attempts to achieve professional unity, as we shall see.

This discussion has by no means exhausted the sociological issues raised by the growth of non-orthodox medical practice. However, it is to be hoped that it will have provided a useful framework for the analysis of my own data, to which I now turn.

7 Practising complementary medicine
A local study

This chapter is based on research into the provision of complementary medicine in Claybury, a Midlands conurbation. Claybury (the name is a pseudonym) is largely industrial in character and has had high levels of unemployment in recent times; it is not the kind of place in which one would expect to find a particularly high demand for non-orthodox medicine, nor indeed for any other kind of private medicine. On the other hand, it is within travelling distance of a well known school of acupuncture and several colleges of homoeopathy, so one might suppose that some kinds of non-orthodox therapy would be known and provided locally. Probably there is no 'typical' locality with respect to the provision and usage of complementary medicine, but it seemed important to me to examine its provision outside those southern areas where it is known to be prolific and well established.

Between August 1988 and January 1990 I interviewed a total of thirty-four practitioners who were in full or part-time practice. I excluded individuals who did not accept payment for their services, regardless of how much time they spent on their healing activities and I confined the interviews to practitioners of those therapies which conform most closely to the model of a 'medical system', as defined in the Introduction of this book. The presence of activities excluded by this definition, such as Alexander Technique or Tai Chi, may be indirectly relevant to the local pattern of complementary medicine – they may help to generate a demand for it and their practitioners may work in close co-operation with certain kinds of non-orthodox medical therapist. Some of the latter have a competence in physiotherapy, massage, Tai Chi or yoga and may integrate such skills into their practice in various ways. My definition of the field is therefore arbitrary but, as I argued earlier, some degree of arbitrariness is unavoidable here.

The geographical delineation of the study was also a problem. Initial enquiries suggested that people who lived in the city were likely to consult practitioners based in one of the small industrial and market towns peripheral to the main conurbation. It would be useful to know more about the way in which markets for non-orthodox medical services are formed, especially their spatial dimensions. Claybury and its hinterland, including a ring of five adjacent towns (having a total population of around 650,000) would seem to have some of the characteristics of a 'natural' region but, here again, no assumptions about typicality can be made.

There is no fool-proof way of discovering the entire range of non-orthodox medical services on offer in a given district, so as to obtain a frame for any kind of sampling. Few orthodox practitioners advertise once they are established, and many are explicitly debarred from doing so by the rules of their professional organisations. Professional registers and the Yellow Pages of the telephone directory yielded a certain amount of information, as did my forays into public libraries and health food stores, contacts with patients' associations, etc. but at no time could I be sure that I had discovered every last practitioner in the area. A further difficulty lay in the fact that the local scene was evidently very fluid. During the period of fieldwork several older practitioners retired, a few moved to other areas (usually south of Claybury) and a number of recently qualified practitioners entered the market for the first time or set up practice independently where they had previously been assistants at a more established practice. I did not interview GPs who practise non-orthodox therapy alongside orthodox medicine (impossible to form an accurate estimate of their local numbers) and it is highly likely that some people who advertise themselves primarily as physiotherapists or masseurs also practise some form of non-orthodox medical therapy subsidiary to their main activity. Another complication is the fact that many therapists practise from more than one address, sometimes helping at another practitioners's

Table 9 Complementary practitioners in the Claybury area, classified by main therapy offered

Acupuncture	7	(6)
Acupressure	1	(1)
Bach Flower Remedies	1	(1)
Chiropractic	1	(1)
Herbalism	5	(4)
Homoeopathy	6	(4)
Hypnotherapy	4	(2)
Osteopathy	13	(10)
Reflexology	5	(5)
Total	43	(34)

(The figures in brackets represent the numbers actually interviewed)

clinic for one or two days a week, or putting in a few afternoons in a clinic or joint practice where several therapies are on offer. In a given locality it is relatively easy to identify those practitioners who have their professional 'home base' there but very difficult to trace all those who offer occasional or part-time services within it whilst carrying out their main work in another area.

I cannot therefore claim that the thirty-four complementary practitioners whom I located (see Table 9) represent the totality of services available in Claybury and its environs. However, the response rate from those whom I was able to locate was excellent (only two declined to participate although seven were either unable to arrange a time for the interview within the period of the project or offered some form of help short of a recorded interview). I am grateful to all those who found time within their very busy schedules – between consultations, during lunch hours or on an afternoon off – to tell me about themselves and about how they practised.

WHO ENTERS COMPLEMENTARY MEDICINE AND WHY?

The question 'why do people become complementary practitioners?' can be answered on at least as many levels as the question 'why do people use complementary medicine?' and we run up against the same methodological problems in reconstructing past decisions from respondents' own recollections and rationalisations. Most interviewees answered in a diffuse way, mentioning a variety of influences and contingencies which they regarded as relevant to their decision to set up practice, and referred to different 'layers' of past experience and motivation. As so many of the practitioners had had some other prior occupation, the decision to become, say, a homoeopath or acupuncturist usually also involved the decision to leave a career already embarked upon, to stop working as a teacher, a nurse or an accountant. This discussion is therefore based on the assumption that it will not be useful to try to produce a straightforward classification of motives.

The substantial presence of women (twenty-seven of the forty-three practitioners located were female, twenty-two of those actually interviewed) suggests that the gender issues here may be quite different from those which operate in orthodox medicine. A woman osteopath told me:

> I was always interested in medicine and learning how the body works. I thought of medicine as a career briefly, also nursing and speech therapy. But a friend told me about osteopathy and I also thought quite a lot about the advantages for a woman in practice. There didn't seem to be the same kind of bias against women that I had been led to believe there was in

medicine. I also felt that if I did at some point get married and have a family it would be a job I could return to and I did not have to think that my career would stop if I did have a family. As a woman it is quite easy to get back into osteopathy which it isn't necessarily with medicine.

Conditions for acceptance on training courses in complementary medicine vary greatly from therapy to therapy and between different etablishments, but non-orthodox medicine obviously provides a route into medical work for women who have not studied science to 'A' level and who therefore would not be eligible for conventional medical training. Those female practitioners who had had children after setting up practice had generally found it possible to vary the hours they worked to suit their family commitments.

There was only one black practitioner among the forty-three whom I identified. This was a Pakistani whom I have classified as a herbalist but who is probably more appropriately regarded as a spiritual healer. Certainly the local Asian population seem to see his skills as spiritual and charismatic rather than technical although he appears to be somewhat eclectic in his practice. I located several other Asians who practised homoeopathy on an occasional basis among friends and kin, but none of these took payment for their services. Unfortunately a small-scale study in an area where black people number no more than around 2 per cent of the total population is unlikely to shed much light on the representation of ethnic minorities in non-orthodox medicine in general.

Table 10 Practitioners' years in practice (Claybury study)

No. of years	Practitioners
Under 5	12
5–9	14
10–19	4
20+	4
Total	34

Whilst the average age of the practitioners I interviewed is around forty-two years old, we can see from Table 10 that most of them had been in practice for less than ten years. Most of them (see Table 11) had worked in some other field before training in complementary medicine. It is difficult to generalise about the career paths of these twenty-two very various people, except to say that in most cases they interpreted their interest in non-orthodox medicine as a direct continuation of interests they had already been develo-

Table 11 Occupation immediately prior to practising complementary medicine (Claybury study)

Beauty therapy	3
Teaching/counselling	6
Healthcare (NHS):	
SRN	7
other	3
Other professional	3
Other manual	2
None	10
Total	34

ping, or as proceeding from a change of direction which had been made well before the actual decision to train. A hypnotherapist had begun to train part-time while employed as an accountant; a personal crisis had made him aware that he desired a total re-orientation of his life. More typical was a reflexologist who had formerly worked as a research scientist; his disillusion with the 'rat race' had already led him to quit his job in industry for a post as warden of a hostel for young men, reflecting his desire to find work which was more directly related to caring for people. Three practitioners had trained in complementary medicine after achieving some success in the world of beauty therapy:

> I am actually a fully qualified (don't laugh!) beauty therapist. I did all the proper courses and studied all the healing aspects, but I sold my business because I realised that this work was not enough for me. I did all the remedial massage and things like that, but I was more interested in the healing side. I realised I didn't want to look after beautiful women, there were other people who needed looking after in the world, and that's why I did it.

> (Female chiropractor)

An acupuncturist who had been a teacher and a counsellor saw a direct line of continuity between her counselling activities and the supportive aspects of the healthcare she now offered. Two manipulators related their interest in non-orthodox medicine to their training in the martial arts; both had acquired skills in oriental healing from Japanese teachers at the same time as they acquired skills in unarmed combat. A former ballet dancer decided to study osteopathy, in part a result of his interest in the kinds of injuries and physical stresses to which dancers are specially prone. Ten interviewees had worked in the NHS, seven as nurses, one in the field of health education, one as a physiotherapist and another as an ambulance driver.

Most of these 'mature entrants' were not graduates, but were well educated and had been holding jobs of professional or semi-professional status and responsibility prior to training as complementary therapists. Most came from middle-class backgrounds; only two of the interviewees were from working-class families.

The substantial number of ex-nurses within this local cohort of practitioners demands our attention. Did they leave nursing because they were dissatisfied with the methods and opportunities offered by orthodox medicine, or were they positively attracted by some aspect of non-orthodox therapies? Certainly several mentioned doubts about some of the kinds of treatment they had witnessed or were required to administer:

> When I worked on the medical ward, I was anxious to do well, first sister's posting, and I was quite young and I wanted to make a success of it.... Many tender-skinned patients had bed sores and I found that the modern creams and things burned the very very tender skins. I had got an old SEN and she said, have you tried comfrey, sister? I was always interested in the natural side of things and we started getting results. I was going down to the lab. and saying have you got this, and they would say, well we could get it, we haven't been asked for this for years. So that is how it started. I decided to train and get back to the individual patient again.
>
> (Female acupuncturist)

> You know, it is a gripe of mine that GPs just stick asthma patients on inhalers. I have seen a four-year-old on an inhaler. I would never stick a kid on one. I think it is immoral because I know that I can cure these kids with acupuncture. I contrast this with the NHS, because I ran a medical ward. I know what the problems are, it is a nonsense, all the money being thrown at it, yet people are so cheaply cured. It is crazy.
>
> (Male acupuncturist)

> I was concerned the way things were going, too technical and too many drugs, getting away from the natural.
>
> (Female acupuncturist)

These quotations recall the qualms expressed by a number of users about over-reliance on drugs in treatment, lack of attention to the individual, etc. (see p. 38). On the other hand, none of these interviewees cited such doubts as his/her main reason for leaving the NHS. Most of the nurses had, by their own accounts, reached fairly senior positions within the hospital or within their chosen specialisms. A training in non-orthodox medicine was not seen as an exit route from NHS employment in the first place, being chosen out of interest or with a view to possible use within the NHS.

> I had no intention of going into acupuncture, it was just one of those things. It took my interest and then it took me over because the results that I was getting and the satisfaction were just phenomenal. I just couldn't believe it. I was getting people better who had long histories of conventional medical treatment.

> (Male acupuncturist)

In this case and in several others, setting up a practice seems to have been a natural progression from the regretful realisation that there was little scope to pursue these interests or skills within the NHS, nor indeed any other means to advance much further on the nursing career ladder. We are not dealing with incompetent defectors from orthodox medicine but with seasoned health professionals who had held responsible positions but decided to use their training in complementary medicine as a means of practising the healing arts more independently or of overcoming institutional limitations to pursuing the concerns they had already developed within their NHS work situations.

The ten practitioners who had begun training as therapists immediately after leaving school or university were mostly osteopaths. A few of these had originally intended to train as doctors but found that they could not get the 'A' level grades necessary to enter a medical school, but most had positively decided on osteopathy as a career:

> I was treated by an osteopath at the age of seventeen and after two treatments I never had asthma once. I had always wanted to help people as a child but I had thought about physiotherapy, pharmacy, that sort of thing. When I went to see him and saw what he did I really decided that this was what I wanted to do if I could, so I just got the information off him about the college he went to and applied to that college.

> (Female osteopath)

Osteopathy has a higher standing with doctors than most other complementary therapies and has modelled its training opportunities mostly closely along the lines of the orthodox medical profession. It is a well established therapy and is therefore more likely to be presented to school or college leavers at careers conventions and by counsellors than other types of non-orthodox medicine. A student is also more likely to obtain a discretionary award for a course in osteopathy than for other therapies. This situation may change in future as more information becomes available to those who advise young people about their careers – Careers Consultants Ltd have already published a booklet on training in complementary medicine (Summerson 1985). At the moment, however, the other therapies do not seem dissatisfied with the predominance of mature candidates graduating from their training schools. Indeed some of the representatives of professional organisations whom I interviewed regarded maturity and experience of life as a desirable, if not essential, qualification in a candidate for training.

Although I did not ask about this directly, eleven of the interviewees spontaneously mentioned illness experiences as having influenced their thinking about sickness and healing.

> I had a serious eye condition of the retina. My sight was going fast. The consultant told me that I must be philosophical, that there was nothing to be done. A friend of ours who is an osteopath suggested that I try a homoeopath who was also an ophthalmologist. I was treated by him and after three months I felt no better. But after six months the condition was stabilised and in a year I was cured. By the time I went to the homoeopath I was ready to go to a witch doctor if I thought it would do any good, I was so desperate. A lot of people get into alternative medicine through experiences like this.
>
> (Female homoeopath, former SRN)

This observation is certainly confirmed by the few available studies of professional motivation among complementary practitioners (White and Skipper 1971: 303, Moore and Stephenson 1962: 299).

We could see this as an example of non-orthodox healers constituting some kind of cult of affliction. One acquires the capacity to heal from having suffered and undergone treatment oneself. The idea of a cult of affliction has been used by anthropologists to describe certain African curative practices (Turner 1968) and could certainly be applied to spiritualist groups in this country, among whom receiving healing is a normal prelude to discovering the capacity to heal in oneself. But although such experiences may well have opened up the individual to an identification with sick people, stamped a remembrance of what it is to suffer illness and disability on their minds at an early age, interviewees did not seem themselves to be making this particular connection. It was more a matter of having been exposed to positive experiences of non-orthodox treatment in their past and therefore being more open than they might otherwise have been to the idea of studying it later in their lives. Some described experiences of inappropriate treatment at the hand of orthodox doctors as having made them receptive to the idea that modern medicine does not have all the answers. These illness episodes seem to have been in the order of 'relevant experiences' rather than 'deciding factors'.

Discussing motivation in terms of typical career contingencies helps us to contextualise the decision to train as a therapist, but does not tell us much about the kind of temperamental drive which might underlie such a decision. Reading through the interview transcripts, I perceived two main themes emerging from what the practitioners said about their own purposes and projects. The first, which is quite unsurprising, is the desire to work with people, to heal and help. Consider the following descriptions of present or former job satisfactions given by interviewees:

I was doing what I wanted to do, which was working with people and I found that I definitely had an interest in counselling... as I went on, people said that they always felt at ease with me, or they felt good talking to me.

(Male reflexologist, talking about the work he did as a counsellor and warden after leaving a job in industry)

I think my counselling helped me most, you know, because I already had the talent and was very aware of being able to listen and try to understand what they (patients) need, what their emotional mood is.

(Female acupuncturist and former counsellor describing her period of training)

I think it is a job with tremendous job satisfaction. It gives me great pleasure when somebody gets better. It's a smug sort of thing, but when loads of other well-known people have had a go and not got them better and I get them better, then that is rather nice. It's nice to see a satisfied patient.

(Male osteopath)

I love to see patients come back and you can tell they are better when you open the door. You can tell they are better because they gleam or their skin is clear and they say, look at me – I feel great! That is the best part for me. That is the main satisfaction for me, more than any money.

(Female iridologist)

I used to do home visits and they were really rewarding because you got people who were so bad they couldn't get to your consulting room and you managed to get them to crawl onto your couch and then they would be a whole lot better when you went.

(Female osteopath)

Allied to the desire to help and heal I often found an interest in people which might be expressed in scientific terms, or in language which is empathic or even spiritual, but which reveals a curiosity about human interaction and psychology:

I find people fascinating anyway, you see, and as a homoeopath you look at people in a very particular way, because you are putting together the pieces in a puzzle.... I find it fascinating watching people as they talk to me because people don't talk like that generally.

(Female homoeopath)

The second theme which manifests itself in many of the interviews is the desire to work independently, or at any rate to be free of bureaucratic restraints. This does not preclude willingness to co-operate with other healers, as we shall see later, but it does suggest a dislike of hierarchy and certain types of organisational formality:

I am too demanding to work with other practitioners... [a joint practice] is nice for the comradeship if you want to call it that, but I don't need it. Other people do. They need a group and they need a coffee room to have a moan or a crow, or whatever they do. But no, I don't feel like that. And I can only guarantee my own work, I do not want to be responsible for other people's. I like to keep everything under my thumb, I want to keep my finger on the pulse.

(Acupuncturist, explaining why she decided not to invite other therapists to set up a joint practice)

I am a free spirit, I don't want to go in a block with everyone else.

(Male osteopath)

Hypnotherapists tend to keep themselves to themselves.... It is nice to be able to pick up a phone and have the back-up and know that the person at the other end knows more than you, but honestly I don't know whether that is true any more. I pick up information from everywhere and my therapy is evolving all the time.... Perhaps I do like being out on a limb, but I don't feel any need to work within an organisation.

(Female hypnotherapist)

Most of us who come into this business have done it off our own bat, put our own money into it and so on, most of us tend to be the type of people who are much more individual, we work in our way and I like to have that sort of freedom.

(Male osteopath)

I was always interested in medicine and how the body works... but one of the things that discouraged me was I didn't want to be dependent on the system to be employed. I wanted to work as independently as possible. I didn't want to think that I was going to train for a long time and then at the end find that my work was going to be subject to policy and really just part of a huge system, a little unit in a huge hospital.

(Female osteopath)

Here is a kind of occupational individualism, founded on a dislike of organisational constraints. Many of the practitioners described how their own therapeutic practice had changed and developed, and stressed that this growth could not have taken place had they not enjoyed the freedom to try new methods, undertake fresh training, take advantage of flexible work conditions, etc. Several attributed those characteristics of orthodox medicine which they found most repellent to the organisational structures within which doctors work rather than to the tenets on which their practice is based. In particular the pressure on GPs' time due to excessive patient loads was deplored:

> Many of my patients are very disillusioned with allopathic medicine, but it may be the fault of the system rather than the GP. You get six minutes with your GP and half of healing is just being able to listen. GPs don't get time to do that.
>
> (Female herbalist/iridologist)

> Quite a lot of people are dissatisfied with normal medical treatment. I feel quite sorry for the GPs because the criticism isn't against them, it's mainly against the system. It has become such a big unruly machine and there is quite a bit of passing the buck and quite a bit of getting bogged down with bureaucracy which you don't get with osteopathy because it is generally a one-man show and osteopaths by nature hate paperwork, so it is kept to a minimum so that there is maximum time with the patient.
>
> (Male osteopath)

PROFESSIONAL VALUES AND MARKET REALITY

In the last chapter I discussed the contrast between the ideal of disinterested service to the public and the commercial norm of profitability implicit in the rhetoric of professionalism. The *Journal of Alternative and Complementary Medicine* runs a regular column on practice management entitled, rather coyly, 'Tom's Tips'. Tom Klosinski certainly assumes that some practitioners will require fairly basic advice on the financial aspects of practice:

> It goes against the grain for most healing professionals to ask for payment for services rendered. But the reality is you are either running a business or you are running a charity,

he states, and then goes on to make suggestions about how patients can be persuaded to pay promptly (*JACM* May 1989: 42). Non-orthodox practitioners such as those whom I studied are actually self-employed and are responsible for building up their own clienteles; indeed we have just seen that many of them seem to be precisely the kind of people who by temperament would abhor the type of employment which would shield them from market forces. Do they see themselves as professionals, and if so, how do they experience the potential tension between professional ideals and the commercial reality of their situation?

Firstly, the majority of these practitioners made a point of distinguishing the genuine (professional) practitioner whose altruistic purpose was to heal the patient from the (unprofessional) 'cowboy' whose purpose was to make money from people's illnesses. A practitioner should not be judged by the amount of money s/he made, and where profits came before patients something had gone badly wrong. A number of interviewees feared the presence within the complementary medicine movement of unscrupulous and sometimes unqualified practitioners whose primary aim was to make money rather than to heal. An acupuncturist was contemptuous of practitioners who took on patients with cancer or degenerative diseases, holding out the promise of a cure that could never be achieved:

> I have had many a patient come through that door and I know that no way will alternative medicine get them better and neither will conventional medicine get them better.... I just say, look I am sorry but there is nothing that can be done for you.... I know it to be a fact, and what concerns me is that a lot of practitioners I know could take on that patient for five or six sessions, deprive them of £70 and at the end of the day say, well I am sorry but it has not really worked. You see, I find that highly immoral.

A homoeopath spoke of her misgivings about a well advertised and evidently well financed complementary health clinic that had been set up in a nearby town:

> Well, there is one part of me that reacts to the centre negatively because they have been doing a tremendous amount of advertising. There have been newspaper articles and they have said we are here to save your children. That really goes against the grain. In one way it is good because they are spreading [complementary medicine] and people will be attracted, but they make it very exclusive, there is nobody quite like us. So that to me it is very commercial, it's very much more like a business and I get the feeling that they wouldn't refer people to practitioners outside of their centre and I think this is a shame. I think it is better if people work together and we are not in competition with each other.

Many interviewees expressed in one way or another the idea that whilst most practitioners of non-orthodox medicine were genuine professionals offering a valuable service to the sick, they knew of a minority whose prime motive was profit rather than healing. Obviously none of my interviewees claimed to be such a person, nor could I expect them to name names and so I felt rather like the anthropologist who studies witchcraft in a community where belief in witchcraft is endemic; everyone believes there are witches, but no-one believes him/herself to be a witch. This is in no way to make light of my interviewees' claims to professionalism, or of witchcraft beliefs. Where witchcraft is believed in, witches are a serious moral menace and where the boundaries of professionalism require protection, control of the 'cowboy' is essential. Or does the cowboy perform a genuine moral function? Could it be that just as it was important for orthodox doctors to distinguish themselves from quacks in the course of their development as a profession, so for non-orthodox practitioners the 'cowboy' fulfils a similar defining and legitimating function?

Whilst there was agreement about the need to control irresponsible and unprofessional practitioners, there was some disagreement as to how they should be identified. To the homoeopath just quoted, it was explicit and competitive appeal to the 'customer' which constituted the shibboleth. Professional associations of non-orthodox therapists generally either outlaw advertising altogether or, more usually, define very strictly the forms which are permissible. But as the notion of commercialism refers to the intent to make profit as much as to content of practice, it is difficult to see how it can be demonstrably excluded from a profession which must rely on patients' fees. As we shall see in the next chapter, this is a problem for those who represent non-orthodox therapies on the national level. To another interviewee, a former nurse, it was the fact that persons with what he considered as inadequate qualifications could set up practice without let or hindrance which was most to be deplored:

> I am very much against alternative practitioners who are housewives [*sic*] gone on a six-week course or weekend course and start to practice hynotherapy, reflexology or whatever. I think they are positively dangerous and I am really set against them. Herbalists – you know, you get these housewives who say they are herbalists, patients come in and they haven't got a clue.
>
> (Male osteopath)

The bumbling amateur is a different sort of enemy to professional aspirations from the cowboy or shark, since it is knowledge which s/he lacks rather than altruism, but an enemy who is perhaps easier to identify. In the next chapter we shall see that the definition of appropriate standards of training and qualification is an issue which all professional organisations in non-orthodox medicine are addressing very seriously at the moment. There is, however, an awareness, both at the national level and expressed by some of my local interviewees that paper qualifications based on standardised professional examinations have limited value if the candidate lacks understanding or empathy, or is not willing to go on learning. And if practitioners without standardised qualifications are ever forbidden to practice, what about the seasoned and skilled healer who is known by his/her peers to act in all ways as a responsible professional but who has somehow never acquired a diploma or certificate of any kind? The idea that a profession is defined by the responsible exercise of skill rather than through common forms of certification was expressed most strongly by the only two interviewees who came from local working-class backgrounds, both of whom had learnt their art through long apprenticeship rather than through attending training school:

> I have got the knowledge gained over a number of years and I know what people are talking about when they come in and describe what is wrong with them. But nothing is a final point, we are always ready to learn. I have been at it since I was fifteen years old and I am still learning, and if I live to be a hundred years old I shall have learnt only one thousandth of what I want to learn.

The same practitioner trained others in his own clinic and was concerned about a trainee who had recently broken away to set up practice on her own:

> You can't learn this in less than twelve years. To me she is a danger because, like in everything else, a little knowledge is dangerous.

If the distinction between professionalism and commercialism is made at the level of 'intent' rather than 'content' of behaviour, then it would be naive to suppose that in the course of a single interview, however long and informal, a researcher would be able to uncover the practitioner's most private aims and values. Examining practitioners' explicit definitions of professional behaviour in yet more detail will probably tell us less about how they deal with the potential tension between professional and commercial values than looking at the ways in which they claim to handle certain practical contingencies, setting fees for instance, or deciding how many patients to take on.

In spite of rejecting commercialism as a motive, most of the practitioners whom I interviewed discussed the day-to-day running of their practices in a way that suggested that they had thought very carefully about the business aspect of their activities. Two had set up practice with the assistance of a government Enterprise Allowance and had attended courses in small business development run in conjunction with this scheme. One had had support from the Prince of Wales Trust and had participated in their annual exhibition. The favourable publicity from this had, she said, given her practice a healthy boost. Most interviewees had had some advice or help on the practical aspects of developing a practice from the training establishments from which they had graduated or from professional associations, especially in matters like arranging insurance. One therapist had attended a course on setting up a small business, run by a local college for evening students. Five had at some time had experience of self-employed professional practice or of running a business before becoming therapists, in the course of which they had already acquired a certain amount of commercial wisdom.

Table 12 Standard first consultation fees (Claybury study)

Fee	No. of practitioners
£10–14	11
£15–19	14
£20 and above	3
'Variable'	6
Total	34

N.B. Fees are those operative 1988–9. Average fee is £15.93.

In spite of this, setting the levels of fees seemed to be the site of some doubts and conflicts. Table 12 shows the range of fees charged by the practitioners whom I interviewed during the period August 1988 to December 1989. These fees represent charges per patient consultation and not charges per hour. Some practitioners charged less for second and subsequent consultations than for first consultations, on the grounds that they were usually shorter. Several practitioners definitely intended to put their fees up in early 1990 in line with inflation, so the general level of charges in the Claybury area will probably be somewhat higher by the time this book is published.

A few interviewees who had not been in practice long seemed a little uncertain as to whether their fees compared favourably with those charged by other practitioners and even hinted to me that they would like comparative information on this point. Most, however, seemed confident about their capacity to arrive at a valuation of their time which was satisfactory to themselves and realistic in terms of the market for their services. Where ambivalence was expressed it was usually in respect to access:

I charge £15 for the initial session and then £12 for subsequent treatments. I am told that is not enough. I mean, a lot of my colleagues are charging more than that, so I am kind of considering what to do about that. But if someone is a student or on unemployment benefit I don't charge them that much, I only charge them half. I wouldn't want someone not to have treatment because of the financial circumstances. But on the other hand I think people benefit more from something they are contributing to. You know, if it is something you really want... but occasionally I mean, it varies, it depends on the person. If I feel that someone needs an extra treatment and I know they can't afford it, then I will do it free of charge. On the other hand, I have got to make my living. I am putting more money back into my training and it costs a lot to do that.

(Female acupuncturist)

Money is something that is an issue to me, it's an area of self-confidence that I need to work on. Up to last week I was charging £10 for an hour and my accountant kept screaming at me and saying you will go out of business if you carry on like this, because all the overheads have gone up. I have forced myself or told myself that it is time I put my fees up to £20 from next week. I have told my patients and funnily enough a lot of people can actually pay that because they know they get value for money when they are here. So what I say to them is, you have to ask yourself two questions – what is your health worth to you, and what am I worth to you? When they think that over they feel okay. But there are certain people that can't afford that, so we negotiate things. I am flexible about it because my motivation behind charging money is that I am putting out that much of my energy, so that I am not left empty at the end of the day, so that I can feed and house and clothe myself but also so that I can continue my studies. I am not in this for a Porsche or elaborate wardrobes, I am in it so that I can continue to learn and reach more people.

(Female reflexologist)

The last extract is perhaps unusual in its overly defensive tone, but the dilemma was a common one. Thirteen of the interviewees claimed to operate some kind of sliding fee scale. In this sample, those who used sliding scales or concessions tended to be either the inexperienced practitioners new to the field (keen to build up a clientele even if the returns are not very great at first) or the very well-established 'old hands' (able to afford to charge less for long-standing patients fallen on hard times). However, the practice is common enough among therapists everywhere, and in London there is even a directory of practitioners who offer concessionary rates for the unwaged.

This ambivalence about putting a price on one's skills could be attributed to the tension between commercial interest and professional altruism already referred to, but it could also stem from the very special kind of therapeutic relationship which many complementary practitioners claim to foster. Holistic healing implies not only an empathic relationship, but a multi-dimensional one in which the healer not only examines and monitors the patient's body, but comes to know a good deal about his/her personal and social circumstances, temperament and interests. With such a therapeutic ideal, may it not be embarrassing to turn to the patient at the end of a lengthy and empathic session to ask for a cheque? Certainly some practitioners claimed to find that exchanges in kind brought a satisfaction of their own. Was this because the transaction then looks more like an exchange of gifts between friends rather than a sale of services?

If people find they can't pay the fees, then we discuss it and we reduce the fee. Sometimes people give me things in exchange, they bring me eggs and cheese, or do building work for me and things like that.

> (Female homoeopath who also exchanged healing services with a group of like-minded practitioners living near to her)

I have patients who have next to no money and we negotiate how they will actually pay me. I am very open to exchanging things. I have some patients who are market gardeners and they bring me loads of carrots and cabbages. That is fine, it is an exchange.

> (Female reflexologist)

I like working in this area because though people have very narrow ideas of health, which makes it very hard work treating them, yet the amount of kindness I receive from people makes me feel it is a worthwhile place to be. I could go to Cheltenham or London where I used to work, but I wouldn't enjoy it so much. It has to do with transactions which are not totally financial, here I am getting transactions which are other than financial. Patients have helped me find a house locally, found me a chimney sweep, an electrician.

It was wonderful. It was like you were a valuable member of the community and people wanted you to stay here.

> (Female herbalist)

In case it should be thought that this attitude was only found among naive idealists, innocent of the enterprise culture, let me point out that the last extract was from an interview with a well-known practitioner who had much business experience and had once run her own very successful company. If she felt cheered by such reciprocity, it was not because she held any illusions about the importance of payment in professional work. Later in the same interview she stressed that an important element in the healing process is the will to get better, testified by preparedness to pay for treatment or to take some trouble over getting it:

In the early days I used to be very idealistic and I used to think I would like to treat people who really deserved it for free, but the extraordinary thing was they never appreciated it and quite often didn't bother to come back for more. If you get something free it's going to be worthless and so now I make sure I charge them, however small the fee, or they are not going to value it.

Another practitioner made a similar point:

Although I would like to have rooms in town so that OAPs and others who are short of money can get to me more easily, there's something about making an effort of will what is a pre-requisite of any healing process – you shouldn't lay everything on for the sufferer... it should not just be a matter of impulse.

(Male reflexologist)

Another area where we might expect to observe the interplay of altruism and commercial motivation is that of decision making about the use of time and about the number of patients which can be fitted into working hours. Only five interviewees, all of whom had set up practice within the last eighteen months, stated or implied that they wished to see more patients than they were seeing at present. I suppose that it is not to be expected that an established practitioner would admit to a decline in demand for his/her services, but in most cases I saw no reason to disbelieve claims to busyness and many practitioners invited me to inspect their appointment books. Once practitioners have enough appointments to fill the hours they choose to work, further demand can only be accommodated by either working longer hours or reducing the average time of consultation. Sick people must otherwise remain unhealed or go to other practitioners and, either way, an opportunity to earn income is lost.

The average length for a first consultation was one hour and for subsequent consultations just under three-quarters of an hour, osteopaths tending to space appointments more closely than other kinds of therapist. But all emphasised the need to make a very thorough investigation of the patient's problem, generally making detailed notes on his/her medical history as well as the symptoms for which treatment was being sought. Assuming a working week of not less than thirty hours, and assuming the average consultation times just given, a full working week might comprehend between thirty and forty patients. In fact most practitioners did not aim to see so many because they needed time for other activities or commitments (lecturing on their therapy, attending advanced courses) or for 'chores' connected with the practice (paperwork, making up medicines).

However, several practitioners mentioned another quite different reason for deliberately restricting the number of patients they saw, even if demand was brisk:

I don't want to see more than twenty-two or twenty-three people a week. I can only see so many. I am amazed at some friends of mine that can see an amazing amount of people in a day, about every half-hour. I need to see the amount of patients I could emotionally handle and I have to have time to do other things, otherwise you get very down, you have nothing to give your patients basically. I am not going to do that (increase the number of patients) and end up completely brain dead, it just goes against the things I am trying to tell the people I treat. It's important to give something to the patients, and it takes an hour at least. Consultations have to be long, although it varies with the length of time the person has had the condition and how deep it has gone. You get really involved with people, you really tune into them, you listen, you try to make a connection as much as you can. So to do that properly – I mean I found that when I was seeing more people I wasn't able to do it, so I had to limit the number.

(Female homoeopath)

I see about ten people a week on average. Ten is a nice number. I did twenty-nine in one week once and it absolutely killed me. I couldn't do it again because I can't give enough time or enough thought to so many people. If I have got too many people I feel as if I am not giving them value for money or spending enough time thinking about that person so as to help them.

(Female hypnotherapist)

The manipulative therapists in the sample tended to have lower consultation times; several pointed out that some of their patients had acute conditions, were in great pain and needed immediate treatment in order to be able to function normally again, and in such circumstances lengthy note taking sessions were less appropriate than quick and effective treatment. Others had fairly minor and straightforward problems for which only limited treatment was necessary. But even here there was a strong recognition that individually tailored therapy cannot but be time-consuming. A male osteopath who claimed to see a maximum of thirty-five patients a week reminisced about an acupuncturist with whom he had formerly worked, who

saw about eighty people a week. With that many people you had like four treatment rooms going and it was sort of, put the needles in somebody and then dash into the next room, it was all juggling, it was someone every twenty minutes. There was more logistics going than therapy, I felt. It got like a production line and there was no time to spend talking and chatting. I really wanted to get at the deeper aspects of ill health.

As one female acupuncturist said:

[Orthodox doctors] do private medicine with the idea of making a lot of money and seeing a lot of people. In complementary medicine you are limited by the number of people you want to see and be fresh for. Our family live in this area and we want to feel we are a success. Not a financial success with a lot of dissatisfied people but a feeling that you can meet your patients in Tesco's and not be accosted by lots of angry people.

Table 13 Practitioners' own estimates of number of patients seen per week (Claybury study)

	No. of practitioners
Fewer than 10 patients per week	2
10–19	6
20–29	3
30–39	5
40–49	4
50–59	2
60+	4
'varies greatly'	8
Total	34

Table 13 shows the numbers of patients seen per week and confirms the findings of national studies that weekly consultation rates vary, but tend to be low. There can be a number of reasons for this – low demand for services in the case of new therapists whose practices are not yet established, in other cases a commitment to other income-generating activities so that practice is effectively part-time. But we have to take seriously the possibility suggested by the examples I have just cited, namely that some practitioners are consciously restricting the number of patients they see, in order to fulfil a therapeutic ideal (time-consuming and highly personalised treatment). They may thereby be limiting what they can earn from their healing activities.

Holding down the number of consultations is not the only way to handle the dilemma of combining access with quality of treatment. The therapist might hire paid help in the form of an assistant in order to either take on more patients, or hire a receptionist who will take care of the routine matters of booking appointments and answering the door to patients when they arrive. In fact only eight employed receptionists themselves or shared paid receptionists with other practitioners, though another four relied on the informal help of wives, husbands or other family members, or had done so in the past. Only two of the interviewees in this study employed a paid assistant to treat patients, although this seems to be a common practice among established osteopaths elsewhere.

Some explicitly stated that while increasing the scale of their activities and taking on staff might add to their earnings, it would be a move away from what they really wanted to do or be. A male hypnotherapist, who seemed to be doing very well judging by the kind of premises he occupied and the fees he charged, told me:

> If I take on a receptionist I would have to cover the cost of their wages and charge more. It just doesn't seem worth it. It would make me more upmarket, I mean I would have to put my best suit on, and get myself a nice dolly bird. I can't be mithered with it. And I would get the wrong kind of people coming here. I know people in this business who are making thousands of pounds a year, but I shan't get within sniffing distance of that.

Another said:

> I don't need anything other than a place to practise and I suppose if you can afford to spend money on a nice property and a receptionist then you can attract better fees. I don't know whether I would alter it though. I have muddled along quite happily and I am quite busy enough as it is.
>
> (Male osteopath)

Many interviewees, as we have already seen, professed to be the kind of people who did not enjoy working within an organisational structure and most seemed to value a certain flexibility in their timetables. Sucessful therapists might have earned more by formalising the practice, taking on more staff so as to see more patients, but they were aware that such a step would probably mean catering for a different kind of market, possibly arousing expectations which they might not be able to fulfil and incurring costs they might not be able to meet. To make more money by taking this path, they would have to make qualitative as well as quantitative changes in the way they worked which might diminish job satisfaction. The only therapist who had a large staff (a herbalist who employed a secretary/receptionist, a pharmacist and a therapist/assistant) was also the only one who appeared to be catering for a regional, even national clientele. I am aware that I might have obtained a very different picture had I interviewed practitioners who serve wider markets and operate from a metropolitan rather than a provincial base. It is also possible that some of the practitioners whom I interviewed might change their priorities in future; a maturing practice and increased self-confidence might persuade some who are presently content with a modest and strictly local practice to attempt a larger scale of operation.

Professional altruism and compassion for the needs of the sick were important components of interviewees' self-image. Yet as self-employed practitioners they were confronted very directly with the fact that their relationship with patients is actually based on money. In the absence of nationally recommended or agreed rates of payment, the individual therapist is obliged to put a cash price to his/her own healing services. In most cases the practitioner is not in a position to distance him/herself from the commercial aspect of the transaction with the patient by delegating the making of bills and receipt of payments to a receptionist or assistant. All seemed aware of this contradiction to some degree, though the means of coming to terms with it varied. For some it sufficed to dissociate themselves morally and professionally from the 'cowboy' or the 'quack', whose only motivation in healing was financial. For others, using sliding scales so as to increase access to their services for the poor alleviated any feeling that one was making a living out of misfortune without doing anything to help the most unfortunate of all. For another group, the realisation that whilst getting paid should not be their own sole motive for healing, making a payment was an important factor in the motivation of the sick person to be healed mitigated their dilemma. However, altruism or idealism are by no means the same as naivety, though they are often so equated in popular discourse. The holistic practice to which most of my interviewees aspired demands considerable insight into motivation, a shrewd understanding of the complexities of human behaviour, and an unsentimental perspicacity where patients' (and one's own) self-delusions are concerned. I would suggest that it is just because most forms of non-orthodox healing require this shrewdness, this hard-nosed understanding of human psychology, that the people who are attracted to it are generally well able to handle the tensions I have described. It is by no means impossible to combine a business-like approach to practice with a humane understanding of sick people's suffering. After all, if the rhetoric of professionalism employs the notion of altruistic public service, remember that in popular speech the term 'professionalism' is often used to refer to a particularly *detached* competence.

TRAINING AND STARTING UP PRACTICE

Training in complementary medicine is far from being standardised, even within the same discipline. Part-time training is probably as common nowadays as full-time training, except in osteopathy and chiropractic. In many disciplines short courses are available for those who already have a medical qualification. Three of the former nurses had taken such a one-year course in acupuncture, designed to build on a basic medical education and a certain amount of conventional clinical experience. Nine practitioners had taken (or were taking) short courses in other therapies besides the one which they regarded as their chief specialism, either out of interest or to improve the range of services they could offer. In most therapies there are regular opportunities for the qualified practitioner to amplify and update her/his knowledge and most of those who had been in practice for more than three years had attended a number of such short courses and weekend schools.

Table 14 Basic qualifications in complementary medicine (Claybury study)

	No. of practitioners	
Duration of course	part-time	full-time
Less than 1 year	2	
1 year	9*	
2 years	4	
3 years	3	
4 years	3	10
No formal qualifications	3	
Total	34	

* This includes 5 nurses who took special 1-year courses designed for students who already have an orthodox medical training.

In Table 14 I have tried to summarise the range of basic qualifications held by interviewees. This may not be a very meaningful exercise in view of the diversity of courses and consequent problems of comparability, but it does demonstrate that very few people were practising with no certification at all. This is consistent with Fulder's findings in a larger study; quackery – the practice of medicine by the untrained for profit – is rare (Fulder 1988: 58). In any case, lack of formal certification does not necessarily mean lack of training. Of the three 'unqualified' practitioners among my interviewees, one homoeopath had become interested in homoeopathy in India and had pursued what might best be described as a two years' apprenticeship with an experienced homoeopath in that country. On return to Britain she joined the British Homoeopathic Society as an associate member and had taken several short courses offered by an extremely eminent British homoeopath. This teacher, she said, had advised her that having got this far, there was little to be gained in devoting time and money to a formal course. Two male practitioners, of whom one described himself as an osteopath and the other practised a Japanese form of healing related to acupressure, claimed to have learnt their skills through long apprenticeship to experts. Both had set up practice only after a fairly long period of part-time work under the direct supervision of the teacher. None of the people I interviewed therefore can be said to be purely self-taught.

Those who had switched to training in non-orthodox medicine after working in some other occupation had almost invariably financed their own training out of savings or part-time earnings, often with additional support from spouse or parents. A nurse had used a small legacy to pay for his training in acupuncture, but a more typical case was that of an educational counsellor who paid for her three-year part-time course in acupuncture from her earnings as a counsellor. As many practitioners pointed out to me, the training is the most expensive part of becoming a therapist. The capital required for setting up in practice is not great, nor are the overheads if one can work from home, as the majority of interviewees had done when they started out.

Seventeen of the interviewees were working from home at the time of the interview, but this is not always a suitable arrangement in the long term; some therapists found a spatial separation of family and professional life preferable even though it put up the running costs of the practice quite sharply. Patients may take to ringing at all times if the therapist is too accessible, or children and spouses may make demands on the therapist which interfere with total concentration on the patient. Much depends on the structure and size of the house and the number of hours the therapist aims to spend in consultations. But suitable rented premises can be hard to find also, and two interviewees had gone back to working from home after bad experiences with premises which were poorly located or too expensive.

Money is not the only kind of resource which is needed when setting up practice, social resources being quite as important. The majority of the practitioners whom I interviewed had always lived in or near the Claybury area, or had been living there when they decided to take up non-orthodox medicine. Several justified their decision to set up practice in this locality in terms of its formerly rather scanty provision of complementary medical services. Most of the practitioners had undertaken their training at a time of life when they already had spouses and children whose own employment and schooling would have been affected if they had decided to set up practice elsewhere. But it was also clear that family and social networks played a positive as well as a negative role in decisions about where to practice. A young osteopath, for instance, had started practice in a house which her husband's grandmother had helped her to buy. Her mother-in-law had acted as informal receptionist at first, answering the phone and sometimes looking after her children while she saw patients. Another osteopath had initially been able to share premises with an aunt who already ran a health and beauty salon:

When I first qualified I worked with an osteopath in London for two days a week, although I was still self-employed and so had to find my own patients. The rest of the time I commuted back here. I was just trying to start up practice here, which meant home visits initially, with a portable couch in the back of the car. I used my aunt's salon as a sort of base. I got a lot of patients through my name being in the Yellow Pages, but I also got a lot through my family and friends. It helps being in an area where you know lots of people anyway.

Informal methods work well for those with roots in the area:

I was born here. I got going with one patient. I just went round the local pubs and told them who I was and what I was doing. That is the way I did it. Word of mouth. Friends and other people helped me out, I was well stocked with good friends.

(Male osteopath)

A male osteopath who had also trained in London came back to Claybury and was invited by his brother, an optician, to take rooms in the same building so that they could share a receptionist. A chiropractor, whose father also practised chiropractic in a town thirty miles away, started practice in a house bought with a bank loan for which her father stood as collateral. The first patients she saw were former patients of her father's who lived near Claybury and whom he had referred to her. Even the two practitioners who were of non-British origin had social or professional connections in the area which stood them in good stead as they developed their practices.

As well as support from family and friends, several practitioners mentioned the help they had received from teachers and students of the establishments where they had trained. An osteopath, brought up in southern England and trained in London, settled near Claybury on the advice of a former teacher who had retired to a town thirty miles south of the conurbation:

He said, if you come up here there is nobody else, you should have no trouble starting a practice. So I came here and started from scratch, phoned him every five minutes with patients where I thought, I have not seen this one before, this one is not in the textbooks. So he was a great help. He is dead now, but he gave me a lot of support.

An acupuncturist decribed the moral and technical support she had had from people at her former college. One of her teachers, who lived nearby, was prepared to advise on cases where she felt a second opinion would be useful, and old students already in practice would refer patients to her – a kind of 'old boys and girls' network. A recently qualified reflexologist spoke glowingly of her former principal:

You can always go back and ask advice. She is very helpful and you can always ring up if you are having difficulties with a patient or if you are unsure about something.

Eleven of the interviewees derived some part of their income from a source other than patients' fees. Five of these had set up practice within the past three years and continued with a part-time job either because they liked it and did not want to give it up or because they needed the income while they built up a clientele. Otherwise this multiplicity of activities was related to professional success rather than professional immaturity. Several experienced practitioners were quite involved in teaching their own discipline. A herbalist spent the equivalent of one whole day a week lecturing at the college where he had trained himself and another was actually helping to set up a new training school for natural therapies. An osteopath who had formerly been a dancer himself, lectured at a dance school on anatomy and physiology. For these practitioners, their other professional activities were not so much a means of hedging their bets in case the practice failed so much as an overflow of educational or entrepreneurial energy. On the other hand, educational work can be used as a way of nourishing a new practice. Several practitioners mentioned that talks and lectures given at local groups helped to generate demand for their form of therapy in general and (to the extent that they were able to put themselves over as trustworthy and sympathetic healers) for their own services in particular. Talks given to women's organisations or evening classes held at the local evening institute might bring low financial rewards but contributed to building a practice.

In Chapter 3 we saw that word of mouth, circulated through local social networks, was a very important source of information about practitioners. Whilst fourteen interviewees had advertised or announced themselves when they first set up practice and a few had advertised subsequently, all the practitioners whom I spoke to confirmed the importance of the local 'grapevine'. Advertisements or announcements in the local paper may help at first, but as the practice develops, satisfied patients bring in more patients:

> It is getting so that probably half the people I see have heard about me specifically. In the end word of mouth is the only thing.
>
> (Female reflexologist in practice for two years)

> It takes some patience to get started because, at first, it entails sitting and waiting until you are known by word of mouth. If you advertise it's expensive and you have to be there to man your phone after an advert has come out, they don't like answering machines.... I think today two-thirds of the people who actually ring up know someone that has been to me.
>
> (Female acupuncturist, in practice for eight years)

A herbalist suggested that patients who came having heard of the practitioner's services from friends or relatives are easier to deal with than patients who are directed through impersonal channels of information, since they already have some idea of what to expect:

I have never advertised. If I were advising practitioners setting up I would say, do not spend a penny on advertising. Word of mouth is going to work excellently for you because you will get the right kind of patient. You will get Auntie Gladys who belongs to nephew Maurice or whatever and he says, she just did a wonderful job with me and I am really much better now. And you get this open and willing patient. I am in the Yellow Pages, that is the only form of advertisement I do. You get all sorts of people with all sorts of odd expectations, whereas the patient who came before and recommends another patient has already done that spadework.

Perhaps it was because the public are more familiar with osteopathy than therapies like homoeopathy or reflexology, and are more confident that they know what it entails, that the osteopaths in my sample did find impersonal information sources like the Yellow Pages a useful way of making themselves known to the public:

You have got to get people to come to you before the word of mouth gets going. I found the Yellow Pages was fifty-two weeks of free advertising because it is a reference point. If people want to find a registered osteo-path... looking in the Yellow Pages is often the immediate thing. If your name is there and you are the nearest, they will come to you.

(Male osteopath in practice for three years)

Proximity seemed to be particularly important where osteopaths' patients were concerned. Most of them were suffering from musculo-skeletal problems of a kind that might be exacerbated by travel. However, nearly all these practitioners' clienteles were fairly localised, although most could cite a few patients who came from far afield. One practitioner with a growing reputation at the national level reckoned that as many as 40 per cent of her patients came from outside the region, otherwise most patients seemed to come from within the thirty miles around Claybury. A clientele that is based primarily on word of mouth need not be highly localised; this will depend on the structure and spread of patients' social networks. The Claybury area used to be known for the compactness of its kin networks and its low population mobility and these factors would lead us to expect geographically restricted clienteles. A regional survey of practitioners would be more suited to identifying the scale and types of market for non-orthodox medical services than a purely local study.

PRACTITIONERS' NETWORKS

Practitioners' professional networks are of interest for several reasons. Firstly, as I have already shown, when therapists describe their own occupational values, they tend to give explicit priority to altruism and patient-centred service rather than competitiveness or entrepreneurial initiative. But they also value working on their own as opposed to working within an institutional structure. How do they deal with the fact that in terms of the market they are, whether they like it or not, in competition with other practitioners offering the same or similar services? Secondly, most complementary therapists do not work within any formal institutional structure. This being so, are there informal links among them, and if not, in what sense do they constitute any kind of professional community? I asked fairly detailed questions about practitioners' relationships with each other and with orthodox health professionals. Such 'links' and 'relationships' might include personal friendship or acquaintance, participation in a joint practice of some kind, referring or receiving referrals, knowing a practitioner well enough to give or receive advice about a case or point of practice, common membership of local professional groups, etc. Interviewees varied widely in these respects (see Tables 15 and 16 for a rough classification) although none claimed to have no social or professional contact with other health professionals whatsoever.

Table 15 Practitioners' links with other complementary therapists (Claybury study)

	In joint practice	In single practice	
'Loners'	0	7	
'Individualists'	4	7	
'Networkers'	7	9	
Totals	11	23	34

Table 16 Practitioners' links with orthodox medical professionals (Claybury study)

	Practitioners		
Degree of contact with orthodox health professionals	*Having orthodox medical training*	*'Lay' therapists*	
None	0	10	
Limited	6	13	
Extensive	3	2	
Totals	9	25	34

Group practice in anything like the sense that the term is used in relation to GPs was not very usual in the Claybury area, though some new practitioners said that they might in the course of time look for another therapist with whom they could work; a joint practice where several people offer a range of services might be more attractive to the patient and also have more public impact than a practitioner working in isolation. However, there are various degrees of 'jointness' corresponding to different modes of co-operation. It is usual, for instance, for a recently qualified osteopath to get experience as assistant to an established osteopath before setting up a practice of his or her own. All the qualified osteopaths whom I interviewed had started out in this way and one woman still worked for two days a week at the consulting rooms of a senior colleague.

Other kinds of joint practice range from the 'entrepreneurial' to the highly co-operative. An example of an 'entrepreneurial' practice was one set up by a man with no formal qualifications in any kind of medicine but some experience as a masseur and a strong interest in sports injuries. Having seen the scope for expanding complementary medical facilities in the Claybury area, he opened two clinics at which he employed various practitioners on a part-time basis, many from outside the area altogether. He saw his role in this project chiefly as a business manager:

I know enough about it (complementary medicine) to know the market. I was saying to (the practitioners), I can market you, all you have got to do is to do your job properly and when you go on courses or take holidays you won't lose money like you would if you are self-employed. And remember that I am financing your start-up, I am capitalising that, which is expensive.

A more common pattern of 'joint' practice was for two or three practitioners to occupy rooms in the same building without necessarily having a close working relationship or knowing each other well beforehand. In such cases, however, a closer relationship would generally develop over time leading to mutual referrals and occasional discussion of cases.

I started taking patients at home after finishing college and then this (consulting) room came vacant. I know one of the three osteopaths who practise here, and after I came here I got friendly with one of the other osteopaths. We do refer people to each other occasionally and we hope to get a few other people in too. My sister is coming in. She is a physiotherapist and she is doing a course on reflex therapy and she is planning on coming in as well.

(Female homoeopath)

Four of my interviewees participated in a joint practice of this kind with a spouse who had been trained in the same or another therapy (e.g. a homoeopath married to a masseur, an acupuncturist who worked with her hypnotherapist husband).

The most integrated kind of 'joint' practice is found where a practitioner, or group of practitioners, deliberately sets out to build a centre where patients can obtain a range of therapies and where the therapists are carefully selected for compatibility of approach. An osteopath decribed to me how he came to set up a joint practice:

> Initially I set up on my own. This was just an osteopathy clinic. During that time I met June (an acupuncturist) and Alex (a homoeopath), those are the other people who actually work in the clinic now, and I met Cathy (a spiritual healer/reflexologist) who is going to come here one day a week. All these were people whom I met through circumstances. I decided that I wouldn't really think of saying, okay, let's open up a clinic jointly and we will all put money in. I started a business like that before and within six months we were all deadly enemies. So I have been through that once before in something I was really dedicated to and put a lot of energy into, and I wanted to avoid that happening. So I decided that if people were going to work here because I had extra room that was available, it had to grow in an organic sort of way. And I find that the best things in my life have happened to me when I allowed them to grow. After I got to the point I wanted to allow an opening, basically it just sort of happened. The acupuncturist and the homoeopath work on their own essentially, but we refer people back and forth and we confer with each other and that sort of thing. But it is more out of a kind of friendly atmosphere that has developed than a structured business.

In another case, a group of lay people who had an interest in holistic healthcare had formed a charitable trust and leased a building in which a group of therapists practised on different days of the week. Although not all of these therapists knew each other well at the outset they had become a very close group, spending time together outside work hours and sharing ideas and problems.

> We work together well, we treat each other for nothing. We have worked fairly closely together for the last three years, believing in what we are doing, trying to keep costs down for the patient. It's good to work together because we have learnt off each other, about the benefits of each discipline and each person brings a bit of themselves that is different. None of us is whole, but we are all learning to become whole. But the learning process will be enriched by someone else's input, whether it's their actual therapy or the way they work with patients. Quite often I think it is the ambience

and the approach of the practitioner that is more important than the therapy.

(Male reflexologist)

Some practitioners evidently found the idea of any kind of joint practice very problematic and espoused a highly individualistic mode of operation in which they were in no way implicated in either the failures or successes of other people. Even those who were more 'clubbable' by temperament found that it took much trust, commitment and commonality of purpose and outlook to develop satisfying modes of co-operation. As a perceptive osteopath remarked, in complementary medicine there are no pre-existing institutional structures to underpin co-operative relationships among practitioners:

> In this kind of work there is only a very loose structure. Now, if I was a doctor you would have locums, you would have nurses, you have got the whole infrastructure of medicine which has already been developed, so that even if you do not get on well with the people personally, you can still work together because there is that structure that you work within.

Most practitioners could claim acquaintance with at least one or two other local non-orthodox practitioners outside their own practice; in general the longer the individual had been in practice, the more extensive such acquaintance would be. These contacts might be people who had qualified at the same training institutions as themselves or belonged to the same professional association, or they might simply be individuals whom they have come to know, or to know about over time:

> If I don't feel that somebody (i.e. a patient) is making enough progress then I will say, have you tried this or have you tried that? I have referred people to Dr X who practises homoeopathy because I have heard very good reports of her and I know a Bach Flower practitioner and if anyone wants it I refer them to him.

(Female hypnotherapist)

> I know a number of practitioners round here. Very often they will refer patients to me and I will refer patients to them. There is an osteopath who used to be a charge nurse at the hospital where I worked. I would refer people to osteopaths number one, then other kinds of manipulation like reflexology.

(Female iridologist/herbalist)

The contacts that led to referrals were almost always with practitioners of some other therapy, and many interviewees stressed the fact that they had to be confident of that person's credentials:

> If I refer someone, I refer them to a particular practitioner. I don't just say, why don't you try homoeopathy? I know a very good acupuncturist whom I trust implicitly. I have known her a very long time and I trust her opinion, so I sometimes send patients to her.
>
> (Female chiropractor)

> Some of the alternative medical people are qualified doctors so I don't have any qualms about referring people to them. But there are some cranks who aren't properly qualified. I tend to try and separate myself from them, not from any snobbish reason, but if they are not properly qualified, then I don't want to get involved in case they do something daft. But there are one or two homoeopaths and some good acupuncturists.
>
> (Male acupressurist)

> We pass a few patients on if we think it is necessary. We are well aware that we are not experienced in everything and some people are able to give kinds of help that we don't give. But we like to think that if we are going to refer someone to someone else it is not just because we know them or that they have been our patient. We like to know all about their treatments, that they are good-living people. We like good practitioners. We pride ourselves on being good practitioners ourselves. As long as a person has a good reputation, then we will send them patients.
>
> (Female acupuncturist in partnership with husband)

Some found that the force of competition was stronger than that of co-operation:

> There is an osteopath who I know quite well and she will refer patients to me if she thinks they need acupuncture. And if I think someone would benefit from herbal treatment or homoeopathy, then I will refer patients on for that. But locally, at a professional level you find that everyone works in an insular way, they don't want to know because they are all frightened of somebody thieving their patients.
>
> (Male acupuncturist)

Co-operative relationships can only be established therefore when there is a certain amount of trust – both in oneself and in others. A practitioner must have faith in the skills of the people to whom s/he refers patients, but also must have the self-confidence to identify the point at which a patient cannot benefit further from his/her own form of treatment and to feel that they can be referred to another person without loss of face.

I identified at least two semi-formal professional networks in the Claybury area which drew together non-orthodox practitioners of different kinds. One was a local cell of the British Holistic Medicine Association, convened by a

GP. This group had a membership of two GPs, seven nurses and midwives, two chiropodists and nine complementary practitioners (mainly osteopaths). It met every month or two at the convenor's health centre to listen to a speaker or to discuss some matter of common interest. During the period of the study these included such issues as the management of childbirth, uses of acupuncture in the relief of pain, science and healing, etc. The members of this group seemed to know each other fairly well and some of them referred patients to each other. The second group had a less formal constitution. It was convened by an osteopath who was interested in the spiritual and psychological dimensions of healing. Local complementary practitioners met at his clinic regularly to offer each other healing and to practice group meditation. I did not attend this group myself but several interviewees claimed that they had found it very supportive as well as providing an opportunity for the exchange of ideas. Some of the members of this network evidently referred patients to each other also.

Table 15 represents a rough and ready typology of interviewees according to the degree of contact which they had with other non-orthodox practitioners. The first group I have called the 'loners', i.e. those who claim to have little or no personal contact with other complementary therapists within the locality and are definitely not seeking to develop such links, either out of temperamental disinclination or because they saw no practical gain from such a move. Secondly there are the 'individualists', people who knew perhaps two or three other local therapists, who may even participate in some form of joint practice but show a low level of actual co-operation with other practitioners outside their own practice. Some of these have been in practice for only a short time and will no doubt develop more extensive contacts in the course of time. Finally there are the 'networkers', the most clubbable of all, those who know more than three local therapists personally and probably also belong to one of the two semi-formal networks I have mentioned. If 'networkers' belong to a joint practice, it will be one of those where there is a good deal of mutual referral, discusssion of patients and other co-operative activities.

Complementary medicine tends to attract people who like autonomy, but this does not mean that they are all unsociable mavericks, eschewing co-operation with other professionals. Whatever their temperamental inclinations, non-orthodox practitioners are, willy-nilly, subject to two opposite kinds of pressure. On the one hand they have a political interest in solidarity with others of their kind, in a united front to make complementary medicine known and respected in the locality. Shared enthusiasms draw them together and often shared ideologies of healing. They have a practical interest in seeking out practitioners of other therapies to whom they can refer patients when they think fit. On the other hand, they have often chosen to become therapists in part because they like working alone, without the control or interference of others. And there is the inescapable fact that even with what appears to be a rapidly expanding market, they are in competition for patients with each other, especially with those who practise the same system of healing. For those who are more clubbable by temperament, the impulse for co-operation may overcome the divisive effects of competition. However, the networks which result are generally loose and based entirely on mutual regard and shared outlook. Practitioners are more likely to co-operate with people who are practising different therapies from their own, and they are inclined to distance themselves from those whose standards or practices they do not approve of, rather than attempt to influence them. They are not therefore the kinds of link which might provide the means for local forms of social or professional control.

The discussion so far has not taken account of participation in professional organisations. All except one of the interviewees were members of at least one such organisation, but not all were active members. This was partly related to 'clubbability' but also to the opportunities for involvement which different associations offered to members; some have regional groups which organise regular meetings and courses, whilst in others a national network is maintained chiefly through newsletters or annual general meetings. Interviewees saw professional membership as a useful means of keeping abreast with developments in their discipline through professional journals, updating seminars and short courses available to members. Ten of the interviewees could be described as playing an active organising role in some aspect of an association's activities, usually at a regional level, although several long-established practitioners claimed to have been more active in the past. Many who had only recently set up in practice claimed that they could not afford to go on expensive courses or travel to conferences in distant parts of the country whilst those whose practices were already flourishing often found that they had little time left over from their patients. Whilst practitioners were very appreciative of the benefits of professional membership, such organisations were not the only or even the main means of building up useful inter-personal networks with other therapists at the local level.

COMPLEMENTARY PRACTITIONERS AND ORTHODOX MEDICINE

The non-orthodox therapies differ considerably among themselves as to whether they regard themselves as self-sufficient systems of medicine, capable of replacing orthodox medicine altogether, or whether they see themselves as specialisms, good for treating certain kinds of problem. Osteopathy in Britain, whatever the original and more expansive claims of its American founder Andrew Taylor Still, tends to represent itself as a discipline which works alongside orthodox medicine, dealing with particular types of problem, mainly those of the musculo-skeletal system. A more extreme professional rhetoric is found among some non-medically qualified homoeopaths, who offer homoeopathy as a system complete in itself. Indeed it is sometimes claimed that orthodox medicine (allopathy) is not just *different* from homoeopathy; its practices can actually be harmful to health insofar as it prescribes strong drugs which suppress symptoms rather than cure persons, and uses vaccines which tamper dangerously with the immune system. Most disciplines stand somewhere in between these poles in terms of their publicly stated claims.

At the local level I found, as I expected, a range of attitudes but not a very wide one. All the interviewees accorded some kind of role to orthodox medicine, and most preferred to describe what they themselves did as 'complementary' rather than 'alternative' to orthodox medicine. At one end of the spectrum was a homoeopath who admitted that orthodox medicine had a role to play in the treatment of acute illness but that:

> I take a lot of work off the GPs' shoulders, especially as preventative work. I empty their waiting rooms, not because my medicine is superior but because we treat things constitutionally. We help people to anticipate and prevent acute conditions.

An acupuncturist who had worked in a large hospital as a physiotherapist expressed a fairly typical, if rather ambivalent viewpoint:

> Well, acupuncture is a totally different system of medicine, there's no doubt about it. I always think that if you try to explain it to anyone you really need to understand some of the philosophy and the concept of the eastern... it's just different but complementary. I don't like alternatives. Well, I have proved to myself that you can combine them quite happily.

Where the term 'alternative' was preferred, it was understood to mean 'alternative from the point of view of the patient' and not in the sense of mutually exclusive at a societal level:

> Homoeopathy is not complementary to orthodox medicine. It is an alternative and the patient has to make the choice. When people come to me about whether they should let their children have the whooping cough vaccine, for instance, I explain both sides, the pros and cons, but it is their decision as to what to choose. I will go along with their choice, whatever it is. But this is time-consuming.
>
> (Homoeopath, former SRN)

If non-orthodox medicine is regarded as complementary then, it is not with any implication of being dependent or subordinate but in the sense of offering something that orthodox medicine does not offer (holism, preventative approach, more natural and less invasive techniques, etc.). Most saw orthodox medicine as a legitimate and valuable tradition of healing whose present shortcomings were due to institutional factors (lack of time to treat patients holistically, pressure from pharmaceutical companies to over-prescribe drugs) rather than being based on incorrect or inadequate knowledge. Several pointed out that, for acute conditions, orthodox medicine might be more appropriate. 'If I had raging pneumonia I wouldn't mess around sticking needles in myself' as one acupuncturist disarmingly remarked. Many stressed that even if orthodox medicine was deficient in its delivery of empathic care for patients, its system of diagnosis was a valuable resource. There was, as might be expected, considerable difference between those who had come into non-orthodox medicine from some branch of orthodox healthcare and those who had not, the former being much more likely to stress the positive aspects of orthodox medicine:

> It is important to make a correct diagnosis and there are some things for which I could pick up early symptoms which a homoeopath without a medical background could miss. This is true of cancer in its early stages. I would not feel happy practising without that diagnostic background.
>
> (Female homoeopath, former SRN)

However, whilst they acknowledged the value of their orthodox medical background in their non-orthodox medical work, the ex-NHS workers were also the ones who resented most strongly the low status they had in the eyes of orthodox doctors:

> We are doing a very valuable job. The doctors wouldn't do it for the same money.

> Conventional medicine looks down its nose at us.

> Mostly the GPs are very high-handed and talk to you as though you have just done a two-week course.

It was this category of practitioners who were most likely to develop successful networks with orthodox doctors, having 'inherited' useful contacts from their former medical activities. Those who had worked in hospitals were often acquainted with consultants with whom they might maintain some professional contact. Several claimed to have received patient referrals from an orthopaedic consultant known to have an interest in certain types of non-orthodox medicine and several said that they had been asked to lecture on the therapy they practised to local groups of doctors.

Those who did not have an orthodox medical background varied considerably in the extent to which they had tried to forge links with orthodox medical professionals. Most had told their own GP of their activities and a few knew local GPs socially. A few, mainly osteopaths, had deliberately set out to make themselves known to local GPs when they first started practice, by sending a card or making a phone call. Practitioners of homoeopathy, acupuncture or reflexology were less likely to be so confident that GPs would welcome their approaches or regard them as competent.

A problem which both medically qualified and other practitioners found was the great diversity of attitudes within the orthodox medical profession. As an acupressurist put it, 'some doctors are broadsighted, others just look down drainpipes'. It was difficult to know whether to brace oneself for a scornful rebuff or anticipate an interested welcome when approaching them. If one knew which to expect one could concentrate on cultivating the doctors with a more positive attitude and not waste time trying to explain what one did to those who would never be convinced of its validity:

> You get doctors who are very easy to talk to but there are others who just contradict everything you say and they really annoy you. I feel I don't want to explain to them, they obviously don't believe a word I say, so what is the point of talking to them?
>
> (Female herbalist, former SRN)

What kinds of co-operation with orthodox doctors were desired? Many claimed that they already received informal referrals from local GPs who knew them personally or by repute. In some cases they suspected that doctors faced with an intractable case might suggest complementary therapy without wishing to take the responsibility of naming a specific practitioner:

> I think some doctors send patients indirectly by sort of saying, well, don't tell anybody I told you but if I were you I would go and see an osteopath.
>
> (Male osteopath)

Whilst practitioners welcomed such signs of professional approval, however guarded, they noted that referrals from GPs only constituted a small proportion of their total clientele. Most gave priority not to referrals but to professional communication. Some pointed out that it would be useful to be able to discuss a patient who had presented symptoms which might be interpreted as indicating cancer or some other serious disease with the patient's GP. They were worried by the fact that many patients did not want their GP to know that they had consulted a complementary therapist, and that therefore it would be impossible for them to approach the GP themselves, even if personally convinced of a favourable reception. Others were troubled by the fact that they were sometimes consulted for problems which (in their view) were better dealt with by orthodox medicine, but which the patient was scared to discuss with the GP:

> They will say, I didn't like to ask the doctor, or perhaps they don't know what to ask the doctor, or they are worried that they did not understand something he said. I urge them to go to their GP if I think it is important. If they still won't, I try to persuade them by saying that I could help them, but it will be very expensive for me to send them for an X-ray or something like that. I try to convince them. I am not hard up, I don't need their £10 if it is going to keep them away from an operation they need.
>
> (Acupuncturist, ex-SRN)

Several pointed out that GPs had, as members of the NHS, access to resources which the non-orthodox practitioner could not so easily obtain for their patients (X-ray facilities, blood testing etc.):

> I will sometimes refer patients back to their doctors for X-rays if the patients can't afford private X-rays. Well I will normally try to get them to do that, but I think that doctors might get a bit cross then, because it's like I am telling them what to do.
>
> (Female osteopath)

A very general view was that patients' GPs should know about non-orthodox treatment they are receiving so that both doctor and therapist can work together and not against each other.

> I have suggested to patients that if they are being treated by their GP they should let him know that they are being treated by me, because they should know they are having some other kind of therapy, otherwise they don't know who is doing what. No GP has ever rung me up and said, what are you doing? I mean, I would be happy to tell them if they did. But I don't think it is my place to push myself in their direction.
>
> (Chiropractor)

The question of clinical responsibility is one which exercises GPs, although they are more likely to identify the problem in terms of incompatible treatment or conflicting advice. Murray and Shepherd, reporting on a study of patients who had used both orthodox and non-orthodox treatments, ask with alarm:

> How can a patient avoid a potential conflict of medical management?

And where the orthodox doctor has not been consulted at all:

> What, for example is the responsible course of action for the general

practitioner who finds that a child is suffering as a result of unorthodox treatment selected by the parents without medical consultation?

(Murray and Shepherd 1988: 513)

Complementary practitioners are less likely to see the problem purely in terms of the allocation of clinical responsibility, being more disposed to accord the patient final responsibility for choice of treatment where more than one possibility is presented. But without good communication among practitioners, it is difficult to create an environment in which the patient can weigh up the advantages of different courses of action or explore ways in which orthodox and non-orthodox treatments might be combined. Some interviewees also pointed out that if GPs did not know that a patient was being treated by a complementary practitioner they might attribute recovery to their own medical procedures or to the spontaneous remission of symptoms when it was non-orthodox therapy which had actually effected the cure. Credit should be given where credit is due!

Complementary practitioners also face dilemmas over conflicting or unsuitable treatments:

I would never contradict what a patient has been told by their doctor. I think in a lot of cases a GP doesn't have a lot of options. He can advise the patient to rest, he can prescribe analgesics. I think most GPs are aware that they they don't necessarily have a lot to offer in terms of musculo-skeletal problems. I might say to the patient, well, have the treatment the doctor suggested first, it will be cheaper for the patient anyway if it is on the NHS, and if there is still a problem afterwards then give me a call. I think it is only confusing for the patient and for practitioners if the patient is having two lots of treatment at once.

(Male osteopath)

I get detailed accounts from patients of their treatments by GPs. I look up the side effects of the drugs they are taking. If the drugs are needed or they can't forgo the support, then I will give them supportive treatment to minimise the side effects. If I feel the drugs are not necessary then I might put it to them. If they are happy with the drugs I will not interfere. It is their own choice. I don't try to make up people's minds for them.

(Female homoeopath)

If a patient comes to me who is on tranquillisers and wants to come off them, I will suggest that they go and see their GP and ask them if they can come off them and tell them they are having acupuncture from me as well, so that we are both working together.

(Female acupuncturist)

Supposing that someone has cancer and the GP says you must have your breast off and that's the best way of dealing with it, then the patient must make up her mind if that is the best way for her. I would work alongside it, helping her to cope and at the same time trying to destroy any other cancers that there may be. I think it would be very foolish to do anything else.

(Female herbalist/iridologist)

Leaving it to the patient to resolve the conflicts between different systems of treatment might seem like an abrogation of responsibility, but it must be remembered that if, as many users and practitioners of non-orthodox medicine (not to mention advocates of the free market) recommend, there should be more patient choice in healthcare, then this will be one kind of choice that will have to be made.

All interviewees claimed that they asked patients about orthodox treatment in respect of the symptoms about which they consulted, especially current medication, and recorded what they had been told. It seemed to me that a major problem here is that many patients have been told very little by their doctors about the treatment they are given, or have not understood what they have been told because the explanation was hasty or not couched in lay language. So the information which the non-orthodox practitioner can get without direct recourse to the GP him/herself is liable to be incomplete or even garbled. I have already argued that it is unlikely that serious illnesses are going undiagnosed as a result of patients consulting complementary practitioners (see p. 58) – indeed it is possible that non-orthodox practitioners sometimes identify symptoms which patients have been scared to confide in their GPs or which they have thought unimportant. However, the absence of institutionalised channels for communication between orthodox and non-orthodox professionals suggests that we should take seriously the fears expressed by both groups that conflicting advice or incompatible treatments may be meted out to the patient. This is no less a problem in a situation where the different kinds of professional are well disposed to each other if they are not in a position to co-operate, nor is there any accepted inter-professional etiquette. A few practitioners had laboured hard to develop such relationships and praised the efforts of some GPs to understand their work, but most felt that there were enormous obstacles still to be overcome.

RELATIONSHIPS WITH PATIENTS

Most interviewees saw their healthcare as being in some sense holistic, dealing with the psycho-social dimensions of the patient's problems, rather than seeing the body as some kind of (faulty) machine. The only exception to this was a rather down-to-earth osteopath who said that he felt he ought to be offering holistic treatment, but the acute cases which he saw usually required swift action to relieve the patients' pain and get them back to work again. Quick attention to the immediate cause of the pain was more appropriate than extensive investigation, although he was well aware that in many cases there were underlying psychological or environmental factors contributing to the patient's problem.

We have already seen that consultations cannot be hurried if a high level of attention is to be given to the particular circumstances and personality of the patient.

> The longer I am in practice, the broader the range of problems I see. It used to be just back problems, now it is elbows and knees. But that's a funny way to talk about people because what is coming into the treatment more and more is a sense of working with the whole being, and I find that I am working more and more on an emotional, a sort of spiritual level, tying it all together and showing people how their physical problems are manifestations of their whole lives.
>
> (Male osteopath)

At the very least this implied attention to the environment in which the patients lived and worked. One osteopath had made a point of inviting himself to a local farm to watch farm labourers at work. He had a number of patients from the farming community and wanted to understand better the kind of stresses to which they were subject in the course of their work. Some therapists found this aspect of their work rather depressing because they knew that in many cases there was little they could do to effect any change. The labourer that came for manipulation for a bad back would get better, but would be obliged to return to the strenuous job which had caused the bad back in the first place. The most one could do was to give the patient some insight into the basic cause of the problem.

At the other end of the spectrum, a number of interviewees said that a holistic approach meant that in practice much treatment consisted of counselling in one form or another.

> Everyone who walks in that door is like a ravelled-up ball of wool. You never know what you are going to find. So reflexology tends to be the 'theme' but as I learn more and more, and as I experience more and more, my philosophy changes and no two consultations are the same. Some people come here and I can teach them to get rid of anger, and I can let them get out grief and stuff like that. I see myself as a catalyst for people getting to know themselves, even though I am more commonly known as a reflexologist.

However the term 'holism' is interpreted, it implies a highly patient-centred approach in which the style of treatment is very much tailored to suit the individual case. But might it not be that this patient-centredness is nothing to do with holism, New Age ideologies of personal development or psychosocial theories of disease, but a simple and straightforward consequence of the fact that the relationship between the patient and practitioner is a market relationship? I have already discussed Freidson's concepts of client control and professional referral (see p. 121). The previous section suggested that complementary practitioners are unlikely to be subject to strong forms of professional control, working as they do in relative isolation. They must sell their therapies to patients who have no strong motivation to continue treatment if they are not pleased with what they are getting and the best way of doing this is surely to provide custom-made treatment for the individual patient, a sure case of client control.

This is probably too cynical a view, and many of my interviewees would totally reject the language of authority and control as a way of describing what they do. Nonetheless the therapist has a strong interest in patient compliance, regardless of his or her professional ideology, if only because s/he has a genuine faith that the regime prescribed will actually benefit the patient and a sincere desire that the patient get well (not to mention a professional investment in a reputation for being able to effect cures). Therefore we need to look at the way in which the inescapably commercial nature of the transaction between practitioner and patient affects the ways in which practitioners can expect to influence the patient within the therapeutic relationship.

Relying mainly on interviews for my data, I had little opportunity to observe this relationship as it actually develops in practice. I decided to ask practitioners about specific situations in which conflict between the patient's and their own views or priorities might potentially be an issue, inviting them to describe how they had handled particular cases if they were prepared to do so.

First there is the matter of selectivity. Are practitioners prepared to refuse to treat cases which they do not feel competent to deal with or for which they think some other kind of treatment is more appropriate? Only two interviewees claimed to exercise conscious selectivity. An acupuncturist who had formerly been a psychiatric nurse claimed to refuse cases which he felt were incurable because it was unfair to take money from people and waste their time when they were never going to achieve more than marginal improvement. A chiropractor claimed that she had learnt not to try to 'walk on water' and to recognise the small percentage of cases which would not respond to her kind of treatment. Both these practitioners appeared by their own accounts and by those of others to be very successful and busy and could no doubt turn a few potential patients away without damage to their practice or reputation.

Most practitioners felt that this was seldom an issue, because they were not approached by people whom they did not feel they could help in any way at all. It was their business to do whatever they could for anyone who brought their suffering to their door and to help them achieve what they could, however little. On the other hand, some of these did feel that they were very much at the mercy of public perceptions of what their particular therapy was good for. Several osteopaths mentioned that they would be interested in treating more cases which were not concerned primarily with musculo-skeletal problems, but this is what the public thinks osteopathy is about. One felt that the media had much to answer for, and found that she had to break it to some patients that a 'wonder' treatment described in a magazine or on a television programme was not appropriate to their particular problem.

A therapist may over time build up a reputation for curing certain kinds of condition, but these need not be the ones which s/he prefers to treat or feels most competent to treat. As one homoeopath said, to the extent that your patients are referred by word of mouth they often come because they think they have got the same illness as their friend or relative who came before, and expect to have the same treatment or to get better at the same rate. But homoeopathy, like many other therapies, treats the patient rather than the disease; two people presenting symptoms which in their own terms amount to the same 'illness' may be offered different treatments and find that their return to health proceeds in quite different ways. Presumably those therapists who are active in educational work or promotional work can hope to influence public attitudes to some extent, but nonetheless unrealistic or inaccurate expectations were sometimes a problem.

What do practitioners do if the patient is clearly not complying with advice or not taking medication provided? No medical practitioner of any kind can enforce compliance, a problem long recognised by orthodox doctors. But the complementary practitioner is in a slightly different position vis-à-vis the non-compliant patient, having even fewer practical sanctions, and being accorded less professional and moral authority by society in general. Only one interviewee, a chiropractor, admitted to taking an explicitly authoritarian line:

> my patients would never dare not comply. I am very serious because I won't have them as patients. It's a very dogmatic and megalomaniac attitude I have, but it is what has actually made the practice work. My attitude is if you do as you are told there is a fair chance that you will get better but don't mess me around. This works because they know that I

care deeply that they get better and what they have not come across (in orthodox treatment) is this care.

So if I yell at the top of my voice down Claybury High Road 'cause I see one of my patients carrying a load heavier than they should have done, they know that it's because I care about them.

However, even this practitioner acknowledged that over time she had discovered what kind of exercises her patients would be likely to follow at home and had learnt not to waste her own time devising regimes that they would find too demanding. An osteopath/naturopath pointed out that there was a major problem when the treatment or advice went counter to local lay conceptions of how the body worked or what was beneficial:

Most will do the exercises I suggest, but hydrotherapy... well, they don't really agree with that, they are not keen on doing that. I am not doing it on any big scale any more, it's more a matter of after I have treated them I will say put a cold compress over the area for twenty minutes. Well, they look at me as if, what is she talking about, why should I do that? If I said to them put a hot water bottle on it they would do that because they relate to that and think that is going to help.

A homoeopath, somewhat more experienced and perhaps more confident in her approach to patients, claimed that she felt that the patient could be encouraged to try new approaches or give up practices which from the homoeopathic point of view were harmful, but that they might need a good deal of moral support from her in the process. A reflexologist, who practised several other therapies and gave dietary advice, claimed that the best way to meet patients' difficulties in making radical changes in life style or complying with exacting regimes was to give them realistic targets and to help them advance a little at a time:

That is why I maybe only give them one herbal formula when they could use four, because I never want people to walk away from here and think, oh it sounds great but it is just too much, I can't do all this.... I give them little goals and I always say we are going to take one step at a time... there is nothing better than feeling that you have accomplished something, you know your sense of self-worth improves a whole lot, even if it is only a tiny step on the ladder like having cut out caffeine. That is how I work with people.

Most interviewees not only denied any claim to moral or professional control over the patient but also complained about the passive unquestioning attitudes to treatment that orthodox medicine encouraged in patients. As one experienced homoeopath said, it is not a matter of how to make the patient comply with a treatment that runs counter to what the doctor has said, but to get patients to a position where they no longer need the prop of any kind of medical authority, and are prepared to take responsibility for their own health.

Achieving compliance with therapeutic advice is generally seen as a matter of negotiation and persuasion and while some practitioners are more prepared than others to temper the wind to the shorn lamb where difficult treatments are concerned, most do not regard it as a major problem. I suspect that sick people who find the treatments offered altogether too bizarre or counter to their own notions of what will make them better, drop out before the treatment has gone far. Others can be cajoled into accepting unfamiliar, time-consuming or even painful regimes because the therapist is prepared to explain the treatment and provide moral support, for which the orthodox doctor has little time and sometimes no inclination.

The doctor, after all, expects adult patients to arrive at the surgery already knowing what to expect and how to behave. Children are subject to deliberate attempts to socialise them into proper modes of patient behaviour and to foster confidence that what is being done to them is indeed for their own good. Mothers try to communicate this to their children and there are special books for children which take them through the experience of going to the surgery or prepare them for a spell in hospital. So even if the patient's expectations about how a consultation will proceed do not entirely co-incide with those of the doctor, it is unlikely that s/he will arrive at the surgery without some fairly well formed notions as to what is likely to happen. This is not the case with non-orthodox medicine. A few patients may have been taken to homoeopaths or naturopaths as children and will be familiar with their diagnostic routines, but at present these are a minority. A new patient may have some theoretical knowledge of homoeopathy but will have no experience of how homoeopaths behave or what their own part in the consultation is likely to consist of. If anyone is going to do any 'socialising' it must be the practitioner him/herself.

But surely the transmission of knowledge to the patient entails some risk to the practitioner? If too little is offered the patient may fail to understand enough of what is going on to co-operate with the treatment. If too much is offered, may not the practitioner undermine his/her own professional position, based on the claim to special knowledge?

Most practitioners saw some sharing of knowledge as beneficial to the relationship between healer and patient and as conducive to the process of recovery. There was an explicit rejection of professional mystique. In the first place, information may be necessary in order that the patient be reassured:

I have got a little pamphlet downstairs which explains a little about what osteopathy is, because I find most people are quite ignorant. Some come and they are scared stiff, they think they are in for three rounds with Mike Tyson. They come in a bit nervous and I do explain to them a little bit about the concept of osteopathy. The patient doesn't need to know, but they generally like to know, even if it is only a rough idea of what is wrong, if only to put their mind at rest.

(Male osteopath)

It's amazing how many people are worrying like mad. I had a patient this morning who had a whiplash injury and all her neck was seized up, and because she was tired and exhausted all the time she was really convinced she had leukaemia. I explained to her about the blood vessels and the blood supply going up the neck to the head and I could see the burden falling off her as I explained.

(Female osteopath)

Several practitioners complained that patients came to them for very simple information which they felt could, and should, have been provided by their doctors; many sufferers had endured unnecessary anxiety simply because no-one had bothered to explain their condition to them or had perhaps tried to explain but had not used language which they could understand.

To the extent that the therapeutic relationship is seen as a contract or a partnership, then, the patients often need briefing before they can play their part in the healing process:

I always explain to people something about what I am doing. It is all education, isn't it, really? They like to be able to go away and tell their friends how it is working. But it's team work really. I mean, they are healing themselves via the acupuncture and I am sort of educating them as to how they can help that process. I put the needles in and then we talk.

(Female acupuncturist)

I think basic instruction and understanding about the condition is half the battle. It relieves anxiety if you can put a name to the problem and if you can explain it. That is why I have models (of the human skeleton) so that I can show people what they have done and they see the light, and then I go on to explain what they shouldn't do and what they should do to help themselves.

(Male osteopath)

But if knowledge is shared it must be to a degree and in a way which is appropriate to the patient's needs and understanding:

I will tell the patient what is relevant for them to know. I will stand up there with my big chart and explain in very basic language, not because I am trying to pretend or hide anything but I don't need the big words. What is the point of saying malleoli when the patient says ankle bone? I mean, in Claybury they think you are stuck up if you talk like that.

(Female chiropractor)

Someone comes in for treatment of hay fever or for asthma and you explain fully what the acupuncture does and the theory behind it, etc. But it is no good explaining to someone who quite honestly hasn't two brain cells to rub together because it is a waste of my time and they are not taking it in, so you just generalise very briefly and say, well we are going to do this and do that. I mean, some people are very inquisitive and I can stand there and give them an hour's seminar if they want.

(Male acupuncturist)

The knowledge which is shared is, however, knowledge of a certain kind. As a chiropractor put it:

I never explain to them what I am doing, but I always tell them why I am doing it.

The homoeopath does not always tell the patient what remedy s/he has prescribed, nor how s/he arrived at the decision that this remedy was the appropriate one, nor do manipulators offer to share their skills. The knowledge that the therapist offers to share is usually either 'general knowledge' about the way the body works and the way the therapy is conceived as acting upon the body, or insights into the nature and circumstances of the particular patient's disease. The practitioner does not convey diagnostic skill, nor therapeutic technique. While the therapist is prepared to share information, the patient is still reliant on him or her for expertise. However, the majority of the therapists advocated a participatory view of the healing process based on the idea that the patients bring important knowledge of themselves and their circumstances to the medical encounter. The skilful practitioner can cultivate the development of this self-knowledge so as to speed the return to health. If practitioners use knowledge as a means of gaining a purchase on a relationship which the patient can terminate at any time, it is perhaps their practical knowledge of how patients 'tick' as much as their professional knowledge of acupuncture, homoeopathy or radionics which enables them to do this.

What happens if the practitioner is unable to effect a cure? My interviewees were, not surprisingly, confident that whilst they might not be able to achieve miracle cures and whilst healing was sometimes slow, their treatment was effective for most people. Yet it was evident from conversations with practitioners that they did have at their disposal explanations for therapeutic failure which make sense in terms of their own theories of healing (the patient was clinging to his/her illness, s/he was not the kind of patient who could easily accept homoeopathy, the patient did not give the treatment long enough to work). Some of these are quite similar to explanations available to orthodox doctors (there were intractable environmental factors which militated against the patient's recovery, the patient did not comply with the treatment prescribed). But there is no guarantee that these rationalisations will be meaningful or acceptable to patients, even patients who have been fairly well 'socialised' into the way in which a particular therapy is practised.

Any system of healing needs to have some way of making sense of therapeutic failure and death (McGuire 1988: 35). Yet in complementary medicine therapeutic failure will not always be manifest to the practitioner. When the patient completes a series of appointments and does not telephone again, there is no way of knowing whether this is because s/he found the treatment successful and does not feel the need for further consultations, or because s/he was disappointed and does not want to waste further time or money. The practitioner may never see or hear from this patient again. Where the patient confronts the practitioner with putative failure the immediate need for the practitioner is less to provide a rationalisation of the failure than to suggest practical action. I suspect that this need to have something further 'up one's sleeve' might be behind the rather frantic acquisition of new qualifications on the part of one or two interviewees. Those with a more thorough grounding in a single therapy obviously valued their contacts with other practitioners as a kind of safety net for the patient who does not make progress or finds the treatment hard to accept:

> I am terribly thorough. I am a cruel, hard manipulator and there is no use patients trotting off to search for other manipulators, because if they find that my manipulation doesn't work it is unlikely that any other manipulation will suit them. So they could try some other therapy. Those therapies would be homoeopathy and acupuncture as far as I can see. I have good reports of a homoeopath near here and I have sent her address to a number of people who asked, and I know an acupuncturist whose opinion I trust implicitly, and I have sent people to her.
>
> (Female chiropractor)

A dominant theme in this chapter has been the extent to which the complementary practitioner's practice is influenced by the fact that complementary medicine is still private medicine, a service sold on the market to patients who have to pay. It would be easier to study this problem if we could compare these private complementary therapists with a suitable group of orthodox practitioners operating in the private sector, or with a group of complementary practitioners working within the NHS. Even then, the matter would not be straightforward; many non-orthodox practitioners tend to see what they do as, if anything, nearer to primary healthcare, whilst patients actually resort to them as they would to a consultant, i.e. after the GP's resources have proved inadequate.

Lacking such opportunities for comparison I can only interpret the internal evidence of the interviews, which suggests to me that the patient-centred approach which all the interviewees claimed to use to one degree or another was more than a mere rationalisation of their practical dependence on the market, more than medical mystification of the need to please the customer. Whilst a few practitioners had, under pressure of strong demand for their services, tended to cut down the amount of time they spent with individual patients and to deal with them in a way more characteristic of orthodox medicine, others had – under equally favourable market conditions – actually cut down the number of patients they saw in order to preserve the therapeutic practice which they felt they had been trained for and which they believed in.

There is every indication that the market is favourable to non-orthodox practitioners in a place like Claybury at the present time. Newly trained therapists are establishing a level of professional activity satisfactory to themselves within a year or two of setting up practice. Whilst practitioners do not attempt crude manipulation of the demand for their services in either direction (they advertise little, they seldom exercise explicit selectivity as to what kind of patients they take on), they strive to ensure the right kind of demand, that is, to attract the kind of patient who will find their therapy congenial, who will be prepared to engage in the kind of (participatory/holistic) therapeutic relationship which they themselves favour and who therefore will (presumably) be more likely to benefit from the treatment. They can do this in various ways; talks and promotional work help to shape potential patients' expectations of what a therapy involves and what it can do, and reliance on local social networks rather than formal channels of advertisements guarantees a flow of new patients who have been already prepared by previous patients.

The position of the non-orthodox practitioner is full of contradictions, no-one being more conscious of these contradictions or more sensitive to their effects than practitioners themselves. They identify with a professional ideal of altruistic public service and yet their services are only accessible to those who can pay. They tend to be the kind of people that like to operate outside structures, yet they need formal structures and channels of communication so as to gain access to facilities for patients, co-operation with orthodox doctors, to build referral systems in case of therapeutic failure. They desire a preventative approach to healthcare, yet operate in isolation, treat individuals and have no collective clout at the community level to change environments or affect public policies. Most of the people whom I interviewed seemed not to be very active in resolving these problems at a political level, probably because their patients and their other professional activities engrossed all their energies. Obviously there are complementary practitioners who are active at the national level, and I turn to their efforts in the next chapter.

8   The politics of complementary medicine

How far has professionalisation advanced among practitioners of complementary medicine and what directions has it taken? What kinds of professional power are they able to exercise, and how is the process of professionalisation likely to proceed in future? From the interview material which I discussed in Chapter 7 it is clear that practitioners do espouse a professional ethic. In describing what they do and how they perceive their relationships with their clients they employ the professional rhetoric of altruistic responsibility, the moralistic rejection of commercialism. The untrained quack who has no real skills, and the unscrupulous 'cowboy', out to make a quick buck from sick people's misfortunes, are both condemned as the antithesis of sober accountability and compassionate healing.

But unlike the NHS doctor they have to live with the contradictory situation that whilst their ideal is ethical and their motivation may indeed be a genuine desire to see the patient walk out from the consulting room happier and healthier than when s/he walked in, they do nonetheless operate within a market in which some sick people will not be able to afford their fees. Unlike the orthodox private consultant, who also sells medical services direct to the patient but who is shielded from the intrusion of commerce into the consulting room, most non-orthodox practitioners confront this contradiction starkly every time they hand a patient a bill; few operate on such a scale as to be able to afford secretaries or office staff to mail bills and monitor payment on their behalf. Most of the practitioners whom I interviewed had faced up to this contradiction and had made decisions about how to balance the altruistic aim of their art with the need to earn income, preferably an income which is recognised as reflecting the skills and knowledge which they claim to possess.

All except one of the practitioners I interviewed belonged to at least one professional organisation, often one associated with the establishment where they had trained. Most interviewees spoke appreciatively of the services and support which they had obtained from their professional associations. It seems likely that the proportion of practitioners who belong to such groups will continue to increase, although some therapies have an ethos more conducive to 'clubbability' than others.

How effective are such associations in defending the boundaries between 'professional' and 'commercial' practice, of which my interviewees were so conscious? Do they actually have sanctions to control the cowboy or the quack? Cases of professional misconduct among orthodox doctors can be dealt with by the General Medical Council, often in a very public manner with detailed reporting in the press, and this may lead to the doctor in question being struck off the list, either permanently or for a time. There have been cases in which non-orthodox practitioners have been disciplined for misconduct by their professional associations but such cases receive less publicity outside the profession unless the details are lurid enough to interest the tabloid press. Also there is little to prevent anyone expelled from a professional group from continuing to practise since registration with a professional association or register does not have the same legal and bureaucratic significance as registration as a doctor. While pan-professional bodies like the Institute of Complementary Medicine (of which more later) are busy compiling general registers of non-orthodox practitioners and while these registers may be useful to members of the public who seek the services of a non-orthodox therapist, the advantages and prestige of being a member are not so dramatic as make de-registration the kind of shameful disaster the untutored public will recognise.

If the problems of sanctioning behaviour within organisations are great, the difficulties of drawing boundaries without the support of national organisations are even greater, as was illustrated by an incident which occurred while I was conducting interviews. In the area I studied there was a well established clinic at which a form of acupressure was practised, along with other 'oriental' techniques. The founder of the clinic had learnt his art from a Japanese instructor in the martial arts and claimed that there were no other clinics in Britain which offered this particular version of the therapy. He belonged to no national organisation, there being no organisation relevant to his work. He trained therapists in his own clinic and employed them when they had attained what he regarded as adequate skills. Normally, he told me, this training would take five years of such apprenticeship at the very least. During the period of fieldwork one of his trainees had decided unilaterally to end her training and set up a practice on her own. The founder of the clinic felt that she was far from ready to undertake healing without supervision. He duplicated a handbill for distribution to patients which explained the situation, disclaiming any responsibility for this therapist and pointing out that she had not completed her full course of training. It is dubious whether such a disclaimer would have much impact on the public, who would be unlikely to have preconceived ideas as to how long the relevant training ought to have taken, and no formal certification was involved anyway.

Professional groups who have the recognition of the state are in a better position to sanction members because more is at stake, de-registration involving a more palpable loss of privilege. Autonomy brings no special prestige to a professional group unless it is autonomy specifically and deliberately bestowed upon it, as opposed to autonomy obtained, as it were, by default. To take a hypothetical example, a group of shamans might band together and define shamanship, ejecting 'sham' shamans from their company. The renegade shaman would suffer little from this exercise of professional autonomy if there were no widely recognised and publicly accepted standards of shamanship, preferably acknowledged directly or indirectly by the state and understood by a knowing public. I cannot help wondering whether the very excited reaction on the part of some complementary practitioners to the formation of the Campaign Against Health Fraud (familiarly known as 'Quackbusters'), which was set up to expose spurious claims to cure on the part of private practitioners, was not grounded in the fear that this organisation (containing many orthodox doctors) would usurp the function of maintaining standards which most professions would wish to exercise for themselves.

This places the professions in a dilemma. State recognition of some kind would resolve this problem, but within the existing legislative framework the kind of registration which could be offered to non-orthodox medicine is not easy to decide. Should they aim for a status like that of dentists or opticians? Or like that of chiropodists or physiotherapists? Any of these solutions will be unacceptable to some groups and unrealistic for others. One of the major problems confronting the complementary medical practitioners is their great diversity both in terms of the actual systems of healing which they adhere to and in terms of the degree of coherence they have achieved as professional groupings.

Another problem is that while most of the practitioners I interviewed had qualifications in one or even several therapies, and while they were conscious of the need to protect the public from untrained practitioners, there is little standardisation of qualifications within the same therapy. Most interviewees had their certificates and diplomas displayed prominently in their waiting rooms or consulting rooms, but whether patients know what level of skill or knowledge such certification might represent is another matter. It would be tempting to see the drive for more standardisation and more definition of educational requirements on the part of professional organisations as a move for closure and social exclusiveness after a period of very rapid growth, but while the groundswell of demand and popularity is so strong closure would not seem an appropriate strategy. There is still much unoccupied territory for practitioners to colonise. Concern with certification is better interpreted as part of an effort to gain publicly recognised status in the face of any changes consequent upon entering the Single European Market in 1992, and some kind of accredited autonomy (as opposed to the ineffectual autonomy of the prophet in the wilderness or the shaman of my hypothetical example). Closure is more of an issue among groups of medically qualified non-orthodox practitioners, some of whom would like to seal their ranks against the penetration of 'lay' practitioners whom they regard as having a lesser entitlement to set up as healers, even as presenting a danger to the public.

It is not possible to give a full account here of the progress and organisation of every non-orthodox medical profession represented in this country. Some have their own historians and the history of others is so young as to be hard to summarise at this stage. I decided instead to give a brief account of developments in three disciplines – homoeopathy, osteopathy and reflexology. These are very different from each other, both in terms of the treatments they offer and in terms of their mode of organisation and development, but between them they exemplify most of the issues which I wish to raise in this chapter.

OSTEOPATHY

Osteopathy had its origins in the ideas of Andrew Taylor Still, an American doctor, who began to propound his theories in Missouri in the 1870s. He founded the first school of osteopathy in 1892. At first he experienced much opposition from conventional doctors, but eventually osteopathy gained a recognised place in healthcare in the United States. Osteopathic training in America today includes much material common to orthodox medical training courses and osteopaths tend to use orthodox forms of medical treatment as well as manipulation. The convergence between osteopathic and orthodox forms of treatment has been less pronounced in this country but it is still probably true to say that osteopathy represents the form of non-orthodox medicine where there is the highest level of mutual understanding between its practitioners and orthodox doctors. Osteopathy was brought to England by Still's pupil Littlejohn who founded the first British training institution, the British School of Osteopathy, in 1913. Fulder estimated that there were about 1139 practising osteopaths in Britain in 1981 (Fulder 1988: 42), but the total will certainly have grown by now, there being at least ten training colleges where osteopathy is the main or only therapy taught. It is one of the best-known and longest established non-orthodox therapies on the British scene.

Osteopathic treatment consists mainly of manual manipulations of different kinds, based on the idea that much pain and disease arise from damage to the function of body structures; dislocations of the musculo-skeletal system, especially the vertebrae, can have an effect on the functioning of other systems of the body, even though the symptoms need not suggest this kind of causation. Some osteopaths have used the idea of the osteopathic 'lesion' – a local imbalance of normal tensions, usually of the spinal column – to describe this kind of causation. Orthodox doctors have been highly critical of this idea, but this is not the only diagnostic vocabulary used by osteopaths today. In Britain most osteopathic consultations are about back problems, but osteopaths claim that their therapy can be used for a much wider range of problems. The actual form of treatment varies according to what the osteopath perceives as the root of the problem. The soft tissue techniques may be experienced by the patient as something like massage, whilst the famous 'high velocity thrust' can make the joint crack suddenly, often with dramatic relief of pain and disfunction.

The publicity material of some professional associations mentions the fact that treatment may be holistic to the extent that it often includes advice about diet and life style as well as 'hands on' manipulation; osteopaths are usually aware of the environmental factors that produce many of the problems they are called upon to treat. However, Baer points out that holism in osteopathy is, in practice, bound to be limited

in that [osteopathy] relies heavily on notions such as the machine analogy and the single causation of disease

and that consequently its ideology is, like that of orthodox medicine and that of chiropractic,

compatible with capitalist ideology in that they depoliticize the sources of disease.

(Baer 1984: 723)

Yet osteopathy has a tradition of hostility to the unnecessary use of drugs and surgical interventions which goes back to Still's objections to the 'heroic' practices of the conventional medicine of his time (osteopathy is taught alongside naturopathy in one major training school). Given what has already been said about public perceptions of the over-technological nature of modern medicine, this may strengthen the popularity of this therapy in future. My interview material confirms that osteopathy is a fairly broad church, as one might expect of such an old and widespread therapy; whilst it has a common core of theory and practice, some of its practitioners lean more to conventional medical approaches, some to more holistic and eclectic therapeutic practice.

At present, however, the organisations representing the professional interests of osteopaths tend to emphasise the compatibility of osteopathy with orthodox medical knowledge and practice rather than the differences. I have already mentioned the convergence between osteopathy and orthodox medical practice which took place in the United States of America. Baer sees the recent revitalisation of osteopathy in America as an indirect consequence of the shortage of primary health care physicians, and an

> indicator of the decline of the professional dominance and autonomy of medicine as well as the ever growing control of health care by the corporate and governmental sectors of the society.
>
> (Baer 1981: 710)

In Britain there has also been considerable convergence, though for different reasons, osteopathy being the form of non-orthodox medicine which is best understood by and most acceptable to orthodox doctors. On the other hand, osteopaths have never claimed competence as primary healthcare substitutes for the GP, nor have they been seen in this light by others. The General Council and Register of Osteopaths claims that

> The osteopathic approach is now accepted as an effective method which can be used either independently or in conjunction with medical treatment. Registered osteopaths do not offer an alternative treatment, but are able to widen the scope of health care available to the public.
>
> (GCRO pamphlet)

Osteopathic education certainly contains much that is also taught to medical students and is almost as long (four years of full-time study for a Diploma in Osteopathy is normal). The British School of Osteopathy now awards a B.Sc. degree approved by the Council for National Academic Awards, chiropractic being the only other non-orthodox therapy in which it is currently possible to obtain a degree. Like several other therapies, osteopathy is practised by some medical doctors as an adjunct to their other forms of treatment, and the London College of Osteopathic Medicine provides courses in osteopathy for doctors only. Osteopaths in Britain, whilst often critical of many aspects of modern medicine and sometimes impatient of the mistrust they still encounter from some doctors at the local level, generally see themselves as working alongside rather than in competition with orthodox doctors.

As with most other non-orthodox therapies, professional organisation at a national level developed out of associations set up by the various training schools for their graduates. The British College of Naturopathy and Osteopathy generated the British Naturopathic and Osteopathic Association, the European School of Osteopathy generated the Society of Osteopaths, the British School of Osteopathy generated the Osteopathic Association of Great Britain, and so forth. As training colleges multiplied, the plethora of organisations has become somewhat confusing. However, in osteopathy the impetus towards professional consolidation and a national definition of standards of training, which is only just beginning to occur among therapies like reflexology or radionics, began as early as 1936 when the General Council and Register of Osteopaths (GCRO) was founded. This register was set up as an independent body (independent, that is, of either the orthodox medical profession or of any particular training school) to regulate standards of training and practice among osteopaths. Currently it recognises the qualifications of graduates of four major schools of osteopathy and hopes that others will become eligible for recognition in future. From the point of view of the GCRO, the chief obstacle to this at present is the need to expand the opportunities for clinical practice which colleges offer to students during training (a common problem in rapidly developing therapies). A member of the British Osteopathic Association (for medically qualified osteopaths only) sits on the board of the GCRO, so there is not a complete disjunction between the medical and the non-medical wings of the profession, although Baer reports a degree of distancing on the part of medically qualified osteopaths from their 'lay' counterparts (Baer 1984: 720).

The GCRO also oversees standards of practice among its members and has developed regular and well tried procedures for hearing cases of breaches of its ethical code, whereby serious cases are passed on to the Professional Ethics Committee. A member who is found guilty of a breach of the Register's code of practice may be reprimanded, fined or even struck off the register, but it is recognised that so long as registration is not a legal requirement for practice, de-registration is not a very effective sanction for the unscrupulous or the inefficient.

Osteopaths have on several occasions sought to consolidate their status in the healthcare system through some kind of state recognition. As early as the 1930s attempts were made to establish a government-sanctioned register, rather like that which is maintained for doctors. These Bills did not get far, but it was this campaign which resulted in the formation of the GCRO (on the advice of a Select Committee of the House of Lords) to act as voluntary, but not state-recognised, agent for the registration of qualified osteopaths. The GCRO continues to seek some kind of statutory position for osteopaths and in 1986 a Private Member's Bill was presented by Roy Galley and a number of Conservative MPs at the request of the GCRO. This did not succeed, but the GCRO intends to continue to campaign for some kind of acceptable statutory recognition. This will not be in terms of registration as a Profession Supplementary to Medicine; what is desired is something more like the status and conditions of practice enjoyed by dentists, although incorporation into the NHS is not sought at present.

Having got this far under its own steam, as it were, it is not surprising that the GCRO does not see membership of one of the pan-professional organisations in the complementary medicine movement as either necessary or beneficial for the professional security of osteopaths. Government insistence that the therapies 'get their act together' did not change their view that they were in the vanguard of the movement and that it was for others to follow and learn from their example. Simon Fielding of the GCRO is reported in the *Journal of Alternative Medicine* as stating that

> It is hoped that the efforts of the osteopathic and chiropractic professions will provide both a precedent and a model for the other major complementary therapies to follow in the future.
>
> (*JAM* November 1986: 8)

This differs from the attitude of some smaller and less established therapies like reflexology, who have placed their hopes for security and (possibly) government recognition in one or other of the various pan-professional organisations described later in this chapter. The GCRO has felt strong enough to do without the help of organisations like the Institute for Complementary Medicine, although it does have links with the Council for Complementary and Alternative Medicine (see below). Some smaller groups of osteopaths have affiliated to one or other of the pan-professional organisations.

This independent insistence of the GCRO on its own role as vanguard of the complementary medicine movement has, not surprisingly, caused irritation amongst those who are trying to unify the professions. The Director of the Institute of Complementary Medicine, for instance, has insisted that

> The idea of state registration should only be considered when the interests of *all* [my emphasis] practitioners have been protected.
>
> (*JAM* November 1986: 1)

This is a major topic of debate among non-orthodox health professionals at present and the GCRO has insisted (even before the government came to accept this view) that where state registration is concerned a 'therapy by therapy' approach is appropriate, with itself as an example of how consolidation and unification can be achieved as the complementary medical professions develop.

HOMOEOPATHY

Homoeopathy had its origin in the thought and experimentation of Samuel Hahnemann (1755–1843), a German doctor who published his *Homoeopathic Materia Medica* in 1811. In his work he elaborated the principle that 'like cures like'; homoeopathic treatment is based on the administration of substances thought to produce similar symptoms to those from which the patient suffers. The substances are dispensed in extremely dilute form, so that no more than microscopic amounts are actually ingested. The dilutions are often based on herbal tinctures, but substances of animal or mineral origin may also be used. Homoeopathy also uses the notion of the constitutional remedy; each person has a characteristic constitution, predispositions to certain kinds of behaviour or tendencies to certain types of symptom, and illness is often treated by the administration of a remedy considered appropriate to the patient's particular constitution. Whichever mode of prescribing is used, the basic idea is that the remedy stimulates the patient's own healing responses, or 'vital force'. Homoeopathy works with the body rather than against the disease.

Homoeopathy very quickly gained a footing in England, where its gentler methods contrasted with the 'heroic' treatments used by other doctors, the drastic purgings and bleedings of the time. Growing disillusion with the violent methods of allopathic medicine contributed to its popularity then, and perhaps the same kind of consideration may account for its revival today, when invasive surgery and the excessive use of drugs with unwanted side effects are being called into question. Homoeopathy and allopathy waged bitter competition for the allegiance of the public during the middle years of the nineteenth century in Britain. In the end, as we have seen, allopathy was to become the form of medicine approved by the state. However, homoeopathy still had much support from people in high places in the mid-nineteenth century, so that when 1858 Medical Act was passed, it was pressure from Lord Grosvenor which ensured that a clause forbidding doctors from practising treatments other than the orthodox allopathic kind was deleted from the original Bill (Nicholls 1988: 144). Allopathy defined its own boundaries very much in relation to homoeopathy at this period, and repeated attempts were made to exclude homoeopaths from the BMA, yet there was in practice much cross-fertilisation of ideas and treatments (Nicholls 1988: 186). With the rise of allopathy as the new medical 'orthodoxy', and with the falling into desuetude of the drastic forms of allopathic treatment which had become repugnant to many patients, homoeopathy suffered eclipse for a time, but its practice never died out in Britain entirely.

The Faculty of Homoeopathy, established in 1844, remained for a long time the only institution where a training in homoeopathy could be obtained, but this training was only available to those who had first trained in orthodox medicine. With the establishment of the NHS in 1948, it was pressure from the Faculty of Homoeopaths and the British Homoeopathic Association which ensured that homoeopathic hospitals would be maintained under the NHS. But whilst the survival of homoeopathy as a valid mode of practice within the NHS was assured, it has received little positive encouragement from the state.

Things changed with the revival in popularity which homoeopathy began to enjoy from about the late 1970s. There was suddenly a proliferation of 'lay' practitioners and colleges providing training for people without medical qualifications. (These practitioners often object to the term 'lay', claiming that it should not be applied to any person properly trained in homoeopathy, only to those untrained enthusiasts who practise out of interest and without payment. I shall use it nonetheless because it is congruent with the use of the term 'lay' in relation to non-medically qualified osteopaths and other complementary practitioners, but the objection is an understandable one.)

Hitherto the conflict between allopathy and homoeopathy had taken the form of debate and competition within the ranks of the medical profession itself. Now there was a proliferation of practitioners with no medical background from whom, on the whole, medical homoeopaths tended to distance themselves. Lay homoeopaths on the other hand were vocal in asserting their right to practise, and stressed the differences in underlying philosophy between their practice and that of allopathy. In osteopathy, as we have seen, there is a distinction between lay and medically qualified osteopaths, but those aspects of Still's ideas which might conflict with the current theories of orthodox medicine have been de-emphasised and students of osteopathy are exposed to many of the ideas and practices to which orthodox medical students are also exposed. Given that lay osteopaths see themselves as working very closely with doctors and complementing their expertise, this division has not been too salient or too troublesome to professional development. In homoeopathy the lay homoeopaths have, on the contrary, tended to stress the different theoretical underpinnings of their practice, a holistic and non-reductionist conception of the human person.

Nicholls has noted the 'Janus faced' nature of homoeopathy:

> In the one direction it has looked toward scientific enquiry and empirical proof, on the other, towards religion, metaphysics and mysticism. The origin of this dialectic lies in the double orientation of Hahnemann's original work: while claiming serious consideration as a rational system of therapeutics based on the observed effects of drugs in health and disease, it also advanced a metaphysical theory of disease and of the action of medicine.
>
> (Nicholls 1988: 259)

For medically qualified homoeopaths this tension has never been so evident as at present. They are not accorded any kind of professional leadership role by the lay homoeopaths, being regarded as too close to the suspect reductionism of allopathic medicine and the modern incarnations of 'heroic' therapy. Many lay homoeopaths also claim that their (usually four-year part-time) training gives them a better grounding in the true principles of homoeopathy than the much shorter courses offered by the Faculty of Homoeopaths. On the other hand, the medical homoeopaths are still marginal to the orthodox medical establishment, in spite of campaigns to introduce courses in homoeopathy into conventional medical training.

Why were the medical homoeopaths so successful in retaining their niche in view of this marginality? Partly no doubt because whilst the general appeal of homoeopathy waned during the mid- to late nineteenth century, it retained an élite clientele, including members of the royal family. Also from its early days a distinctive feature of homoeopathy was its capacity to generate support groups such as the British Homoeopathic Association (which supports the Faculty of Homoeopathy) and the Friends of Homoeopathy (associated with the lay professional organisation, the Society of Homoeopaths) and many smaller groups at the local level. These both propagated knowledge about homoeopathy and acted as campaigning and fund-raising groups on its behalf. More conspicuously than other forms of non-orthodox medicine, homoeopathy seems to have enjoyed the support of enthusiastic evangelists, grateful patients, 'stable users'. It is also a form of medicine which can be used on a 'do-it-yourself' basis. Whilst the intricacies of homoeopathic prescribing can only be mastered after long study, there are many simple remedies which can be used for every-day complaints and for first aid without consultation, and which can be obtained over the counter in many high street chemists' shops. There is therefore a familiarity with homoeopathic remedies diffused among the general population.

Whilst some medical homoeopaths have been sympathetic to the ideas of Steiner and his anthroposophical medicine, they did not readily align themselves with other forms of non-orthodox medicine, and dissociated themselves from disciplines like osteopathy. Yet homoeopathic remedies are widely used by 'lay' practitioners of other kinds of complementary medicine and may be practised in conjunction with radionics, Bach Flower Remedies, and other therapies. In recognition of this the Society of Homoeopaths, the main professional organisation of lay homoeopaths, has restricted its membership to practitioners who offer homoeopathy as their main form of therapy. The Society, however, does recognise that homoeopaths share some common concerns with practitioners of other complementary therapies, and has affiliated to the Council for Complementary and Alternative Medicine (see below).

The Society of Homoeopaths was established in 1978 to give professional unity to non-medically qualified practitioners and it is now the main organisation in Britain for lay homoeopaths, having 1380 members in 1990. Members of the Faculty of Homoeopaths can join, but so long as they remain registered as doctors they do not have voting rights, an arrangement designed to prevent any 'take-over' by doctors. The Society of Homoeopaths was never, like some professional organisations, associated with any particular training college. That is, such associations exist in homoeopathy but unity at a national level has not grown from the coalescence of such associations as it has in many therapies. So homoeopaths are distributed among fewer separate organisations than, say, acupuncturists. However, the British Society of Homoeopaths faces the tricky task of establishing professional credibility and unity in a therapy which has grown very fast and where there is much scope for divergent and individualistic interpretations of the tenets of the founder. In 1988 the Society instituted a complaints procedure with a formally constituted adjudication board to enforce its code of ethics. A few cases have been heard already, but lay homoeopaths have the problem which faces all the other non-orthodox medical professions, i.e. until some form of state registration is compulsory for practitioners, even the threat of being struck off the Society's register has no 'teeth'.

On the matter of standards of training, the Society of Homoeopaths has close links with the Organisation of Independent Homoeopathic Colleges, set up in response to the perceived need to moderate standards among the rapidly proliferating colleges. Graduates of these colleges are normally acceptable for membership of the Society of Homoeopaths, but others may join if they can pass a qualifying examination. The Society of Homoeopaths has set up a working party (which includes one member from the Faculty of Homoeopathy) to look into the scope for setting up a general accreditation board, and although degree status for homoeopathy is not imminent as I write, it is being looked at as a possibility for the future. Homoeopathy has not gone as far down this road as the osteopaths and the chiropractors as yet but the progress that has been made has taken place very rapidly.

An issue which bedevils any attempt to develop a uniform understanding of what a trained homoeopath should have learnt is the matter of purity of practice and faithfulness to Hahnemann's principles. Homoeopathy has been practised in conjunction with orthodox medicine since the nineteenth century and it is sometimes practised in conjunction with other therapies such as radionics or naturopathy by non-orthodox practitioners. From time to time there have been attempts to return to a stricter interpretation of Hahnemann's classical doctrines and to purify homoeopathy of what are seen as modifications of his doctrines or illegitimate admixtures. The Society of Homoeopaths seems to have overcome or avoided such doctrinal divisions to date, but has found it necessary to restrict membership to those who practise homoeopathy as their main therapy. At a professional level, differences in interpretation of Hahnemannian principles do not seem to have been too divisive so far, but agreement has sometimes been precarious.

Unlike the osteopaths, the homoeopaths have not sought state registration, nor do they seem likely to press for this in the very near future, but this may become a goal when professional unification and consolidation have progressed somewhat further.

REFLEXOLOGY

Reflexology has its origins in Chinese medical thought and practice, although it came to Britain via America in the 1960s. It works on principles comparable to those of acupuncture or acupressure inasmuch as pressure on one part of the body (in this case the foot or occasionally the hand) is held to have an effect on another part of the body through a system of internal correspondences. According to the theory of reflexology, energy channels link the various zones of the body to the 'terminal' on the feet. Reflexology largely consists of identifying and treating imbalances in the body through massage of these corresponding areas of the feet. Dr William Fitzgerald expounded these theories in the United States of America in the 1930s and his ideas were taken up and popularised by Eunice Ingham. One of Eunice Ingham's students, Doreen Bayly, was responsible for bringing reflexology to Britain. She set up the Bayly School of Reflexology in 1968, since which time training courses have proliferated.

Although reflexology (or zone therapy as it is known in some European countries) has attracted the interest of some doctors and nurses, as a profession it does not have a large 'medical wing'. It does not therefore enjoy the advantage of influential advocates within the medical profession, but neither does it experience the problem of integrating a 'lay' and a 'medical' group, each with its own experiences, outlook and interpretation of the therapy. In this respect it differs from both homoeopathy and osteopathy. Although some reflexologists will make quite wide claims for their system, regarding it as efficacious in the treatment of all kinds of disorders, as a professional group reflexologists have been modest in their therapeutic claims. The code of ethics of the Association of Reflexologists, one of the major professional organisations, states that

> Members should not diagnose a medical condition, prescribe or treat a specific ailment in connection with Reflexology treatment, or use implements.

Members are also required to refer patients whom they suspect of having any serious disorder to a medical practitioner. On the whole, reflexology aims to treat disease holistically by bringing about a general improvement of energy levels, locating and eliminating imbalances in the body, rather than by targeting and curing particular ailments.

As with homoeopathy and osteopathy, the first stage in professionalisation took place when the various training colleges set up organisations for their ex-students, helping them to arrange insurance, defining codes of proper therapeutic procedure and giving support to new practitioners, as well as promoting public understanding and acceptance of the therapy. The British Reflexology Association was founded in 1985 and is the professional organisation associated with the oldest training school, the Bayly School. It has about two hundred full members and around another hundred student members. The other large group in England (there is another organisation for Scotland) is the Association of Reflexologists, started in 1984, with a current membership of 234. Unlike the British Reflexology Association, the Association of Reflexologists is not associated with any particular training school, but recognises the qualifications of nineteen different training establishments (including the Bayly School). It distinguishes itself from the British Reflexology Association as a constituted organisation with an elected council, and aims to represent the interests of the profession as a whole. On its initiative the Council for Reflexology was set up, with the brief to work towards the standardisation of qualifications and training in reflexology. A total of nine organisations representing reflexologists participated in this initiative which, however, did not survive more than eighteen months. It collapsed in December 1990, apparently due to the fact that very few of the organisations representing reflexologists were acceptable to the Council as 'democratic and properly constituted' (*JACM* January 1991: 11).

Both the major professional organisations in England have codes of ethics and machinery to enforce them, though perhaps it is too early to say how effective these will be as a means of defining professional boundaries and competence. A problem which faces reflexologists more than osteopaths, though homoeopaths have it to some extent, is the problem of marking the boundaries between reflexology and other therapies. Reflexology is taught in many training schools which do not specialise in this therapy alone and it is practised by many whose main therapy is not reflexology. Conversely, many who do regard reflexology as their main activity offer other therapies as well (such as aromatherapy, Bach Flower Remedies, etc.). The code of ethics of the Association of Reflexologists lays down that

> If a member practises other therapies it should be made clear to the patient that they form no part of Reflexology treatment.

There is always the potential problem that a patient might claim malpractice or misconduct on the part of a registered reflexologist in respect of activities which the Association would not define as reflexology. It would not be realistic, however, for the reflexologists to deny membership of their professional associations to those who practise other therapies, since this would remove control over and deny support to such a large number of reflexologists.

A salient feature of the registers of both major associations in reflexology is the predominance of women, especially married women. Reflexologists with whom I discussed this generally attributed it to the accessibility of reflexology training. The training schools vary in what they demand and what they offer, but in general a certificate in reflexology can be obtained after a year of part-time study and the requirements for clinical experience are not onerous. This enables women with young children to combine study with care of their families or other commitments. Reflexology is the kind of therapy which does not require a great deal of capital equipment and which can easily be practised from the home on a part-time basis. These observations apply of course to a number of therapies. However, the interesting thing about reflexology is that not only is its membership predominantly female, but the schools and organisations seem to have (and to have always had) a correspondingly large female presence. In osteopathy the number of women who train and enter practice is increasing and in homoeopathy the intake of some of the 'lay' training schools is predominantly female, yet women seem less conspicuous in the leadership of these professions at the present time, though of course this could change in future.

A major problem facing reflexology is the division of its profesional membership between two major national organisations and registers with (in practice) very little overlap of membership. It is difficult for an outsider to say how far this cleavage relates to different understandings of what reflexology is or should be, or how far it is purely historical and organisational in origin. The division is exacerbated at present by the fact that where political action at the pan-professional level is concerned, the British Reflexology Association favours the approach of the Institute of Complementary Medicine, with whom it works closely and which is regarded by its president as more professional in its methods. The Association of Reflexologists, on the other hand, favours the political style of the National Consultative Council for Alternative and Complementary Medicine to which it is affiliated, regarding this national body as more democratic.

FISSION AND FUSION

These accounts have been no more than schematic and there will be organisations and developments that I have failed to mention, but they illustrate the general problems facing practitioners in terms of consolidating their professional credibility and status. However, they also show that each group has its own peculiar history, giving rise to particular strengths or cleavages. In no two groups is the mix of centripetal and centrifugal forces quite the same.

As one might expect in a situation where the professional works very much on his or her own, with little in the way of direct bureaucratic or peer group pressure, there is much scope for practitioners to develop their own creative elaborations of the therapies in which they were trained, based on their own ideas or clinical experiences. When some subsequently found training schools based on these individual perspectives they demonstrate the vigour of their therapeutic traditions and help to satisfy the enormous demand for training in non-orthodox therapies, but they also give impetus to the centrifugal tendencies bound to be present in dispersed professional groups subject to little external control. On the other hand, there has been consider- able organisational convergence among some of these historically distinct professional groups, stimulated by a strong realisation of their common political interests. Government exhortation that complementary therapies 'get their act together' before any official recognition can be bestowed upon them, together with apprehension that 1992 will bring danger from which they can only defend themselves by a united front have had the effect of forcing the pace of this convergence. The tendencies to fission and fusion are precariously balanced at the moment, but I would hazard a guess that the forces of fusion will have prevailed in most therapies by the end of this century.

In disciplines like reflexology and homoeopathy the proliferation of training schools has taken place particularly suddenly, ahead of the develop- ment of any well established national professional organisation capable of co-ordinating an agreed system of accreditation and regulation of standards. In reflexology (as in many other therapies, including osteopathy at an earlier phase) the different training schools then set up their own professional organisations for their alumni and the problem facing such groups is to overcome the results of this reduplication of efforts whilst allowing for a tolerable diversity in therapeutic practice. In groups such as homoeopathy and acupuncture, a greater obstacle to unity within the profession has been the division between medically qualified and 'lay' practitioners. Where the medically qualified still see themselves as firmly located within the orthodox medical profession (even where, as in the case of the homoeopaths, the relationship has been antagonistic) it has been hard for them to make common cause with lay practitioners, who may seek parity of prestige with doctors but are less likely to treat the medical profession as their primary reference group. Differences in styles of training and in clinical context are further obstacles to the growth of a common political and professional culture. A further source of tension in several groups has been the question of how far the original principles of the therapy (however these are perceived) can legitimately be modified by admixture with medical practices such as orthodox drug therapy, other non-orthodox treatments or any other kind of accommodation or reformulation. Homoeopathy, acupuncture and many of the mind–body therapies have all had their classical purists and their revisionists.

The drive for fusion, powered by a perception of the political weakness of a divided profession, has been more successful in some professional groups than in others. Osteopathy seems to be doing well on this front and the GCRO seems to have gained some recognition of its claim to speak on behalf of osteopathy in general, even though a considerable number of osteopaths are registered with other groups. But reflexologists, though working hard at the issue, are divided by the very forces that sought to unite them, being affiliated to different pan-professional groupings. The emergence of any group in the near future which can claim to speak for the entire community of homoeopaths seems improbable, doctrinal and lay/medical divisions being too profound, although considerable progress is being made.

Most professions, like the ones I have described, have by now taken some steps towards coalescence. In 1989 the Confederation of Radionic and Radiesthetic Organisations was established to unite practitioners of medical dowsing and distance healing through radionics, and to co-ordinate training in these therapies. A Council for Acupuncture now exists to regulate standards of training in acupuncture. Among spiritual healers there have been two broad groupings – the British Alliance of Healing Associations and the somewhat more medically oriented Confederation of Healing Organisations, to which the Alliance is now affiliated. Both have concerned themselves with the development of proper standards of conduct and training in healing. The Confederation claims to be working towards a standard professional qualification with national recognition. (It thus has the curious task of attempting to professionalise an activity which is often not practised as professional work at all, but either as an extension of spiritual ministry or as the expression of a mysterious natural gift.) In a number of professions, international federations or pressure groups have been established to encourage communication between those who practise the same therapy in different countries and to care for the interests of practitioners at a European level.

But even if each form of non-orthodox medicine were united in a single undisputed professional grouping, this would not dispose of the problems presented by the fact that the therapies which can be classified as non-orthodox have highly diverse origins and highly diverse therapeutic procedures. In the last decade there have been several attempts to promote the interests of practitioners of all the therapies on a broad front. I have already described the British Holistic Medical Association (see p. 110) which does not aim to represent the professional interests of non-orthodox medicine, but which has certainly done a great deal to promote their use within the NHS and to encourage links with the orthodox medical profession. In 1982 the Research Council for Complementary Medicine was established, with a brief to encourage and fund research in the complementary therapies. The RCCM has sponsored some substantial research projects into both the clinical and the social aspects of complementary medicine, and has taken a special interest in the development of research methodology which is appropriate to the nature of complementary medicine yet rigorous enough to have scientific credibility.

However, only three organisations can be regarded (or would regard themselves) as in any sense tackling the problem of the political and professional unification of all the non-orthodox therapies. Of these the Council for Complementary and Alternative Medicine (CCAM), established in 1985 in the wake of the BMA report on alternative therapies, has perhaps the most modest claims. This group consists of nine member organisations representing most of the well-known therapies and aims to help secure the position of complementary medicine in this country and to provide a forum for practitioners. Whilst many of the member organisations will include medical doctors, the CCAM has avoided medical domination. Its chairman Ken Shifrin claims that

> we do not intend to have our professions run by doctors – but that means we have to demonstrate we don't need doctors running them. When the government wants advice on medical matters it goes to the doctors and asks them. We know what will happen if they go to the doctors and ask them to advise them on us. So we have to put forward a coherent case of why we should be listened to as independent professionals.
>
> (Thomas 1990a: 23)

The response of the CCAM to the setting up of two other pan-professional organisations, the Institute of Complementary Medicine (ICM) and the National Consultative Council (NCC), has been to resist ceding its claim to act as a national forum for the different kinds of complementary medicine in their search for forms of state recognition which suit their needs and for a more uniform definition of standards of training and practice. It has, however, concentrated on consolidating progress and consensus among existing member organisations. Ken Shifrin explained why the CCAM has not attempted to expand its original membership:

> Well, we've never wanted to, to be honest. We've never tried to act as an umbrella organisation. It has never been our policy to be that. Most of us can remember other attempts to create umbrella organisations and how

they all foundered as the result of arguments and ego trips. That has made us very cautious. We don't want to make the same mistake.... We saw a danger in what we were trying to do becoming unworkable if we took on new members. We really aren't anything more than a convenient meeting point or focus if you like. We don't believe in the need for an umbrella organisation. The movement is too diverse and its membership is too diverse.

(Thomas 1990b: 20)

Since it claims to act as a forum and a channel of communication for (rather than as a political representative of) the non-orthodox medical professions, the CCAM does not have a general policy as to how these professions should be integrated into the national provision of healthcare:

CCAM is fully committed to assisting whichever therapies choose, in their own time, to seek statutory registration and also to promote the cause, in whichever ways are appropriate, of any therapy that decides not to seek registration in the foreseeable future.

(*CCAM News* January 1988: 1)

The CCAM has therefore tended to see itself as facilitator of the process by which the diverse complementary therapies choose the paths they find most appropriate in order to achieve greater professional unity, rather than as an overseeing regulating body.

The Institute for Complementary Medicine was established as an independent charity in 1982. Like the CCAM, it claims to be independent of the orthodox medical profession. Its director Anthony Baird claims that:

There's no institutionalised contact between us and medical organisations. They've still got to come to terms with what we're offering. The only regular contact we have is with individual doctors or doctor's practices contact us for advice and information.

(*JACM* February 1990: 27)

Compared with the CCAM, however, the ICM seems to have set itself much broader goals. It clearly works on a much larger scale of funding, and publishes its own journal, the *Journal of Complementary Medicine*. While the ICM does have pan-professional aspirations, it is constituted as a charity rather than a professional association or council. It does run an Association for Complementary Medicine for individual practitioners and sympathisers, but this is not the best-known of its activities. It also supports research into non-orthodox medicine but again, is less well known for this kind of activity than the RCCM. Where it has made a very distinctive contribution is as a public information service. It has always attached great importance to its role as a source of independent information about complementary medicine in general or about specific therapies in particular for members of the public who might wish to use them, and lately it has set up 'Public Information Points' (PIPS) in a number of areas. It also runs many short courses on particular therapies or aspects of complementary healthcare for practitioners, members of the medical and paramedical professions and for the public.

An issue which the ICM has seen as particularly urgent in view of its director's perception of what is likely to happen in 1992 has been the development of a general register of complementary practitioners. These practitioners have to meet standards of training defined by the ICM, and the register is therefore independent of the registers of particular professions. Volunteers who agree to operate local Public Information Points can only disseminate the names of practitioners already on this register. In the area where I conducted my study of practitioners very few had actually registered, although probably many would have qualified for inclusion in terms of their experience and qualifications. This could be because established practitioners do not usually have problems in attracting patients and they are generally already registered with one or more national professional associations. Presumably therefore they see less advantage in this arrangement than might members of the public (among whom, as we have also seen, there is a great demand for such information).

Training standards are a crucial issue if any system of registration (whether government-recognised or independent) is to gain the confidence of the public and the ICM has set itself the ambitious task of establishing national educational standards for the complementary therapies. Recognising that complementary therapies are very diverse and that uniform qualifications for the whole lot would be impracticable, the ICM's long-term aim has been to establish a British Council of Complementary Medicine which would oversee standards of training and practice, each therapy being represented on the Council. The current disunity of the professions is of course a major obstacle to this end and the ICM has attempted to facilitate the coming together of fragmented groups representing the same or closely related disciplines. It claims some credit for the establishment of the Confederation of Healing Organisations (*Complementary Medicine Supplement* July 1987: 4) and has stimulated the formation of the Association of Osteopathic Practitioners, a union of osteopathic groups outside the GCRO. Another major objective of the ICM has been the setting up of a university of complementary medicine which will offer training in the natural therapies to degree standard. This is expected to open in the London Docklands in 1996.

So far as professionalisation is concerned, the ICM, like the CCAM, has described its role as a facilitating one, assisting groups to realise aims appropriate to the kinds of therapies they practice. The ICM, however, has developed a different political style from that of the CCAM, partly no doubt (as its director Anthony Baird claims) as a result of its having been set up originally as a charity rather than a professional organisation or council. Whilst the CCAM sees itself as a forum for different organisations to meet and air common problems, the ICM has tended to see itself as occupying what might be called an independent leadership role. Anthony Baird states:

> What we have been arguing – as we have done for years, and done it very successfully – is to come to us and we will help you find your feet, put you on the way. We don't care who does it as long as it gets done.
>
> (Thomas 1990b: 27)

This approach has led to accusations that the ICM is undemocratic, that it claims to lead the complementary therapies while not allowing for direct and formal representation from them. The ICM, unlike the CCAM, does not invite affiliation from organisations as such, but tends to work through informal contacts in the different organisations, giving advice and encouraging the development of unified professional aims. As far as I know, there is nothing very secret about these contacts, but the fact that the ICM chooses itself whom to deal with, rather than letting organisations themselves choose who will advise on a particular therapy, is the source of some resentment and misunderstanding. Certainly it has laid itself open to accusations of paternalism. Denis Haviland, Chair of the Confederation of Healing Organisations, refers to the 'obscurity of ICM leadership' and stresses that what is needed is a democratically organised council to defend complementary therapies and safeguard their interests (Haviland 1989: 12). A letter in the *Journal of Alternative and Complementary Medicine* from the President of the Association of Qualified Curative Hypnotherapists voices more specific doubts:

> When the ICM decided to start a 'register of hypnotherapists' we were not advised, invited or informed in any way.... We had (and still have) no knowledge of the methods of hypnosis utilised or the standards of treatment advocated by the 'advisers' who are making decisions regarding inclusion in, or exclusion from, this 'register'.
>
> (*JACM* January 1990: 9)

Evidently some organisations sense (and resent) an implication that they are not capable of setting national standards themselves for their own practitioners.

In the ICM and the CCAM we find two different models for pan-professional unification. In the ICM we have the model of the independent advisory body which can mediate both among the therapies and organisations themselves and also between therapies and the government, being in a position to offer objective advice about standards etc. In the CCAM we have the model of the representative council generated by demand from the therapies themselves, not in a position or even wishing to lay down standards but assisting particular groups to realise their own aims and addressing matters of common concern. These models typify a dilemma which remains to be solved, namely how to hasten the unification of a profession which is really a conglomeration of separate and specialised professions, each with its own history. It is not even clear that all these groups will wish to aim for the same kind of professional status, starting as they do from different historical positions and being driven by different contingencies. Even assuming common aims, the different groups of practitioners are too diverse in aims and history to unite under their own impetus as yet, but any independent body which attempts this work on their behalf is liable to be regarded as at worst dictatorial, and at best dilettante. The CCAM regards the ICM as undemocratic and the ICM regards the CCAM as ineffective and both these criticisms have been made by outside commentators as well:

> CCAM... has no structure, no charisma and no money (or not enough). ICM... aspires to lead, decide standards and campaigns. But it also has money problems, is prone to dictate and is unaccountable.
>
> (*JACM* leader August 1989: 5)

The division within the movement has been deplored by those who are not exclusively committed to either group, though usually with some understanding of the historical and practical circumstances which have brought this state of affairs about and not without appreciation of the work which both organisations have done. Supporting the newly formed National Consultative Council, Paul Webster comments that:

> The (ICM and CCAM) have both done more than most to advance many aspects of natural medicine and they both have much to offer. I am sure that by using the best of both organisations to support a new larger body something worthwhile could be created.... Before the leading players actually destroy the business they play in, is it too late for dedicated and enthusiastic 'outsiders' to offer advice which could save them from themselves? Is it impossible to find ways of fitting both ICM and the CCAM into an enlarged scheme of things?
>
> (Letter in *JACM* October 1989: 9)

The National Consultative Council for Alternative and Complementary Medicine was born from the Working Party on Alternative and Complementary Medicine, itself a product of the British Congress of Complementary and Alternative Practitioners, an exhibition-cum-professional meet organised by Swan House Events which is now an annual event in London.

In October 1989 a meeting of representatives of practitioners' organisations met in London, convened by the BRICAPP Working Party. An interim executive council was formed pending the proper election of an executive council in January 1990. Its newly elected president, Maurice Newbound, described the aims of the NCC as to promote inter-organisational co-operation, to attend to the matter of the standardisation of education and training and to disseminate information about complementary medicine. These aims do not seem too different from those of the other 'pan-professional' organisations, but Newbound stressed that

> we are the first attempt to create a single political umbrella organisation in this country based on the democratic procedures of the recognised electoral process and as such we believe that we have the best chance yet of succeeding where no previous attempts have succeeded.... We invite all healthcare organisations to sit down and talk with us on how we can provide the best service for the public and such talks need not intrude in the internal affairs of these organisations unless they ask us.
>
> (Thomas 1990c: 11)

Membership of the NCC is composed of organisations only, and claims a total membership of forty groups at the time of writing. The NCC now represents a way out of the organisational impasse to many people in the complementary medicine movement although it remains to be seen whether it will obtain the widespread support it needs in order to transcend efforts of the other two pan-professional organisations or whether it will have an even more divisive effect by simply constituting a third group parallel to the others. It has not been welcomed without reservation. As we might expect, the ICM has remained aloof and the CCAM uncommitted. As yet the GCRO have not associated themselves with it, seeing no need for any kind of umbrella grouping and the BHMA has not come out in explicit favour at the time of writing. It may also turn out that the government's apparent recent change of mind regarding the need for the complementary therapies to form a united grouping will take some of the impetus from this attempt to overcome inter-professional divisions.

In Chapter 6 I pointed out that as well as the non-orthodox medical professions, each with its own degree of coherence and organisation, there is a wider complementary medicine movement, which includes not only the practitioners themselves but those members of the public who support them and value their services, those with a material interest in their prosperity (such as manufacturers of herbal and homoeopathic medicine and other 'natural' health products and equipment), and sympathetic members of the orthodox medical and paramedical professions. Members of these wider constituencies have an interest in the unification of the professions insofar as this unification is necessary if their survival is to be ensured. Yet they cannot do much to hasten this process themselves, hence the frustration of many well-wishers who observe the sometimes rather unedifying wrangles that have taken place over the rightful leadership of the pan-professional effort. Fear of what 1992 might bring and ideological warfare with the more rigid sections of the orthodox medical profession has created a situation in which members of the movement perceive a need to professionalise more rapidly than might have been the 'natural' pace.

But is there ever a 'natural' pace of professionalisation? Do not the histories of professions like orthodox medicine and nursing demonstrate that mobilisation usually takes place when there are particular prizes to be won, privileges or boundaries to defend? The history of acknowledged professions has shown that even when they are generally desired, unity and univocality are not always achieved unaided. Wakley, Warburton and others were campaigning for the unification of the medical profession for thirty years before the 1858 Act was passed and this gestation period also saw the gradual development of a general professional association, the British Medical Association, which enabled doctors of different kinds to speak with a single voice. The divisions of interest within the medical world were by no means eliminated in the course of this process, but whether doctors would have achieved the unity they did without the interest of the state is doubtful. The emergence of a unified profession served the interests of the state in the prosecution of a concept of public health in which the state had a right and a duty to intervene in such issues as the control of contagious diseases, public sanitation and the regulation of the poor, especially those poor people who were unable to work because they were sick or mentally ill. The legislation which both endowed the medical profession with state-sanctioned authority and provided an integrated system of registration represented a convergence of the interests of the medical profession(s) and the state.

In the present situation there are no obvious issues around which the interests of the state and those of the non-orthodox medical professions might converge so as to hasten unification, or at any rate none that both parties recognise. Conceivable scenarios in which such a convergence might take place would be if (on the negative side) there were a number of public scandals in which, say, patients of non-orthodox practitioners died through malpractice or inefficiency, or (on the positive side) if it were proved that some branch of complementary medicine had developed a major break-through in the treatment or prevention of AIDS. In the absence of such conditions, the non-orthodox medical professions are left to themselves to negotiate their historical and ideological differences. Professionalisation is accepted as a goal but takes place perforce in the space left by earlier waves of medical professionalisation.

But this space is a very oddly shaped one, and full of contradictions. At the moment, non-orthodox medicine operates from a position of strength so far as the market is concerned, or so it would seem. It has captured an important part of the market for medical services, especially for holistic healthcare. Non-orthodox practitioners are strong in terms of demand for their services but conscious that this purchase on the market might be transient. The most obvious threat is from orthodox medicine, not just in the sense that this profession might attempt (or might collude with attempts) to outlaw their practice or marginalise it further. As we have seen, both holistic healthcare and non-orthodox therapies are practised by some orthodox doctors and there is always the possibility that orthodox doctors might capture these markets for themselves. This may explain the fears expressed by many of my interviewees about doctors who practise acupuncture or homoeopathy after completing short courses or with superficial qualifications. To obtain some kind of recognised and reasonably stable professional status is therefore understandably high on the agenda of most groups of complementary practitioners, though there is not always agreement as to the best means to achieve this security.

It is doubtful whether any strategy for professionalisation could ever be a comfortable and conflict-free process for any occupational group. The particular problem which the non-orthodox medical professions face is that whilst they have managed to capture a very substantial share of the market for healthcare, this very success has entailed the over-rapid increase in more or less autonomous practitioners and training institutions. This share of the market can only be defended if these practitioners and institutions are prepared to yield some of the free-wheeling autonomy they enjoy, whether to the state or to some state-approved unifying agency. The trouble is that autonomy is indeed a very enjoyable condition, and generally neither individuals nor organisations are persuaded to cede it readily.

Conclusion

Why did complementary medicine become so popular in the late seventies and eighties, and will this popularity continue into the nineties and the next century? If it does continue, does anything need to be 'done' about complementary medicine, and by whom – or is its present status and practice satisfactory?

To answer the first question, let me recapitulate the sociological argument which has been developed over the earlier chapters. The use of complementary medicine is not restricted to any one group in the population, but probably its increase has been greatest among those broad sectors of the middle class and upper working class whose standards of living have risen continually, if rather jerkily, over the past three decades. The generation of working men and women who were raising families just after the Second World War gratefully accepted the public medicine offered by the NHS. Many of their sons and daughters can now afford to pay for some private medicine and some of them choose non-orthodox medicine, especially for problems which orthodox medicine cannot cure but only 'manage'. For this generation, brought up to take the existence of the NHS for granted and indeed to value its services highly, using private medicine with any regularity involves quite an important change in habit – it is not just a question of having more money to dispose of but of altering patterns of expenditure, making changes in the allocation of personal or household resources. Users of complementary medicine like Mrs Peake, whose case I discussed in Chapter 4, were aware of the fact that whilst they themselves felt that good healthcare was worth budgeting for, even if it meant sacrificing some other items of consumption, many of their friends and peers were not yet prepared to make this change; healthcare for them was something which should always be free and for which the individual or household should not have to earmark funds.

In general, the policy of the present government has been to encourage people to make this shift, mainly by privileging expenditure on private health insurance schemes. Certainly spending on medicines and medical fees and services, as measured by the government's Family Expenditure Survey, has risen in relation to total household expenditure during the past ten years. Whether or not this change in household budgeting is entirely the result of Conservative policy, and how permanent it is likely to be in view of current inflation rates, I am not qualified to say. But some of this increase in expenditure certainly goes on non-orthodox healthcare, and it is likely that in families where complementary medicine has been found to be really helpful, this experience will have enduring effects on the consumption culture of the household.

But economic arguments only explain the increased use of private medicine in a general way. They tell us nothing about why complementary medicine in particular should have grown so dramatically. Most attempts to answer this question (see Taylor 1984, Fulder 1988) refer to perceived inadequacies in orthodox medicine, especially as delivered by the NHS, and my own research largely confirms this view of the matter.

Private affluence often goes with public squalor; it would be unkind to call the NHS squalid, but its underfunding has led to problems of which the public is only too conscious, although some groups are affected more than others. Long waiting lists for treatment affect those with chronic conditions most, and services like physiotherapy (which involve personal labour rather than high technology) are in short supply. It is not at all difficult to account for the demand for private medicine in areas like the treatment of chronic musculo-skeletal problems where the inadequacies of public provision are particularly obvious.

But these deficiencies relate to the nature of modern medical science and practice as much as to problems of funding. Orthodox medicine has become ever more technological in its approach, favouring interventions based on 'objective' knowledge about the patient, or rather his/her body, which take no account of the subjective and social experience of illness. The physician increasingly handles and interprets the products of all kinds of mechanical 'scanning' of the sick person's body and prescribes technical interventions. Dialogue about what either symptoms or interventions might mean to the patient takes place (if it takes place at all) predominantly with nurses, counsellors, social workers – paramedical or non-medical professionals. In short, cure has increasingly become detached from care, especially in the context of the hospital.

In some areas, especially in cases of acute disease or malfunction, such modes of treatment have been very successful and are much appreciated by the public who will eagerly participate in efforts to raise funds for new scanning devices or incubators, or in locating suitable bone marrow donors. There are many areas, however, where this kind of heroic expertise is either unavailable at the present time, or is much less appropriate. The problem of senile dementia does not lend itself to the magic bullet approach and the technological approach to childbirth is not acceptable to all parturient women. Further doubts have been generated at the level of primary health-care. Much primary healthcare is experienced by patients as simply the dispensation of drugs, often without any proper explanation of their side effects and with little attention to those personal and social circumstances of the individual which might be highly relevant to his/her illness. Many users of the GP's services will be forgiving to a doctor whom they like and who they know tries to deliver as sympathetic a service as is possible under the circumstances. But the culture of orthodox medical science is such that the solution to the problem of a crowded surgery is likely to be seen in terms of the delivery of yet more drugs, more 'objective' scans and more technical monitoring of the body with even less attention to the social and spiritual person of the sufferer. The attachment of community nurses or social workers to some health centres represents an attempt to rescue 'care' from the over-riding focus on 'cure', but cure and care remain hard to integrate.

There is still a large category of (mainly chronic) diseases for which doctors cannot even provide an unambiguous cure, AIDS being the egregious example. Many, however, are diseases of varying seriousness which have been with us for a long time, such as the common cold or psoriasis. Some are perceived as 'modern' diseases – ME, for instance or the increasingly reported childhood allergies. Whether conditions like these are really new diseases is not the issue here. At the public level they raise anxiety as to whether modern medicine is really in 'control' of disease. For the individual patient they are experienced as interfering with ordinary work and leisure no less because they are chronic and undramatic rather than acute.

Not all people who are discontented with any of these aspects of orthodox NHS medicine will resort to complementary medicine. There are many responses, both political and personal, active and passive, to such disillusion. Some discontents will, however, stray into the territory of non-orthodox medicine as a result of their inability to get the kind of cure/care they want from orthodox medicine and some, having strayed, will stick with it. I use the term 'stray' to indicate that such pathways to complementary medicine often exhibit a large element of the random and the fortuitous – the patient *happened* to have a colleague who had used an osteopath and recommended him/her to the sufferer, a chiropractor *turned out to be* the nearest practitioner. When we look at sufferers' own accounts of their efforts to get well, such as I discussed in Chapter 3, terms like 'planned expedition' or 'purposeful foray' seem more appropriate to describe the total effort, characterised as they are by singular determination and systematic attempts to assemble all relevant information on their disease and to explore all possible treatments.

Some have seen this increased resort to complementary medicine as evidence of an important cultural shift in thinking about health, the person and the body (see Coward 1989). Many complementary therapies certainly marry a New Age concern with personal development with a stress on the responsibility of the individual for his or her own healthcare. They recommend their methods not just as a technical deviation from orthodox medicine, but as embodying a quite different concept of healing and of the roles which healer and sufferer play in this process. This concept of the individual's ultimate responsibility for his/her own health appears like an echo of an idea very explicitly expressed by Conservative politicians and ideologists, that it is time for people in Britain to depend less on the state and more on themselves. In the field of healthcare this translates into a concern with preventive health which is focussed on individuals (eating the right food, getting regular health checks, not indulging in sexual or recreational activities which are defined as 'risky') rather than on environments (eliminating stressful or dangerous conditions at work, reducing the chances of picking up infections in hospital, improving the housing of the poor). The resemblance between these modes of thinking is superficial (New Age therapy aims to wean the patient from dependence on medical authority, Conservative ideology speaks of the individual's independence of the state) but probably not fortuitous. I view both New Age rhetoric and Conservative ideology as modern transformations of an individualism which is very fundamental to English cultural life, but the renewed expression of this individualism is certainly having an important effect on current public discourse about health.

On the basis of my research on patients, I observed that new users of non-orthodox medicine seemed impelled by a pragmatic concern to get relief from a specific disease on terms that were acceptable to themselves. The explicit pursuit of cultural ideals about healthcare did not much enter into their stories of the decisions that had led them to the consulting room of a complementary therapist in the first place. In the practitioners' narratives however, ideas about what healthcare should be like were very articulately and spontaneously expressed. Allowing for a considerable range of values and viewpoints among a fairly diverse group of therapists, a desire to redefine the patient–therapist relationship emerged as a constant theme. The ideal of holistic treatment, in which the therapist deals with the patient not merely as a physical body but as a social and spiritual being, was widely subscribed to, even though some therapists admitted that they could not achieve it in their own practice. An essential aspect of holistic healing as conceived by these practitioners is the active and participatory role of the patient, who should be encouraged to make choices and to understand what is going on. Most practitioners claimed that they did try to communicate this to patients and to educate them in self-responsibility, and the accounts of patients themselves indicate awareness (and usually appreciation) of this communication. So whilst most patients are probably not motivated by a positive concern to redefine healthcare and the therapeutic relationship in the first place, what the complementary therapist tells them or does with them may well make sense of their unsatisfactory experience as patients of orthodox medicine, and dispose them to further experimentation with the non-orthodox. I have tended to be cautious of purely cultural interpretations of the rise of complementary medicine on the grounds that there is plenty of empirical evidence for mundane institutional origins – deficiencies in the delivery of orthodox medicine, for instance, or the expansion of consumerism. But cultural innovation often takes place in the space provided by institutional deficiency; exposure to non-orthodox thinking about healthcare and therapy will encourage and reinforce such shifts in patients' expectations even if the original reasons for consultation were pragmatic and situational.

The demand for complementary medicine is therefore constructed out of various specific demands – for more caring delivery of medical services, for cures for intractable diseases, for more participation in healthcare choices, for a more preventive approach to health. All of these demands could be met by changes in the way in which orthodox medicine is practised. However, if there are neither radical changes within the orthodox medical camp nor a major recession affecting the spending power of the classes where use of complementary medicine is widespread, those for whom some kind of non-orthodox healthcare has proved satisfactory will probably use it more and more. Whilst my own research suggests that wholesale rejection of orthodox medicine is very unlikely, the demand for complementary medicine will certainly continue in the foreseeable future because the conditions which helped to create it have not gone away (although its actual rate of growth may be affected by all kinds of other factors). This being so, we cannot ignore the problems which it presents.

POLICY PROBLEMS

These problems, and the responsibility for solving them, are defined differently by the various actors on the medical scene. So far as orthodox medicine is concerned, complementary medicine presents a threat to its credibility and professional position. To doctors who have some interest in and sympathy with non-orthodox therapies the chief problem is one for doctors themselves to solve:

How can we change our own practice so as to incorporate the features which patients of complementary medicine have found lacking in it?

To those members of the medical profession who are either uncommitted or unsympathetic, the chief problem is one for complementary medicine itself to solve:

Can non-orthodox medicine prove itself to be efficacious in terms which modern scientific medicine approves and understands?

For the public who use the services of healthcare professionals of various kinds, the most pressing problem is:

How can we be sure that we receive proper information about complementary medicine and are protected from the unqualified and the quack?

This is a problem which can be resolved in part through the initiative of 'consumers' themselves or their representatives, to the extent that information about complementary medicine can be (and is being) collected and disseminated to the public at large by non-statutory organisations and commercial agencies. Quality control and reassurance, whether it took the form of state registration or the official accreditation of training in non-orthodox medicine, would have to be the result of action on the part of the government and the complementary medical professions themselves.

For those of the public who are convinced that complementary medicine is generally beneficial, a major question is:

How can this form of medicine be made more accessible?

This, again, is a problem which would require the initiative of the government and the professions, although pressure groups can campaign for this availability.

From the point of view of the practitioners themselves, we have seen that the most pressing problem is that of professional security:

How can we ensure that in 1992 we are not overtaken by events in the absence of either any provision for statutory registration or of uniform and publicly accredited standards of training?

This is a problem which the complementary professions are attempting to solve under their own steam, while feeling somewhat hampered by government inactivity.

For the state's view of the situation has been:

Complementary medicine does not present any problems at the present time which demand our initiative.

This is only a very sketchy summary of the situation but it will be perfectly clear that not only is there conflict as to what the main problems consist of, but much disagreement about whose responsibility it is to solve them.

EFFICACY

Representatives of orthodox medicine have asserted time and again that before there can be any question of professional rapprochement between orthodox and non-orthodox medicine the latter must prove its efficacy scientifically. Some complementary practitioners regard this as mere professional defensiveness on the part of doctors. What is so great about science anyway, and why should it be the only touchstone of truth? Indeed, may not the definitions of science and scientificity with which doctors work be very limited ones, doggedly Newtonian compared with the most recent developments in the thinking of physicists (Graham 1990: 38ff)?

'Scientificity' is a debatable, even manipulable concept, but nevertheless I do not think that this demand for scientific proof should be dismissed as rhetoric. The culture of modern medicine is, in its own terms, highly scientific – both its weakness and its strength, some might say. Some doctors, such as those involved in the holistic health movement, find it possible to discourse about medical practice outside this idiom, but in general medical institutions and outlook make this difficult. Also, scientific discourse is not the prerogative of doctors; its language enables them to communicate with other scientists and to secure credibility with a public which very largely approves of science in principle even if it does not always understand it.

For many individual complementary practitioners this is not seen as an urgent question. They feel that they know from experience that their treatments work. Scientific proof might appease others, but it is not necessary to their own self-confidence. Nor is it necessary to ensure clientele, since for many patients the question of scientific proof is equally irrelevant. They have already tried orthodox remedies which are supposed to have been subjected to such rigorous testing but which have not worked for them. This has taught them that statistical rates of efficacy are less important than finding the treatment that works for the particular individual, who may or may not represent any kind of norm.

Both the practitioner and the patient are concerned with the individual, and this is what renders complementary medicine attractive to many. It also makes it difficult to devise tests of efficacy which would apply to large groups of people, let alone whole populations. The homoeopathic practitioner does not prescribe for hay fever or for arthritis but for a particular patient who describes his/her symptoms in terms of hay fever or arthritis. Where treatment does not involve the taking of drugs or medicine, there is also the problem of how to devise double blind trials. You can compare acupuncture treatment which uses the meridian points which acupuncturists themselves regard as genuinely significant with a 'dummy' treatment, inserting needles in a random way. To the extent that most western patients will not normally be aware of where the correct points are, they need not know which is the 'real' treatment and the strength of the 'placebo effect' can be measured if nothing else. But one can hardly simulate osteopathic or chiropractic manipulation, or at least not without the danger of harm to the patient. (These are only some of the practical and ethical issues involved in devising suitable trials for non-orthodox treatments; for more detailed discussions see BMA 1986: 79ff, Conway 1986, Watt and Wood 1988.)

Notwithstanding these problems, many members of the complementary health movement think that the quest for a scientific methodology for evaluating complementary therapies should be taken very seriously. Though research in this area is, as I have already pointed out, underfunded and can only progress slowly, there is a growing literature on such trials. The Research Council for Complementary Medicine, one of whose major objectives is to develop methods of evaluation appropriate to non-orthodox medical treatments, holds regular methodology conferences and has funded a number of research projects in this area.

Is this effort appropriately directed, or should we agree with those supporters of complementary medicine who see it as simply toadying to the demands of the orthodox medical profession, who will never accept them on equal terms anyway? The demand that complementary medicine prove its worth in some objective way seems to me to be quite fair. Public claims should be supported with evidence that the public can understand and approve. A patient should be able to embark upon a treatment with some rough idea of the chances of its success, based on more than the practitioner's individual evaluation and perhaps selective recall of its effects on other patients. Certainly if complementary practitioners claim to provide a service which is *better* than that of orthodox medicine they should be prepared to demonstrate that this is the case in a systematic way. Anecdotal evidence is relevant, considered as evidence, but it cannot be regarded as proof, nor does it tell us anything about the likely rates of success for a particular treatment. It may be unrealistic to expect the non-orthodox professions to meet all such demands, given the underprivileged situation which they enjoy in relation to orthodox medicine, especially with regard to research funding, but the desire for proof is not in itself unreasonable.

On the other hand, the patient is not offered proof of efficacy in the case of all orthodox treatments. Not all orthodox medical procedures have been subjected to comparative clinical trial; where they have, there is not always unequivocal agreement among doctors as to what the best orthodox treatment for a particular problem should be, nor is the patient invariably counselled about the relative success rates of different treatments or precedures for the same problem, or even involved in decisions about which procedure might be suitable in his/her case. There is the suspicion that many procedures are used because the technology is available and somebody's job is the more secure if this technology is used.

In any case, is not the concept of efficacy used in orthodox medicine too narrow? Efficacy must be a necessary condition for the decision to use a particular procedure or treatment, but sometimes it is not the only condition to be met. Removing a woman's breast may be an efficacious way of eliminating breast cancer, but it does not follow that it is the best treatment for a particular woman. My own interviews with patients showed only too clearly that efficacy in this narrow sense is not the only criterion for judging treatments where patients are concerned. A study of patients involved in a clinical trial of Hyperbaric Oxygen treatment (HBO) for Multiple Sclerosis showed that patients themselves had their own practical criteria for judging the treatment and deciding whether they would continue with HBO after the trial, which were not based purely on the kind of medical 'efficacy' which the trial was designed to establish. These judgements were based on their own subjective assessments of any changes discerned in the symptoms they experienced, their expectations about how long any improvement due to the treatment ought to take to manifest itself, and a consideration of what the treatment involved in terms of the social and economic costs or benefits involved in frequent hospital attendance:

> The 'effects' of HBO would be that which remained when the effects of the negative factors were balanced out in an equation against the positive. In the assessment of this equation, it made no sense to consider HBO 'as such', as if its effectiveness could be separated from the mode of its delivery.
>
> (Wynne 1989: 1294)

The side effects or discomforts of a treatment that is indubitably 'efficacious' may render it less acceptable to a particular patient than one which is not so 'efficacious'. The involvement and attention of the therapist is probably another major component in patient 'satisfaction' and affects the way in which treatments are compared and evaluated by patients (see Booker: 1988). Points such as these should be borne in mind when considering the recent interim report on the survival rates of cancer patients at the Bristol Cancer Help Centre.

Where choice is possible, good medical practice demands that the patient be given the treatment which is best suited to his/her criteria and situation; the actual organisation of the orthodox health services ensures that what the patient is actually offered is determined by institutional, financial or bureaucratic considerations as much as anything. Many patients get 'efficacious' treatments which they regard as unsuitable or invasive. If the orthodox medical profession operates with a narrow and often inappropriate definition of therapeutic efficacy, why should we demand that the non-orthodox professions play the same mad game?

Another way of looking at the matter, and one with which I have much sympathy, is that it is more a question of protecting the public against treatments that definitely do not work or are dangerous rather than proving which work best. This, of course, is an important aspect of the testing of drugs for the market. The frequently made claim that 'if it [complementary treatment] does not do you any good, it will not do you any harm either' may be true in many cases, but implies very low expectations. There is perhaps no harm in patients whom orthodox medicine cannot cure paying money for treatment which is seldom or never efficacious in the narrow technical sense, provided that they have sufficient information to assess the risk they are taking in advance. They may then decide to take it out of desperation or because they like the therapist's bedside manner. But they can never be in a position to make this judgement if they do not have the necessary information. Here again we meet the problem of devising trials which are relevant to the way in which complementary practitioners actually operate, as opposed to the way in which orthodox practitioners think they operate. It is all very well to prove that ingesting enormous quantities of comfrey will cause damage to the liver (Stalker and Glymour 1989: 328). The limits of safety need to be established and this information is rightly demanded in the case of products sold over the counter. But the hazards of misuse are easy to prove and apply to orthodox medicine as much as to non-orthodox medicine. What should also be tested is the use of comfrey (or whatever) in the quantities in which herbalists generally administer it, with a view to establishing whether or not, used in this way, it has the therapeutic effects claimed, because this is what the client of a herbalist needs to know.

I would agree with Duncan Campbell (see p. 100) that the stricture *caveat emptor* is insufficient guarantee of safety in the case of any kind of healthcare. Most complementary medicine is available on the market, but it is a market which is quite different from that in, say, used cars or sports equipment. Appropriate and objective testing is therefore to be desired and should be encouraged – a government grant to the Research Council for Complementary Medicine might be a good way of expediting this. Where I would disagree with the orthodox medical profession is in their stipulation that there can be no further discussion of the statutory position of complementary medicine until such scientific validation has taken place to its own satisfaction. If we insist on this, we shall be overtaken by events. If the present popularity of non-orthodox medicine continues, millions of patients will have used complementary medicine (for good or ill) before this happens, and thousands of therapists (good and bad) will have set up practice before even one half of the treatments which they commonly use have been subjected to clinical trials.

ACCESSIBILITY OF COMPLEMENTARY THERAPIES: PUBLIC OR PRIVATE MEDICINE?

It is likely that more people approve of complementary medicine than are actually using it. The MORI opinion poll conducted in 1989 showed that whilst 27 per cent of the sample claimed to have used a form of complementary medicine at some time or other, as many as 73 per cent 'would seriously consider' using one of the therapies cited and 74 per cent gave some degree of support to the idea of their inclusion in the NHS. Probably some people do not use complementary medicine because they cannot find a therapist through their own lay information systems and mistrust public ones. Some do not use it because there are few practitioners working near to where they live, others because they cannot afford to. I have already discussed the question of public information (see p.46) and suggested that statutory bodies like CHCs could do more to inform the public about complementary therapists in their localities. But even if such bodies could be persuaded to take responsibility for informing the public about non-orthodox medicine at all, it is unlikely that they will feel happy about doing it in the absence of any system of official registration. No organisation can be expected to promulgate the names of practitioners without some assurance of their reputability, yet they cannot be expected to conduct investigations into the diverse qualifications and experience of each and every practitioner themselves.

One way of making complementary medicine accessible to more people would be to make it available under the NHS. A limited amount of non-orthodox treatment is already available under the NHS (see Chapter 5) and it is likely that this will expand. This expansion will probably remain patchy and dependent on the policies and priorities of local (orthodox) medical personnel and their NHS managers. Would it be possible or desirable to incorporate non-orthodox medicine into the NHS more systematically, according to some concerted national plan?

This could certainly be argued politically in terms of demand; many citizens would certainly like to see it available as part of the public health system. Yet the fact that a large number of people need or want a service, however, has never been accepted as a sufficient reason for the state providing it in capitalist societies. The arguments that complementary healthcare is very cost-effective, that it concentrates on preventative care, that it cures problems that orthodox medicine cannot deal with, are as much arguments for the reform of orthodox medicine as for the incorporation of yet another set of services into the over-stretched NHS.

Underlying public health policy in Britain, as in most capitalist countries, has been the assumption that a distinction can be made between health services which are vital to the individual citizen's welfare and conducive to reasonable standards of public hygiene, and services which might certainly be beneficial to the individual, but which the state should not normally be expected to pay for – such as cosmetic surgery of various kinds, 'non-essential' physiotherapy, education in stress management, etc. Within the 'essential' public health sector further priorities may be defined so as to switch funds to or from services such as cytology or family planning. The borderline between 'essential' and 'non-essential' healthcare is of course flexible and open to manipulation. A decade of Conservative government has seen the transfer of much ophthalmic and dental care from the category of the essential (paid for by the state) to that of the non-essential (paid for by the individual citizen) categories. 'Community care' represents a similar transfer of certain health services which were formerly performed by nurses and other employees of the public sector to the domestic sector of the economy. Both the 'cure' and the 'care' aspects of medicine are subject to such redefinition.

This would seem to be no very favourable climate in which to introduce the claim that complementary medicine represents a basic form of healthcare which the state should pay for. The best that can be hoped for in the short run is that under the new NHS organisation some GPs and some hospital managers will find the hire of complementary therapists cheap enough to justify switching funds within their budgets from some more expensive services.

Many of the practitioners whom I interviewed queried whether complementary medicine could be offered as part of a state system of healthcare and retain those characteristics which make it so satisfactory to many patients. Complementary medicine is labour-intensive rather than capital-intensive; consultations take time if they are to lead to successful treatment. Would not the pressure upon therapists' time which would certainly result from making their services publicly available force them to curtail consultation time, thereby making them less effective? More than this, in much complementary medicine the conception of the patient–practitioner relationship is quite different from that which is implicit in most orthodox medical practice. The therapeutic process is sustained not just by the therapist's expertise and specialised knowledge, but also by the active involvement and effort of the patient. In a public healthcare system the patient does not pay directly for the therapy and has not sought the particular practitioner out as part of an active quest for healing, often arriving at the consulting room through a process of bureaucratic referral. Under such circumstances, might not the treatment be less satisfactory, the motivation of both patient and therapist being different?

One of the themes which recurred time and again while I was writing the chapters on practitioners was the tension between the conception of medicine as a commercial enterprise, the sale of services which can be quantified and priced, and the conception of healing as a transaction between two persons in which the quality and circumstances of their relationship and interaction is crucial. In Chapter 7 I showed how individual practitioners dealt with the contradiction between the fact that they operated within a medical market (which from many points of view they found very satisfactory) and their view of healing as predicated on care for and of the patient – a care which could be corrupted once it was given a price. All good healing depends on a blend between what I shall call *scientia* – knowledge, learning, expertise, technique – and *caritas* – loving care, commitment to the patient's wellbeing. When medical care is bought and sold this does not make the exercise of *caritas* impossible, but it means that it cannot be extended to the impecunious or underprivileged, another contradiction which troubled many of my practitioner interviewees.

On the other hand, non-commercial models for the delivery of healthcare in a complex society bear problems of their own. To expect healthcare professionals to practise for nothing, is unrealistic; indeed the kind of healing which truly conjoins *caritas* and *scientia* is peculiarly demanding of the healer. Several interviewees remarked on the fact that true commitment to the cure of the patient was incompatible with a large patient-load. It is true that a good deal of healing is performed free of charge by spiritual healers and students of complementary medicine, or at extremely low cost by therapists who waive charges for patients of long standing or limited means, but this will never do as a means for making the benefits of complementary medicine regularly available to the masses.

In the public sector medical care is delivered within a relationship which is neither purely commercial nor purely personal, but is best described as bureaucratic. At its best this institutional form allows space for both *caritas* and for *scientia*, both care and cure. Under pressure – when pressure on services increases or when funding is deliberately restricted – it is the exercise of holistic care which is likely to founder first. *Scientia* wins every time – or rather a particular kind of *scientia*, the specialised technical expertise which is most compatible with bureaucratic 'efficiency'.

This all sounds very negative, but I do not therefore conclude that some complementary healthcare cannot be incorporated into the NHS. The best of non-orthodox medicine offers healing services which are good for patients' mental and physical health and which therefore should be available to all, not just those who can afford it. But the best of this medicine also involves an investment on the part of the practitioner which is not just a matter of *scientia*; if non-orthodox therapists are forced to practise under conditions which are not conducive to this, then they will only replicate what is already available under the NHS in a different technical form.

Not much thought has been given to how such an integration might be organised, mainly I think because most of the non-orthodox professions do not regard incorporation into the NHS as the most urgent issue facing them at the moment. The present trend, i.e. the hire of specific services provided by non-orthodox practitioners in pain clinics, geriatric wards, orthopaedic clinics, etc., could be continued with benefit. Another possibility is that some therapies could be provided on a similar basis to that on which dental care is delivered. That is, the practitioner would be more or less self-employed but the state would re-imburse all or part of the patients' fees at standardised rates.

However, a major obstacle to any such provision at present is the attitude of the orthodox medical profession. I do not see how complementary medicine could be made available as part of the public healthcare system without some formalisation of the relationship between orthodox and non-orthodox practitioners, unless we were to have two entirely independent public health sectors. Non-orthodox healthcare could be made available on referral from orthodox doctors, either at the primary healthcare level or some other level, which would be easy where doctors are favourable to and knowledgeable about complementary medicine, but impossible where they are not. Or some system of patient choice could be instituted, patients deciding for themselves whether, for instance, they would prefer to use pain killers for back trouble or the services of an osteopath. A degree of public sector pluralism exists for instance in India, where the government funds education in cosmopolitan medicine, homoeopathy and Ayurveda. Patients have some choice of treatment, although cosmopolitan biomedicine dominates in the public sector and all types may not be equally available in a given area. Indeed, in some areas very little professional medicine of any kind at all is readily accessible to the sick. This pluralism is institutionally feasible because the organisation of primary healthcare (where it exists at all) is quite different from that which obtains in Britain. The patient does not gain access to healthcare by virtue of being officially registered with a particular GP who then constitutes the bureaucratic gatekeeper for access to more specialised care. The under-bureaucratisation of the citizen/patient in India is probably more an effect of underdevelopment of the economy than of any deliberate attempt to foster patient choice; can the self-responsibility with regard to healthcare which people in underdeveloped countries exercise perforce as a consequence of poverty be introduced into the public healthcare systems of industrialised countries as a positive value?

Both Conservative rhetoric and many non-orthodox therapists approve of the principle that people should be encouraged to take more and more responsibility for their own healthcare. For complementary practitioners this means encouraging the patient to make appropriate choices for him/herself, furnishing him/her with the information necessary for such choices. One major obstacle to this lies in the culture of orthodox medicine, which regards the physician as having a relation of control and authority over the patient by virtue of superior knowledge of the body, so that the informed and empowered patient is seen as a potential problem (see Blair 1985). Another obstacle lies in the culture of bureaucracies. State medicine is delivered through a bureaucratic system where therapeutic and other responsibilities are well defined and not negotiable. The popularity of complementary medicine raises the question of how the GP's responsibility for his/her patients could possibly be shared with practitioners outside the bureaucracy altogether (see Murray and Shepherd 1988 for a discussion of this from the orthodox doctor's point of view). GPs are now permitted by the General Medical Council to refer patients to non-orthodox practitioners, but they do not thereby cede ultimate responsibility for the patient's medical care, so formal referral is not a very attractive option even for GPs who are well disposed to complementary medicine and know something about it. Bureaucracies are also hierarchically organised. A bureaucracy where the person at the lowest point in the pyramid (the patient) makes the critical choices would be difficult to conceive. If we take the view that public medicine is, amongst other things, a system of state control, then it is even more difficult to see how the state could possibly be persuaded to maintain a public health system in which responsibilities were flexible and where much discretion was vested in the patient.

The institutional obstacles to any kind of integration of orthodox with non-orthodox medicine are deep-seated and not such as to be overcome by good intentions alone, but there is cause for optimism in the fact that some constructive experimentation with new forms of collaboration and communication is going on. At the Marylebone Health Centre in London Dr Peter Reason is conducting an inquiry into modes of co-operation among different kinds of practitioner (*Holistic Health* Spring 1990), and the Norwegian researchers Vigdis Christie and Edwin Sandberg report on a 'dialogue group' of orthodox and non-orthodox practitioners which they helped to set up in Oslo (Christie and Sandberg 1989). It is to be hoped that such experiments will generate ideas which can be tried out on a wider scale.

REGISTRATION AND THE STANDARDISATION OF TRAINING

We have already seen that most of the organisations representing non-orthodox medical practitioners accord high priority to this issue because they see it as the chief guarantee that their statutory freedom to practise will not be eroded with the coming of the Single European Market, or indeed any other political eventuality. But there are other reasons for approving their pre-occupation with this issue.

It is not realistic to suppose that any of the desirable reforms which I have discussed above could possibly come about in the absence of some system by which the qualified and responsible practitioners are seen to be distinguished from the unqualified and unscrupulous ones. The state will not deal with a profession which is not well delineated, nor will other professions. A major problem here, as many supporters of complementary medicine have pointed out, is that there are many experienced and skilful practitioners around who have no formal qualification to their name but who may perform more valuable services and show more medical wisdom than many who do.

However any discussion of state registration is premature while practitioner education remains unstandardised. As we saw in Chapter 8, the complementary professional organisations are putting their minds to this problem, some having made more progress than others. One of the difficulties is that some non-orthodox disciplines embrace several different schools of thought, each with its own interpretation of the therapy's basic ideas, and in some cases, each with its own claims to purity of doctrine. Some of the major professional organisations are confined to ex-students of a particular training establishment, or have their origins in such organisations, and have not hitherto been required to think in terms of the profession as a whole. Within most of the major disciplines there are institutionalised divisions between those who see an orthodox medical education as essential and those who are vehemently opposed to such a requirement. And each therapy has its own historical relationship to orthodox medicine and to other forms of non-orthodox medicine.

The orthodox medical profession took time to grow from an association of several professions, each formerly having its own separate institutions and interests. Is it realistic to expect the non-orthodox professions to achieve the same degree of unity in a shorter space of time, especially when faced with an otiose government and defensive or even hostile doctors? The struggles of a diversity of groups pursuing different strategies of professionalisation (and at different stages in their various struggles) to achieve some degree of joint organisation has led to unedifying wrangling as to whose voice is legitimate and where the initiative for such unification should come from. Different groups have sought accreditation through different statutory channels and some, such as the osteopaths, are ambivalent about the extent to which they wish to identify themselves with or co-operate with the other non-orthodox medical professions at all. Most professions are well on the way to achieving some degree of coherence and unity but some conflict between established bodies is only to be expected. It is to be hoped that this coalescence will proceed more briskly in future since protracted dissent can breed antagonisms which are slower to heal than those which result from the sharp professional skirmish.

THE INTERESTS OF PATIENTS MUST PREVAIL

It would be very satisfying to end this book with a nice package of policy recommendations which administrators and healthcare professionals could take away to think about and debate. I have concentrated on clarifying priorities, indicating the order in which things need to be done and whose interests they ought to serve, rather than proposed detailed schemes of action. The reason for this is that, as I hope the foregoing discussion has shown, a number of issues of principle need to be reflected upon before concrete proposals could ever be agreed. To what extent can or should a public health system incorporate care as well as cure? Within what kind of institutional context can medical *scientia* and *caritas* be integrated? How can communication between different (even presently conflicting) professions be organised so that the interest of the patient prevails? Is the principle of the self-responsible patient compatible with the delivery of heathcare in a non-market situation?

If change is going to require such profound re-considerations, then why opt for change? Is not the *status quo* satisfactory in many respects? Many individual non-orthodox practitioners would agree with such a proposition; they have no shortage of patients, they are free to practise as they wish, their remuneration is reasonable and their work is deeply satisfying to them. Assured that these conditions would continue, they would ask for little more. In my view there are two reasons why the *status quo* is not satisfactory and these derive from the interests of the patients, whose needs must be paramount in any system of healthcare.

Firstly, there is reason to believe that the best of non-orthodox medicine does help to produce good health for many patients. It can promote intelligent self-care, encourage sensible attention to diet and life style, foster the positive confidence which aids healing and reduce the distress and pessimism which hinder it. (Note that I am not talking about efficacy in its narrow sense here.) There is also much that is wrong with orthodox medicine as it is practised today – its over-reliance on technological solutions, its impersonality, its stress on physician authority rather than patient responsibility. These defects are widely recognised, and not just by advocates of complementary medicine. They have produced a disaffection with, though not disaffiliation from, the public health sector on the part of many categories of patient. Orthodox doctors are fond of pointing out that non-orthodox medicine cannot claim to have any monopoly of the ideal of holistic and caring treatment. In this they are quite correct, but if non-orthodox medicine is perceived as being able to deliver this kind of treatment and orthodox medicine is not, then it behoves the doctor to be willing to learn from the complementary therapist as to how these ideals can better be realised. If professional *amour propre* permits nothing else, orthodox doctors could begin by listening more closely to those within their own ranks who practise holistic and complementary medicine. If only orthodox medicine can revise its own priorities in the light of such lessons and develop a more whole-patient-centred approach, then many of the issues I have discussed in this chapter will become much less urgent.

Secondly, any activity or therapy which is productive of good health should be as widely available as possible. At present many people who suffer from diseases regarded as incurable by orthodox medicine, or who are undergoing orthodox treatment which they find unacceptable, are denied the opportunity to seek alternative healthcare. Whilst many non-orthodox practitioners are doing a good job of encouraging better health practices in patients, developing their confidence and sense of wellbeing, the circumstances in which they operate ensure that they make little impact on national health inequalities, which largely mirror other social inequalities. Change is desirable therefore in order that complementary healthcare is accessible to all those who can benefit from its particular strengths.

And here I rest my case, in the hope that Hippocratic and political wisdom will prevail.

Glossary

This glossary is intended to provide a key to the names of therapies and related terms used in the text of this book. It is not meant to be an exhaustive list of complementary therapies nor to provide more than the very briefest definition of those included. For fuller accounts of these and other therapies see Fulder (1988), Stanway (1986), Inglis and West(1983).

Acupressure Similar to acupuncture, but pressure is applied to meridian points with fingers (q.v.).

Acupuncture This is an ancient Chinese system of medicine which holds that meridians, or energy channels, link inner organs and external points of the body. The acupuncturist applies fine steel needles at external points along these meridians (or sometimes burns tiny cones of herbal material over these points) to stimulate healing.

Alexander technique A system of instruction having its origin in the work of F. Matthias Alexander (1869–1955). The Alexander teacher encourages the pupil to develop more efficient modes of posture and more economical use of the body. It is not a therapy as such so much as a process of learning, but has some therapeutic applications, especially to musculo-skeletal problems.

Allopathy A term applied mainly by homoeopaths to refer to orthodox medicine, referring to the fact that (unlike homoeopathy) it is based on the principle of countering disease with substances that are held to produce effects *unlike* the symptoms of the disease itself.

Anthroposophical medicine Developed by the thinker Rudolf Steiner (1861–1925) in conjunction with medical associates. It was intended to extend conventional medicine rather than to establish an alternative system. It is based on a broad spiritual view of the human individual and uses a variety of therapeutic techniques including the use of herbal medicines, art therapy and eurythmy.

Aromatherapy Based on the healing properties of fragrant oils. These may affect both emotional mood and the physiological processes of the body. The essential oils are derived from plants of different kinds and are most commonly applied externally through massage of the skin.

Ayurveda   An ancient Hindu system of medicine, based on a humoral and constitutional conception of the body. Health is conceived as a state in which the forces within the body are in a state of balance. A range of therapeutic measures may be used (medication, massage, surgery, exercises). Medicines are prepared from a variety of mainly herbal materials. A practitioner of Ayurveda is called a Vaid.

Bach Flower Remedies   Edward Bach (1880–1936) believed in the healing properties of trees and flowers. Flowers are immersed in spring water and this water is taken by the patient. These remedies are held to be particularly effective for emotional and mental problems.

Biomedicine   When doctors refer to 'medicine' they are generally referring to a particular kind of medicine. Sociologists and social anthropologists need a term which distinguishes the system of medicine regarded as conventional or orthodox in the West, and supported by the state in many countries, from other systems of medicine and healing. 'Biomedicine' is one such term. 'Cosmopolitan' medicine is also used in the same sense, or 'western' medicine, and there are other possibilities. Occasionally the term allopathy is used by non-homoeopaths in this sense.

Chiropractic   A system of manipulation founded in 1895 by D. D. Palmer, a Canadian doctor who believed that the majority of diseases could be traced to 'subluxations' or maladjustments of the vertebrae which interfere with the healthy working of the nervous system. The **Chiropractor** manipulates joints and may also give advice on exercise, diet, posture, etc.

Dowsing/medical dowsing   (also called Radiesthesia). The dowser uses a pendulum and a 'witness', a small piece of the patient's nail clippings, for instance. S/he 'reads' or divines the patient's problem by holding the pendulum over the witness and observing how it oscillates in reponse to questions. Dowsers usually prescribe homoeopathic remedies to treat patients.

Hakim   Someone who practices the **Unani** system of medicine (q.v.).

Healing   This term is often used by complementary therapists and others to refer specifically to spiritual or psychic healing. Spiritual healers may use the 'laying on of hands' or simply place their hands over the patient's body without touching it, in order to channel healing energies, however these are conceived. Distance healing does not even require the presence of the recipient and may be achieved through prayer or other kinds of mindful attention to the recipient. Sociologists sometimes use the term healing to refer to the entire process by which a sick person is restored to health (not just the bodily intervention of the doctor).

Herbalism   Many, probably most systems of medicine make therapeutic use of herbal substances. In the context of discussion of complementary medicine in contemporary Britain, the term herbalism (or medical herbalism) usually denotes the system of herbal medicine used in western Europe, based on a pharmacopoeia which is more ancient than that of biomedicine.

Heroic remedies/treatment   The violent remedies used by doctors in the early and mid-nineteenth century, involving purging, bleeding and other drastic measures.

Homoeopathy   The system of medicine founded by Samuel Hahnemann (b. 1755) based on the principle 'let like be cured by like'. The body is conceived as having a vital force which tends to self-healing. The cure of symptoms and the eventual achievement of good health is brought about by administering substances which are deemed to produce symptoms similar to those which the patient experiences. These stimulate the body's capacity to mend itself. The substances (which may be animal, vegetable or mineral) are, however, adminstered in highly dilute form, so dilute that it is arguable whether any molecules of the original tincture or substance could be present in the pills which the patient ingests.

Hypnotherapy   The therapeutic use of hypnosis. Hypnotherapy is widely used to control or change undesirable behaviour patterns, such as smoking or over-eating, but can also be used in the treatments of many organic disorders and in pain relief. Under hypnosis the patient can be encouraged to uncover the roots of fears and hopelessness in past experience and to develop positive attitudes and health-promoting confidence.

Iridology   This is a system of diagnosis. The condition of the iris of the eye is held to provide indications as to the condition of other parts of the body; each section of the iris corresponds to particular organs or body systems. The iridologist examines an enlarged photograph of the patient's eye in order to make a diagnosis and further photographs may be taken in order to monitor the effectiveness of treatment. This form of diagnosis can be used in conjunction with a variety of different therapies. In my experience it is most commonly used with medical herbalism.

Naturopathy   Like homoeopathy, naturopathy holds that the best therapy consists of mobilising the body's capacity to heal itself and, like homoeopathy, naturopathy treats the patient rather than the disease. Naturopaths, however, stress that a major cause of illness is imbalance within the body, especially accumulations of toxins. Orthodox medical treatment is held to suppress the symptoms thereby disturbing the body's ability to correct its own malfunction. Naturopaths use a range of therapeutic programmes, especially dietary adjustment and fasting, but hydrotherapy and exercise regimes may also be used.

New Age A term used rather imprecisely to describe a broad group of contemporary movements, therapies and quasi-religious groups which have in common a concern with personal self-realisation, liberation or fulfilment. Some explicitly draw on eastern or other non-European spiritual traditions and most could be described as rejecting the dualistic mind–body distinction which underlies much western thinking about the human person.

Osteopathy Osteopathy was founded by Andrew Taylor Still (1828–1912), an American doctor. Like chiropractic, osteopathy attends particularly to the musculo-skeletal system. 'Osteopathic lesions' are local imbalances in the normal tension of the spinal column which, through their effect on the nervous system, may be the origin of discomfort or malfunction elsewhere in the body. These and other abnormalities in the functioning of the musculo-skeletal system are treated through a range of mainly manipulative techniques.

Psionic medicine This was developed by George Laurence, a retired GP, in the 1950s and 1960s. Psionic medicine employs many of the ideas and diagnostic techniques of orthodox medicine, but rejects its reductionism, drawing extensively on the concept of the hereditary miasm. This idea has its origin in the work of Hahnemann, founder of homoeopathy. Besides the usual diagnostic techniques of orthodox medicine, the psionic doctor may also use radiesthetic diagnosis through the use of 'witnesses' (see **Dowsing**).

Radionics A sytem of diagnosis developed in America originally by Dr Albert Abrams and subsequently by Ruth Drown. As in dowsing and psionic medicine, diagnosis can take place at a distance. It generally involves the subjection of a 'witness' – such as a blood spot or a length of hair taken from the patient – to testing, often using special kinds of instrument regarded as measuring electromagnetic radiation or other forms of energy. A variety of therapies may be used – some of these operate at a distance just like the diagnosis.

Reflexology This system of diagnosis and treatment may have very ancient origins, but was first popularised in the West in the 1930s by Dr William Fitzgerald and Eunice Ingham, both Americans. Different areas of the feet are held to correspond to other parts of the body through a system of internal connections. Massage of the appropriate area of the foot will stimulate healing in the corresponding organ or part of the body.

Shiatsu A Japanese system of treatment which has a similar basis to Chinese acupuncture and acupressure. Pressure with the finger on the meridian points is used with therapeutic effect. Some techniques can be learnt for self-help or first aid by the lay person.

Tai Chi   A traditional Chinese system of exercises or movements practised in order to cultivate the co-ordination of mind, body and soul.

Unani Tibb   A traditional system of medicine practised mainly among Muslim communities in South Asia. It has some affinities with Ayurveda, although the term Unani actually means 'Greek'. A variety of medications of herbal and mineral origin are used. A practitioner of this system of medicine is popularly known as a **Hakim**.

Bibliography

Aldridge, D. (1989) 'Europe looks at complementary medicine', *BMJ* 299: 1121–2.

Allen, I. (1988) *Doctors and their Careers*, London: Policy Studies Institute.

Anderson, E. and Anderson, P. (1987) 'General practitioners and alternative medicine', *Journal of the Royal College of General Practitioners* 37: 52–5.

Anderson, R. and Bury, M. (1988) *Living with Chronic Illness. The Experience of Patients and their Families*, London: Unwin Hyman.

Arluke, A. (1977) 'Social control rituals in medicine', in R. Dingwall, C. Heath, M. Reid and M. Stacey (eds) *Health Care and Health Knowledge*, London: Croom Helm.

Aslam, M. (1979) 'The Practice of Asian Medicine in the U.K.' Unpublished Ph.D. thesis. University of Nottingham.

Association of Community Health Councils for England and Wales (1988) *The State of Non-Conventional Medicine – The Consumer View*.

Avina, R. and Schneiderman, L. (1978) 'Why patients use homoeopathy', *Western Journal of Medicine* 128: 366–9.

Baer, H. (1981) 'The organizational rejuvenation of osteopathy: a reflection of the decline of professional dominance in medicine', *Soc Sci and Med* 15A: 701–11.

—— (1984) 'The drive for professionalization in British osteopathy', *Soc Sci and Med* 19, 7: 717–25.

Barnes, B. (1974) *Scientific Knowledge and Sociological Theory*, London: Routledge and Kegan Paul.

Beals, A. (1976) 'Strategies of resort to curers in South India', in C. Leslie (ed.) *Asian Medical Systems*, Berkeley: University of California Press.

Beier, L. McCray (1981) 'The creation of the medical fringe 1500–1700', *Bulletin of the Society for the Social History of Medicine* 33: 29–31.

Blair, P. (1985) 'The informed patient: burden or ally?', *Modern Medicine* November 1985: 28–32.

Blaxter, M. and Patterson, E. (1982) *Mothers and Daughters: A Three Generational Study of Health Attitudes and Behaviour*, London: Heinemann Educational Books.

Booker, C. Kerry (1988) 'Patient satisfaction. The Surrey project: new models of the therapeutic process', *Complementary Medical Research* 3, 1: 71–88.

Boven, R., Genn, C., Lupton, G., Payne, S., Sheehan, M., and Western, J. (1977) *New Patients to Alternative Medicine. Western Report No. 1*. Appendix to Report of the Committee of Enquiry on Chiropractic, Osteopathy, Homoeopathy and Naturopathy. Parliamentary Paper No. 102, Government of Australia.

British Medical Association (1986) *Alternative Therapy.* Report of the Board of Science and Education, London: BMA.

BMJ Editorial (1980) 'The flight from science', *BMJ* 5 January 1980: 1–2.

Canter, D. and Booker, C. Kerry (1987) 'Multiple consultations as a basis for classifying patients' use of conventional and unconventional medical practice', *Complementary Medical Research* 2, 2: 141–60.

Cartwright, A. and Anderson, R. (1981) *General Practice Revisited: a Second Study of Patients and their Doctors*, London: Tavistock.

Charles, N. and Kerr, M. (1988) *Women, Food and Families*, Manchester: Manchester University Press.

Christie, V. n.d. 'Alternative medicine as a reflection of modern allopathic medicine: an investigation into the use of alternative practitioners in Norway'. Unpublished paper.

Christie, V. and Sandberg, E. (1989) 'A dialogue between practitioners of alternative (traditional) and modern (school) medicine in Norway'. Paper presented at the Eleventh International Conference on Social Science and Medicine.

Comaroff, J. (1976) 'A bitter pill to swallow', *Sociological Review* 24: 79–96.

Commission for Racial Equality (1988) *Medical Schools Admissions. Report of a Formal Investigation into St George's Hospital Medical School.* London: CRE.

Conway, A. (1986) 'Assessment of complementary medicine – revolution or evolution', *Complementary Medical Research* 3: 47–51.

Cooter, R. (ed.) (1988) *Studies in the History of Alternative Medicine*, London: Macmillan.

Cornwell, J. (1984) *Hard Earned Lives*, London: Tavistock.

Coward, R. (1989) *The Whole Truth: The Myth of Alternative Health*, London: Faber and Faber.

Davies, P. (1984) *Report on Trends in Complementary Medicine*, London: ICM.

Donnelly, W., Spykerboer, J., and Thong, Y. (1985) 'Are patients who use alternative medicine dissatisfied with orthodox medicine?', *Medical Journal of Australia* 142: 539–41.

Donovan, J. (1986) *We Don't Buy Sickness, It Just Comes*, Aldershot: Gower.

Freidson, E. (1960) 'Client control and medical practice', *American Journal of Sociology* 65: 374–82.

—— (1961) *Patients' Views of Medical Practice – A Study of Subscribers to a Prepaid Medical Plan in the Bronx*, New York: Russell Sage Foundation.

—— (1975) *The Profession of Medicine*, New York: Dodd, Mead and Co.

—— (1986) *Professional Powers. A Study of the Institutionalization of Formal Knowledge*, Chicago: University of Chicago Press.

Fulder, S. (1988) *The Handbook of Complementary Medicine*, Sevenoaks: Coronet Books (second edition).

Fulder, S. and Munro, R. (1982) *The Status of Complementary Medicine in the United Kingdom*, London: Threshold Foundation.

—— (1985) 'Complementary medicine in the United Kingdom: patients, practitioners and consultations', *Lancet* 8454: 542–5.

Furnham, A. and Smith, C. (1988) 'Choosing alternative medicine: a comparison of the beliefs of patients visiting a GP and a homoeopath', *Soc Sci and Med* 26, 7: 685–9.

Graham, H. (1985) 'Providers, negotiators and mediators: women as the hidden carers', in E. Lewin and V. Oleson (eds) *Women, Health and Healing, Towards a New Perspective*, London: Tavistock.

Graham, H. (1990) *Time, Energy and Healing*, London: Jessica Kingsley.

Hansard (House of Lords) 11 November 1987 Debate on Complementary Medicine, Columns 1379–416.

—— 9 May 1990 Debate on Complementary and Conventional Treatments, Columns 1400–36.

Haviland, D. (1989) 'We must support a democratic umbrella', (open letter) *JACM* 7, 7: 12.

Health Matters Winter 1988 'In search of the holistic grail' (Report by Charles O'Brien), Pilot Issue: 9.

—— April/May 1989 Editorial: 'Health off the shelf', issue 1: 1.

Here's Health (1990) 'Nurses take in alternatives' (Report by Sara Martin), February issue: 18–22.

Higgins, J. (1988) *The Business of Medicine*, London: Macmillan.

HMSO (1989) *Working for Patients. The Health Service – Caring for the 1990s*. London.

Holistic Health (1988) 'The Secretary's Column', 21: 4–6 (Winter issue).

—— (1989) 'Something borrowed, something new' (Report on St Marylebone Healing and Counselling Centre, by Maureen Green), 22: 5 (Spring issue).

—— (1990) 'A collaborative enquiry' (Report by Dr Peter Reason), 26: 14 (Spring issue).

Homoeopathy (1990) 'Homoeopath study reveals 750, 000 treatments a year' (Report by Celia Hall), February: 14–16.

Horne, D. A. (1984) 'A survey of patients in the private sector', *Hospital and Health Services Review* March: 70–2.

Huggon, T. (1990a) 'Rule by Brussels – liberation or liquidation for natural medicine?' *JACM* 8, 1: 13–16.

—— (1990b) 'Brussels post-1992: protector or persecutor?' *JACM* 8, 2: 13–15.

Inglis, B. and West, R. (1983) *The Alternative Health Guide*, London: Michael Joseph.

JACM (1989) 'In Parliament' (Comment by Bill Cash, M.P. on NHS re-organisation) 7, 5: 10 (May issue).

—— (1989) 'Why I will bust quacks' (Interview with Michael Baum) 7, 6: 12 (June issue).

—— (1989) 'In Parliament' (Comment by Lord Colwyn) 7, 10: 10 (October issue).

—— (1989) 'Why I am Quackbusting' (Comment by Duncan Campbell) 7, 11: 13 (November issue).

—— (1990) 'Patronising dictator – or misunderstood benefactor?' (Interview with Anthony Baird and Michael Endacott of the ICM) 8, 2: 25–30 (February issue).

James, R., Fox, M., and Taheri, G. (1983) 'Who goes to a natural therapist? Why', *Australian Family Physician* 12, 5: 383–6.

Janzen, J. (with the collaboration of W. Arkinstall) (1978) *The Quest for Therapy in Lower Zaire*, Berkeley: University of California Press .

Johnson, T. (1972) *Professions and Power*, Macmillan: London.

Jones, M. G. and Gardner, G. (1976) *Consumerism. A New Force in Society*, Lexington, Massachusetts: Lexington Books.

Kempson, E. (1987) *Informing Health Consumers: A Review of Health Information Needs and Services*, London: College of Health.

Kronenfeld, J. K. and Wasner, C. (1982) 'The use of unorthodox therapies and marginal practitioners', *Soc Sci and Med* 16: 1119–25.

Kuhn, T. (1962) *The Structure of Scientific Revolutions*, Chicago: University of Chicago Press.

Larkin, G. (1987) *Occupational Monopoly and Modern Medicine*, Tavistock: London.

Larson, M. S. (1977) *The Rise of Professionalism: A Sociological Analysis*, Berkeley: University of California Press.

Lasker, J. (1981) 'Choosing among therapies: illness behavior in the Ivory Coast', *Soc Sci and Med* 15A: 157–68.

Leslie, C. (1980) 'Medical pluralism in world perspective', *Soc Sci and Med* 14B: 191–5.

Lodge, D. (1988) *Nice Work*, London: Secker and Warburg.

MacEoin, D. (1990) 'The myth of clinical trials', *JACM* 8, 8: 15–18.

McGuire, M. (with the assistance of Debra Kantor) (1988) *Ritual Healing in Suburban America*, New Brunswick: Rutgers University Press.

McKinlay, J. (1973) 'Social networks, lay consultation and help-seeking behaviour', *Social Forces* 51: 275–92.

Marcovitch, H. (1989) 'Some implications of the White Paper', *Holistic Health* 23: 1, 4–5.

Minocha, A. (1980) 'Medical pluralism and health services', *Soc Sci and Med* 14B: 217–23.

Moore, J., Phipps, K., and Marcer, D. (1985) 'Why do people seek treatment by alternative medicine?', *BMJ* 290: 28–9 (5 January).

Moore, M. and Stephenson, J. (1962) 'A motivational and sociological analysis of homoeopathic physicians in the USA and the UK', *British Homoeopathic Journal* 51: 297–303.

Morgan, M., Calnan, M., and Manning, N. (1985) *Sociological Approaches to Health and Medicine*, London: Croom Helm.

MORI (Market and Opinion Research International) (1989) *Research on Alternative Medicine* (conducted for *The Times* newspaper).

Murray, J. and Shepherd, S. (1988) 'Alternative or additional medicine? A new dilemma for the doctor', *Journal of the Royal College of General Practitioners* 38: 511–14.

National Consumer Council (1976) *Consumers and the Nationalised Industries. Report by the NCC to the Secretary of State for Prices and Consumer Protection*, London: HMSO.

Nicholls, P. (1988) *Homoeopathy and the Medical Profession*, London: Croom Helm.

Nicholls, P. and Luton, J. (1986) *Doctors and Complementary Medicine: a Survey of General Practitioners in the Potteries*, Occasional Paper No.2, Department of Sociology, Staffordshire Polytechnic.

NMS Newsletter (1989) 'Natural medicines penalised again' (Report on cost of medicine-licensing procedures for natural medicines) 11: 1 (Summer issue).

—— (1989) 'It's a herbal nightmare' (Report on DHSS licensing review of herbal medicines) 12: 1 (Winter issue).

—— (1990) 'The draft EEC Directive on Homoeopathic Medicine' (Report by Tom Huggon) 13: 1 (March issue).

Ooijendijk, W., Mackenbach, J., and Limberger, H. (1981) *What is Better?* Netherlands Institute of Preventive Medicine and the Technical Industrial Organisation. London: Translated and published by Threshold Foundation.

Parker, G. and Tupling, H. (1976) 'The chiropractic patient: psycho-social aspects', *Medical Journal of Australia* 2, 10: 373–9.

Parry, N. and Parry, J. (1976) *The Rise of the Medical Profession*, London: Croom Helm.

Parsons, T. (1951) *The Social System*, London: Routledge and Kegan Paul.

Porter, R. (1983) 'The language of quackery', *Bulletin of the Society for the Social History of Medicine* 33: 68.

Reilly, D. Taylor (1983) 'Young doctors' views on alternative medicine', *BMJ* 287: 337–9.

Research Surveys of Great Britain (1984) *Omnibus Survey on Alternative Medicine* (Prepared for Swan House Special Events), London.

Ritchie, J., Jacoby, A., and Bone, M. (1981) *Access to Primary Health Care. An enquiry carried out on behalf of the United Kingdom Health Department*. OPCS Social Survey Division.

Robinson, D. (1971) *The Process of Becoming Ill*, London: Routledge and Kegan Paul.

Romanucci-Schwartz, L. (1969) 'The hierarchy of resort in curative practices: the Admiralty Islands, Melanesia', *Journal of Health and Social Behaviour* 10: 201–9.

Rothstein, W. (1973) 'Professionalisation and employer demands: the cases of homoeopathy and psychoanalysis in the United States', in P. Halmos (ed.) 'Professionalisation and Social Change', *Sociological Review Monograph*, No. 20: 158–76.

Sermeus, G. (1987) *Alternative Medicine in Europe. A Quantitative Comparison of the Use and Knowledge of Alternative Medicine and Patient Profiles in Nine European Countries*, Brussels: Belgian Consumers' Association.

Stacey, M. (1976) 'The Health Service consumer: a sociological misconception', in M. Stacey (ed.) 'The Sociology of the NHS', *Sociological Review Monograph*, No. 22: 194–200.

—— (1988) *The Sociology of Health and Healing*, London: Unwin Hyman.

—— (1989a) 'The NHS Review: whither health care in Britain?', *Caduceus* 7: 7–8.

—— (1989b) 'The NHS White Paper: implications for alternative and complementary medicine', *Caduceus* 8: 32–5.

Stalker, D. and Glymour, C. (1989) *Examining Holistic Medicine*, New York: Prometheus Books.

Stanway, A. (1986) *Alternative Medicine. A Guide to Natural Therapies*, Harmondsworth: Penguin Books.

Stimson, G. and Webb, B. (1975) *Going to see the Doctor: The Consultation Process in General Practice*, London: Routledge and Kegan Paul.

Summerson, E. J. (1985) *Getting into Alternative Medicine and Therapies*, London: Careers Consultants Ltd.

Taylor, C. R. (1984) 'Alternative medicine and the medical encounter in Britain and the United States', in J. Warren Salmon (ed.) *Alternative Medicines. Popular and Policy Perspectives*, London: Tavistock.

Thomas, R. (1990a) 'Guardians of Britain's unique freedoms – or élite club?', (interview with Ken Shifrin) *JACM* 8, 1: 19–24.

—— (1990b) 'Patronising dictator – or misunderstood benefactor?', (interview with Anthony Baird) *JACM* 8, 2: 25–30.

—— (1990c) 'Newbound beats Langford to head up first NCC Council', *JACM* 8, 2: 11.

Trumpington, Baroness (1988) 'Alternative medicine and therapies and the DHSS', in J. Watt and C. Wood (eds) *Talking Health. Conventional and Complementary Approaches*, London: Royal Society of Medicine.

Turner, V. (1968) *The Drums of Affliction, a Study of the Religious Processes of the Ndembu of Zambia*, Oxford: Clarendon Press.

Wallis, R. and Morley, P. (eds) (1976) *Marginal Medicine*, London: Peter Owen.

Watt, J. and Wood, C. (eds) (1988) *Talking Health. Conventional and Complementary Approaches*, London: Royal Society of Medicine.

Weisburg, D. (1982) 'Northern Thai health care alternatives: patient control and the structure of medical pluralism', *Soc Sci and Med* 16: 1507–17.

Wharton, R. and Lewith, G. (1986) 'Complementary medicine and the general practitioner', *BMJ* 292: 1498–1500.

Which (1986) 'Magic or medicine?' October issue: 443–7.

White, M. and Skipper, J. K. (1971) 'The chiropractic physician: a study of contingencies', *Journal of Health and Social Behaviour* 12: 300–6.

Wilkinson, P. (1971) *Social Movements*, London: Pall Mall Press.

Witz, A. (1990) 'Patriarchy and Professions: The gendered politics of occupational closure', *Sociology* 24, 4: 675–90.

Wynne, A. (1989) 'Is it any good? The evaluation of therapy by participants in a clinical trial', *Soc Sci and Med* 29, 11: 1289–97.

Zola, I. (1978) 'Pathways to the doctor – from person to patient', in D. Tuckett and J. Kaufert, *Basic Readings in Medical Sociology*, London: Tavistock.

Name index

Subject index